Think Kingdom.
Be Family.

Missional Family Wholeness, Characteristics, and Mobilization

By
Mark Jacob Coté

Lisa,

May God continue to fill you with hope in His mission!

~ Mark Coté

xulon
PRESS

Think Kingdom. Be Family.
Missional Family Wholeness, Characteristics, and Mobilization
by Mark Jacob Coté

Printed in the United States of America

ISBN 9781629521985

Unless otherwise indicated, Bible quotations are taken from The New American Standard Bible. Copyright © 1995 by The Lockman Foundation.

www.xulonpress.com

To the glory of God and in gratitude for Victoria Grace Coté, my daughter and His beautiful servant, whose brief life has eternally blessed our family and others throughout the world.

Acknowledgements

Thank you to my wife, Kristin, and our children, Caleb, Jacob, and Rachel for the joyous fellowship that we share in Jesus and His mission by thinking kingdom and being family. Thank you to Kristin, for your constant love and friendship, as well as your support during the writing process through patience, proofreading, and analysis.

Thank you to Drs. Joseph Umidi, James Flynn, James Bowers, and S. David Moore for your wisdom and guidance that have greatly benefited me and others through this project.

Thank you to my editor, Erica Deiter, and to my proofreaders, Anne Marie Walny and Mary Elizabeth Weaver, for you have served the readers well.

Thank you to my parents, Steve and Joyce Coté, family members, and extended family for faithfully walking alongside of us through brokenness into blessing.

Thank you to my spiritual grandfather and namesake, Rev. Dr. Jacob Wagner, for your loving interest and sincere support for my life and calling.

Thank you to the Zion Church of Millersville family for the honor of serving you, and for allowing your storied living through participation in this project to be shared with others.

Thank you to the Lancaster County Christian School community for the mission of equipping students for God's call through *Living Education*.

Thank you to those who partner with our service and Victoria's Little Lambs Fund, and to those in our Peruvian family whose fellowship helped begin and advance this vision. . .

Contents

—∞∞∞—

Figures

⸻

Appendixes

—∞∞∞—

Introduction to The Think Kingdom–Be Family Project

Overview

This project identifies the elements that characterize missional families and how a model based upon family-with-family consociation can effectively mobilize them. Consociation means families sharing life with families. The problem is that ministry models inadvertently divide a family by its individual members and segregate families from families, thus hindering a family's corporate sense of mission that can be discovered with other families. This is particularly relevant in North American churches where programmatic approaches to spiritual formation are common. As a result, churches need to embrace the challenge of mobilizing families according to their collective identity and purpose in Christ.

The relational nature of discerning identity and purpose is the rationale for this research project. Identity and purpose correspond to a family's flow from its being into doing. In its broadest context, when a family's unique story aligns with the identity and story of God, the family joins God in His mission.

A single, average-sized congregation, Zion Church of Millersville, PA, represents the local context for detailing the limitations and scope of the project. This section surveys the congregation's background, the number of participants, definition of terms, and concepts related to the project's methodology.

The description of the ministry project defines its name, The Think Kingdom–Be Family (TKBF) Project (or Initiative). The roles of facilitators and participants are detailed, as well as the selection and training of the facilitators. This section also explains further the project's focused time period of family-with-family consociation.

There is a section that frames the project's ethnographic methodological approach in the context of practical theology. It includes an overview of the two measurement tools I developed for the project: *Missional Family Wholeness* and *Missional Family Characteristics*. Families evaluated themselves with questionnaires based upon these tools.

The closing sections preview the results and contributions that The TKBF Project can model for other churches and their families. It also previews the approach used for evaluating the project. From the project's inception to evaluation, a vision emerged for mobilizing Zion's families alongside the church's participation in God's story.

The Problem of Families
Without Identity and Purpose

What elements constitute a missional family, and how can a model based upon family-with-family consociation effectively mobilize such missional families? According to Günter Krallmann's exegetically-based research of Jesus' pedagogy, "consociation" is a key term to describe the approach He employed with His disciples; Krallmann defines this in short with his own term, "with-ness."[1] According to Webster's dictionary, consociation is "association in fellowship or alliance," even with "churches or religious societies" in view. To consociate is "to associate especially in fellowship or partnership."[2]

---

[1]   Günter Krallmann, *Mentoring for Mission: A Handbook on Leadership Principles Exemplified by Jesus Christ* (Waynesboro, GA: Gabriel Publishing, 2002), 53-54.

[2]   *Merriam Webster's Collegiate Dictionary*, 10th ed. (Springfield, MA: Merriam Webster, 1997), 247.

Families sharing life with other families serves as a relational context for focusing on the presence of Jesus in their midst and discovering their unique opportunity to join His mission.

This fellowship between families reflects a widespread opportunity for cultivating intergenerational relationships and mission through the church. Based upon his extensive research related to young Christians leaving the church in North America, David Kinnaman corrects the view that generations are divided age-groups, which leads to the assumption that "the church exists to prepare the next generation to fulfill God's purposes." Instead, Kinnaman asserts that "the church is a partnership of generations fulfilling God's purpose in their time"[3] [italics added]:

> The Christian community is one of the few places on earth where those who represent the full scope of human life, literally from the cradle to the grave, come together with a singular motive and mission. . .Flourishing intergenerational relationships should distinguish the church from other cultural institutions. The concept of dividing people into various segments based on their birth years is a very modern contrivance, emerging in part from the needs of the marketplace over the last hundred years. As goods were mass-produced, marketers sought new and effective ways to connect a given product or service to a specific niche or segment. Age (or generation) became one of those helpful 'hooks'–a way to pitch, advertise, or attract a certain kind of buyer of one's wares. *In a misguided abdication of our prophetic calling, many churches have allowed themselves to become internally segregated by age.* Most began with the valuable goal that their teaching be age appropriate but

---

[3]   David Kinnaman, *You Lost Me: Why Young Christians Are Leaving Church. . .And Rethinking Faith* (Grand Rapids: Baker Books, 2011), 203.

went on to create a systematized method of discipleship akin to the instructional model of public schools, which requires each age-group be its own learning cohort. Thus many churches and parishes segregate by age-group and, in doing so, unintentionally contribute to the rising tide of alienation that defines our times. As a by-product of this approach, the next generation's enthusiasm and vitality have been separated from the wisdom and experience of their elders. Just to be clear, I am not saying that we should suddenly do away with children's Sunday school or programs for youth. I am saying that *our programs need to be re-evaluated and revamped where necessary to make intergenerational relationships a priority.*[4]

New approaches need to be developed that prioritize intergenerational relationships. Family ministry is one area where this can be explored. North American Christian families live in this context of an individualistic society, which has led to an individualistic approach to discipleship within the church. The conventional method is communicating a message. Family members are divided into age-appropriate, and sometimes gender- and role-specific groups, for teaching and fellowship. This programmatic discipleship approach segregates family members, thus hindering a family from fellowship within itself and among other families. As a result, families lack a collective sense of identity and purpose.

When a family's cohesiveness is diffused, a sense of collective identity can be supplanted by individuals' searches for identity. Rather than persist in professionally-led ministry models that perpetuate these unintended consequences, what would it look like for churches to programmatically decentralize so that families are relationally and holistically equipped with a sense of identity in Christ and missional

---

[4]   Kinnaman, 203-204.

purpose? Whatever shape this takes for the family, it must happen within the context of the church. This is not an attempt to separate the family from the church. Rodney Clapp emphasizes the role of the church: "Restoring and redeeming the family, then, does not begin with the nation or the family itself. It begins with the church."[5]

The redemptive possibility for family is conducive for implementing mission. Steve Saint, a missionary leader who exemplifies holistic, multi-generational family involvement in missions, supports this connection of effective mission with the principles that operate within a healthy family. In critiquing the well-meaning but often limiting efforts of North American mission ventures, he asserts, "When we think missions I suggest we think family."[6] The foundation and framework of healthy families could be a critical lens through which the church re-thinks the design and effectiveness of current family ministry models.

There are blessings to be experienced when families exhibit healthy relationships, so it is understandable that a church's family ministry tends to focus on the family itself. Furthermore, the disorder characterizing many homes requires such a focus of the church's ministry energy. Yet what might it look like to pursue another end in family ministry that reaches beyond the family itself? Zion Church desires to explore the possibilities of family ministry that lifts the family's focus beyond itself. In other words, instead of making the wholeness of the family a goal, the family's wholeness becomes an important means to another end–the family's missional calling. A key outcome for this research was how this approach leads to changes for families at Zion Church who embrace a missional calling.

As a pastor and elder at the church, I serve alongside my dad, Pastor Stephen Coté, who has led the church through significant changes in nearly four decades of pastoral leadership. These changes include a departure from a mainline

---

[5]   Rodney Clapp, *Families At The Crossroads: Beyond Traditional and Modern Options* (Downers Grove, IL: InterVarsity Press, 1993), 47.

[6]   Steve Saint, *Missions Dilemma: Workbook* (USA: I-TEC, 2009), 38.

denomination, an integration of renewal theology and practice, and a transition from congregational polity to elder governance. I grew up in the midst of these transitions and their accompanying conflict. My decade-plus of pastoral ministry with my dad has been framed by the completion of two transformational educational experiences at Regent University–the Master of Divinity program at the outset and the Doctor of Ministry program, which has resulted in this project. During this decade, we established the foundation for Zion's mission: "Think kingdom. Be family."[7]

Thinking kingdom is a biblical theological mindset centered on Jesus Christ and the gospel of the kingdom of God. This perspective traces the reign and rule of God from creation, through the fall, to the hope for restoration based upon God's redemptive work. The nature of this belief and experience in the kingdom of God is revelatory by God's Spirit.

Being family is sharing life together within the story of God. It is characterized by enjoying the blessing of relationship with God and one another, as well as extending His love to others. Being family is shaped within the larger purpose of God on mission with His people, particularly expressed in several commissions recorded in scripture (Gen 1:28; 12:1-3; and Matt 28:18-20).

Central to the experience for my wife and me during this decade of ministry has been the birth of our four children and the death of our third-born and first daughter, Victoria Grace. Her life has served our family and church family as a testimony of God's victory by His grace. She is a portrait of what it means to be His servant–belonging to Him first and foremost before doing anything for Him. Victoria could only belong to the Father. Though her life was shortened because of a physical defect with her brain, her life continues to serve God's purposes to this day through our family, church family, and Victoria's Little Lambs Fund (a ministry fund through

---

[7]   Zion Church of Millersville, Online:
       http://www.zionchurchmillersville.com/?page_id=7 [2013].

Zion Church that provides medicine for sick children in Peru, Ethiopia, Mexico, and Bolivia).

Out of this formative experience, my study in the Doctor of Ministry program at Regent University converged with the opportunity to lead families at Zion Church into a life filled with Christ's presence and purpose. My vision was to develop a biblically-grounded, research-based, and relationally-delivered discipleship approach for mobilizing families into missional living, through Christ-centered family-with-family consociation.

Based upon the kingdom mindset and commitment to fellowship that was already established, the immediate impact in view with this project was to mobilize Zion's families in mission. Beyond this immediate goal, the initiative also provides an effective paradigm that can inspire and inform others. Addressing the problem of families lacking both a sense of identity in Christ and a missional purpose is thus focused: What elements constitute an effective model of family-with-family consociation to mobilize missional families at Zion Church of Millersville, PA?

The Rationale of Being Before Doing

Developing an approach to family-centered discipleship begins with the nature of the family's fellowship and continues with the family's activities. True maturity for families, including individuals and churches, does not begin with mastery of "doing." Rather, what is needed is fullness in a family's "being" that pours out "doing," which begins by belonging to God. Jesus' life exemplifies this dynamic. Stephen Seamands indicates that "Jesus is declared to be the Father's beloved Son in whom he is well pleased *before* he begins to preach, teach and heal. His mighty works and laying His life down. . .flow out of his fullness of being."[8]

---

[8] Stephen Seamands, *Ministry in the Image of God: The Trinitarian Shape of Christian Service* (Downers Grove, IL: IVP Books, 2005), 64.

This is the message of the life of my daughter, Victoria Grace, as previously noted. The prayer on our hearts was that she would be God's "beautiful servant." This was our prayer before we knew anything about her, including her gender, let alone her physical condition. As evidenced in Victoria's life, her belonging as her state of "being" yielded a "doing" that has reached far beyond her brief life on earth.

The proper flow for discipleship begins from "being" that consists of the indwelling presence of Jesus and continues by "doing" His mission with Him. Scott Boren comments on the priority of being: "Because God's mission flows from his heart, we must allow the Holy Spirit to lead us into communion with the Father to understand that mission. This is the first calling of the church. We are invited into a way of being with God before we are to do ministry."[9]

Peter Scazzero sees this approach as a balance between the emotional and spiritual spheres: "Emotional health and spiritual maturity are inseparable. It is not possible to be spiritually mature while remaining emotionally immature."[10] By aiming for emotional and spiritual health in families, becoming missional itself is a transformational process. Scazzero remembers his own transformation toward emotional and spiritual health: "I understood what it meant to minister out of who you are, not what you do."[11] The hope is for family members to transform from "human doings" into "human beings."[12]

This requires vulnerability. Larry Crabb describes his realization as a counselor of "how terrified I am to simply *be* in someone else's presence. There's no power to my being." He explains the allusion of security in relying on his doing, "It's my training, my giftedness, my experience that makes a

---

[9] M. Scott Boren, *The Relational Way* (Houston: TOUCH® Publications, 2007), 254.

[10] Peter Scazzero with Warren Bird, *The Emotionally Healthy Church: A Strategy for Discipleship that Actually Changes Lives,* Updated and Expanded Edition (Grand Rapids: Zondervan, 2010), 10.

[11] Scazzero, 34.

[12] Ibid.

difference. And besides, if you reject my wisdom, I can study more, read more, think more. But if you reject *me* there's no place to hide."[13] In another circumstance he had the same realization: "if anything good happens in our conversation, it will have more to do with who I am than what I can do."[14] Doing in the form of "advice, insight, and friendly encourage-ment" has its place, but it is when families determine simply to be present with one another that true connecting occurs, which Crabb indicates is "the absolute center of all powerful attempts to impact people."[15] This is the heart of consociation.

Henri Nouwen's testimony serves as a profound example of a life trajectory re-orienting around being. Burned out from his life of high-profile ministry in the church and academy, he heard God say, "Go and live among the poor in spirit, and they will heal you."[16] Seamands explains the possibility of holistic being to be found in such community: "The being of a person is therefore being-in-relationship. Moreover, relat-edness to others is two-dimensional: vertical (relatedness to God) and horizontal (relatedness to other humans and the rest of creation)."[17]

According to Seamands, "the implications for relational personhood" necessitate a tri-fold commitment. The first is "a commitment to wholeness in our interpersonal relationships." This is followed by "involvement in close-knit small group fellowship." Finally, there must be "a commitment to healthy family relationships."[18]

Relational identity supported by these relational commit-ments thrives on an inner-outward flow that is a central core

---

[13] Larry Crabb, *Connecting: Healing for Ourselves and Our Relationships* (Nashville: W Publishing Group, 2005), 42.

[14] Larry Crabb, *Becoming a True Spiritual Community: A Profound Vision of What the Church Can Be* (Nashville: Thomas Nelson, 1999), 23.

[15] Crabb, *Connecting*, 43.

[16] Henri J.M. Nouwen, *In the Name of Jesus: Reflections on Christian Leadership* (New York: Crossroad, 2000), 10-11.

[17] Seamands, 35.

[18] Ibid., 40.

to spiritual formation. James Wilhoit reiterates its centrality: "Often an early victory in proper spiritual listening occurs when Christians give attention to the affirming voice of God calling his beloved to creative service, which fits who they uniquely are."[19] Doing is shaped by a distinct identity of being. He also frames the nature of discipleship in light of this reality:

> In considering how to pattern our lives after Christ, we need to realize the power of our core being (in biblical language, heart, soul, mind, will) to shape our lives. The biblical writers continually give attention to the interior: In fact, 'root' is one of the primary images of the hidden but essential spiritual life. Those who trust the Lord are like a well-rooted tree planted by a stream (Jer. 17:7-8). Even during hot weather and drought, the leaves of this deeply rooted tree remain green, and it continues to produce fruit. Believers are to remain rooted in the Lord Jesus (Col. 2:7) and his great love (Eph. 3:17-19) so that they might remain stable. A basic spiritual principle emerges: the aspects of spiritual life that are out of sight deserve our highest attention.[20]

This project explores how consociation between families focused on Jesus Christ can be a context in which this proper understanding of "being" can be embraced. To remain healthy, it is important to guard against the common human default toward striving. When human striving is leading the way, something less than missional is occurring. Crabb cautions, "Our most difficult work in forming spiritual community is to

---

[19] James C. Wilhoit, *Spiritual Formation as if the Church Mattered: Growing in Christ through Community* (Grand Rapids: Baker Academic, 2008), 150.

[20] Wilhoit, 164.

stop working so hard."[21] Ed Stetzer and Philip Nation clarify the source of missional engagement: "missional ministry is not about our abilities. It is about presenting God's presence to the people of our world. If it becomes something besides that, then all we've done is create a new idol."[22]

Hence, striving to perform mission is a serious mistake. Avoiding this in a busy and performance-oriented world is a counter-cultural goal for families, even within the church. Speaking of how cluttered churches have become, Rainer and Geiger conclude "that many people are busy *doing* church instead of *being* the church."[23] In fact, they believe "we are losing ground not *despite* our overabundance of activity but *because* of it."[24]

Intergenerational community, as experienced in some churches and families, helps sustain focus in a culture that is increasingly fragmented. Family in the Hebrew culture can be understood as a household, which included multi-genera-tions of relatives as well as others absorbed into the family's fellowship.[25] Fellowship like this combines the wisdom of the older generation with the opportunities of the younger generation.

Perspective is a key aspect of the older generation's wisdom. Among mature followers of Jesus, such perspective is evident in a simple yet profound focus on His presence and purpose. Surrender to Him is where life is found. In the words of Nouwen, who sees maturity for leaders as being led through surrender, "Powerlessness and humility in the spiritual life. . .refer to people who are so deeply in love with

---

21 Crabb, *Becoming a True Spiritual Community*, 127-128.

22 Ed Stetzer and Philip Nation, *Compelled: Living The Mission Of God* (Birmingham: New Hope Publishers, 2012), 87.

23 Thom S. Rainer and Eric Geiger, *Simple Church: Returning to God's Process for Making Disciples* (Nashville: B&H Publishing Group, 2006), 19.

24 Rainer, 20.

25 Jeffrey L. Myers, "Cultivate – Church Version," Draft Manuscript May 3, 2011, In author's possession, 1.

Jesus that they are ready to follow him wherever he guides them, always trusting that, with him, they will find life and find it abundantly."[26] Families need this focus in a distracted and disjointed society in order to follow Jesus in His mission. The beginning and end of human-centered religion is striving, whereas Jesus is the beginning and end of God-centered restoration (Rev 22:13).

A foundational rationale for the project, for what has already been described and what is to follow, is that mission itself flows from God's being and is carried out as His doing. Seamands articulates "the *missio Dei* (mission of God):"

> Mission, then, was first an attribute of God before it was an activity of individual Christians or the church. It is derived from God's triune nature, from the *sending* of God, and should be grounded primarily in the doctrine of God...the church is an instrument of God's mission, but God's mission precedes, initiates, defines and sustains the church in mission. Consequently, there is not mission because there is church; there is church because there is mission already – the mission of the triune God. Mission, then, is not essentially a human activity undertaken by the church and its leaders out of obligation to the Great Commission, gratitude for what God has done for us, and the desperate plight of the world. It is God's own mission in which we are invited to participate.[27]

For the past decade, the vision of Zion Church of Millersville has been, "Our Focus is on Jesus, Beholding His Glory, Building His Body, Blessing His World."[28] Through

---

[26]   Nouwen, *In the Name of Jesus*, 63-64.

[27]   Seamands, 160-161.

[28]   Zion Church of Millersville, Online: http://www.zionchurchmillersville.com/?page_id=7 [2013].

this foremost focus on Christ and His glory, He has been revealing His mission and inviting the church to follow Him. Accordingly, members view worship as a lifestyle in Jesus' kingdom of loving Him and neighbor. Subsequently, they have experienced a family-like environment while growing in awareness of and involvement with the mission field locally and internationally. As this vision has developed, Zion began articulating its aforementioned mission, "Think kingdom. Be family." Zion built its strategy for mission upon the revelation of the kingdom of God and the fellowship with Him as part of His mission. Therefore, it is an opportune time to take mea-surable steps in the congregation's maturity in understanding the indwelling life of Christ (being), which in turn mobilizes families together in the mission of God (doing). Rather than burden the congregation to stir up missionary zeal through their own efforts, Seamands proposes a question to free the congregation to enter into a mission that is already in motion: "What's hindering us from joining the mission in which the Father, Son and Holy Spirit are already engaged?"[29]

The Focused Scope of the Project

The context for the project was one average-sized congre-gation. It was neither field-tested in large congregations nor in multiple congregations. The research focused on the concepts, detailed in sections to follow, of *Missional Family Wholeness* and the *Missional Family Characteristics*, with a relational and qualitative methodology. I am one of two ordained pastors at the church and one of six individuals with seminary edu-cation who serve in various capacities. The church operates with bi-vocational pastors.

There are certain dynamics within the congregation that supported a project of this nature. The "soil" had been cultivated over a decade with consistent biblical theological preaching, teaching, and discipleship. Relational trust is embedded within the familial environment, which was a key

---

[29]   Seamands, 169.

ingredient for effectiveness. Maximizing this trust depended on a certain degree of restraint to keep the initiative from becoming prescriptive and overly programmatic. Hence, within this contextual framework of Zion Church's congregation, the project was carried out in hope of learning the elements of a missional family and an effective way to mobilize families accordingly.

In this conceptual purpose and framework, the project is transportable to other contexts outside of Zion Church of Millersville, such as other churches, small groups, Christian schools, and ministry and mission organizations that work with families. Each context is circumstantially unique. Factors to consider in accommodating this principle-based family-with-family discipleship initiative may include but are not limited to the types of families, the size and staffing of the church, the quality of relational trust between leaders and among congregants, and theological and missiological understanding and practice. Cultural values related to varying approaches to ministry, hospitality, community engagement, and the typical experience of family life are also unique from region to region and even from church to church within the same region. In short, some dynamics are normative for churches and families and some are contextual and require adaptability.

There are further details to consider as contextual assumptions related to Zion's congregation. Families' structures at Zion reflect varying degrees of division and togetherness like the surrounding society, and a value for family life is generally regarded in the congregation. It is a friendly congregation where sharing life together in and out of the church building is expected and comfortable for many members, though not all. The congregation is accustomed to a non-programmatic approach to discipleship. The hospitality rendered is highly relational. Community engagement is encouraged and modeled more as an individual than a group initiative. For example, my dad, the lead pastor, serves in a variety of local emergency responder chaplain capacities. The church also participates frequently in cross-cultural mission trips, both through large teams and increasingly through smaller groups and more specialized arrangements.

Zion is located in Lancaster County, which is generally a religiously conservative region where family, faith, and work ethic are highly regarded. The county spans from the rural and agrarian settings to the multi-cultural urban setting that is focused on revitalizing local business, the arts, and a sense of community. Zion's immediate context is that of a suburban college town, with both urban and rural settings just a few miles away.

In order to strengthen the project's potential general applicability, especially for the variety of types of families, twenty families were involved in the research. This was a larger group than a case study approach would have utilized. Recruiting the participating families was accomplished by building upon existing relationships within church life and small groups. Once a group of facilitators agreed to serve in the initiative, they worked with me to personally invite other families to participate. In order to create space in schedules, small groups were suspended during the project.

Regarding the variety of forms that families take, it is clear that not all families conform to a traditional structure. Emphasizing adherence to a particular form would have hindered the scope of the project's impact. A key assumption is that the term "family" is flexible and can take shape in the broader sense of a household. Such an understanding of family can include multiple generations, extended family members, and friends and others that a family includes in its fellowship. This assumption views family through a Hebraic lens. Marvin R. Wilson contends for this necessary Hebraic vantage point over a Greek one, saying, "the authors of God's Word–virtually every one of them a Jew–have a profoundly Hebraic perspective on life and the world. If we are to interpret the Bible correctly, we must become attuned to this Hebraic setting in the ancient Near East. Thus we must look primarily not to Athens but to Jerusalem for this biblical view of reality."[30]

One of the more compelling New Testament examples of the extension of the household is how homes hosted church gatherings. Gerhard Lohfink elaborates:

> Early Christian 'house churches' were the place where, in addition to itinerant missionaries and their supporters, Christian brotherhood could be realized concretely. In each city where Christians lived one or more families made their homes available for the assembly of the community (cf. Acts 12:12; Rom. 16:5, 23; 1 Cor. 16:15, 19; Col. 4:15; Philemon 2). The owners of the homes (such as Prisca and Aquila) often conducted vital missionary activity; with self-sacrificing hospitality they made their house both the center of community life and a place of support for Christians who were traveling. This involved not only hosting missionaries traveling on behalf of a congregation. . .but also welcoming Christians underway on their own accord, for example for business reasons.[31]

For the purposes of this project, a family minimally referred to two family members in the same home. It could be a married couple, a parent and child, a grandparent and grandchild, two grown siblings, an aunt and niece, etc. It certainly included families with more than two family members as well, such as married couples with children, and a grandparent or other relative that lives in the home. Single friends of the family (other senior adults, adults, or children) that are not relatives were also involved in the project. This will be explained in a

---

[30]   Marvin R. Wilson, *Our Father Abraham* (Grand Rapids: Eerdmans, 1989), 9.

[31]   Gerhard Lohfink, *Jesus and Community* (Philadelphia: Fortress Press, 1984), 107.

following section. Key factors that impact family fellowship in this study included marital and intergenerational relationships. The primary intergenerational relationships consisted of parents and children, though grandparents were welcomed participants as previously noted.

Regarding the methods for family discipleship, I assume with Krallmann that Jesus' "perception and practice of discipling were so comprehensive that they encompassed essential connotations of current designations like 'mentoring,' 'leadership training' and coaching.'"[32] The use of "consociation" inter-relates with these concepts.

Description of The TKBF Project

This was a practical theological research project according to John Swinton and Harriet Mowat's description: "Practical Theology is critical, theological reflection on the practices of the Church as they interact with the practices of the world, with a view to ensuring and enabling faithful participation in God's redemptive practices in, to, and for the world."[33] With Zion Church as the particular church in view, the reflection focused on identifying elements of a missional family as the church practices the mobilization of these families. Our view was toward faithful obedience in the mission of God.

Such a discipleship process involves teaching that is relational and community-based. The Hebrew philosophy of education includes the notion expressed in Proverbs 22:6 that training is not based on the parents' prescription but "according to the child's way. . .in keeping with the child's unique God-given bent, disposition, talents, and gifts."[34] This project approached missional family mobilization with a similar philosophy as that applied to the Hebrew child. Families have a unique design and mission capability that emanates

---

[32] Krallmann, 14.

[33] John Swinton and Harriet Mowat, *Practical Theology and Qualitative Research* (London: SCM Press, 2006), 6.

[34] Wilson, 203.

from the unity of its unique members in Christ, within the church, and with one another.

No defined mission activity that can be placed upon every family. The opportunities, gifts, and passions of each family create a unique opportunity for that family to be a blessing. This uniqueness of each family reflects the relationship and work of the Father, Son, and Holy Spirit as well as a parallel understanding to the unity and diversity of the Body of Christ (1 Cor 12:14-31).

Both in prescription and strategy, it was necessary for Zion Church's leadership to exercise restraint. Our vision for mobilizing missional families is neither a quantitative church growth plan nor a highly structured ministry program. It flows from a kingdom-first mentality with a commitment to living as families within a church family as part of God's mission on earth. Zion's missional families can affirm Newbigin's conviction that the way "to represent the reign of God in the world in the way Jesus did" is the local congregation, which is "the primary reality. . .in seeking for a Christian impact on public life;" indeed, "Jesus. . .did not write a book but formed a community."[35] As previously noted, Lohfink identifies this community as a "new family."[36]

Relationship was critical to the origin, means, and end in view for this initiative. Consociation between facilitating and participating families was the contextual foundation for this project. This family-with-family fellowship is understood in the framework of Jesus' shared life with His followers. Krallmann describes Jesus' approach alongside of His disciples as "with-ness for formation."[37] "To put it another way, Jesus opened up to them countless occasions to move with him in consociation. . .it accentuates the aspect of togetherness."[38] Relationship is a central methodology for spiritual

---

[35] Leslie Newbigin, *The Gospel in a Pluralist Society* (Grand Rapids: Eerdmans Publishing Co., 1989), 226-227.

[36] Lohfink, 41.

[37] Krallmann, 33.

[38] Ibid., 53.

formation and mission cultivation. Boren captures this thrust in his book, *The Relational Way*:

> In the life of the church today, such an imagination can only be cultivated as those within the church re-learn what it means to live in vital relationships with one another. As we relate to God and each other through the power and inspiration of the Holy Spirit, an organic mission will arise that will foster a new future for the church. Mission and the relational way cannot work without one another. Mission without relationships results in an army. Relational Christianity without mission will only produce a country club. When mission and relationality join forces, God's plans for the church generate hope, just as Jeremiah foretold.[39]

Life coaching, often used with individuals, can also effectively cultivate "organic mission" in a family. This type of mission rises from the unique weaknesses, capabilities, opportunities, and dreams that reside within a family. Joseph Umidi offers the following definition of a coach:

> . . .a transformational coach is one who does not try to export what has not already been imported, but is a person who has experienced themselves the power of transformational conversations, transformational friendships, transparent relationships, and now has the ability to know how to bring that about, how to replicate that in the lives of others. Good transformational coaches are people who bring about great things in the lives of others.[40]

---

[39] Boren, 116.

[40] Joseph Umidi, *Transformational Coaching* (Virginia Beach: Xulon Press, 2005), 28.

This profile is consistent with the function of facilitators in this project. Each facilitator in their unique way nurtured a sense of identity[41] in Christ which shaped ministry to others. Coaching dynamics sustained a necessary flexibility to focus on each family's unique weaknesses and strengths, growth potential, and opportunities for mission. Hence, coaching complemented the project's relational approach.

The project's name comes from the mission of Zion Church: "Think kingdom. Be family." Abbreviated references throughout the book include: The TKBF Project, The TKBF Initiative, or simply TKBF. The kingdom of God is the theological foundation from the biblical narrative of redemption. Jesus proclaimed the kingdom as the heart of the gospel (Mark 1:15). Family characterizes the community that forms around Jesus' mission.

More than a ministry tool or program, the heart behind the initiative was that the context of family-with-family fellowship serves as a catalyst for nurturing the revelation of God's Spirit indwelling a family and releasing them into His mission. It called for a relational commitment of Zion's leaders to mobilize families in their God-inspired vision for mission. Again, this mobilization is a result of understanding Jesus' presence as the source of fellowship and obedience. Otherwise, it defaults to striving that leads to weariness.

The participants in The TKBF Initiative included both families and individuals, both singles and family members who participated as individuals. Families embraced individuals in their circle of fellowship. While the focus of the project was the missional mobilization of families, the context of a church family includes family units as well as individuals. TKBF honored the make-up of God's family, not as a concession, but because of the mutual benefit between families and singles. In Clapp's words, "singles and marrieds have complementary missionary advantages." He specifies these advantages as hospitality for families and mobility for singles.[42] Mobilization

---

41   Umidi, 27.

42   Clapp, 106.

through The TKBF Project impacted families and individuals alongside one another, because it enriched the consociation and missional outgrowth for all. In other words, a community made up of both families and singles best cultivates missional thinking and doing.

The focus of this research, in theory and measurement, was families. Beyond the research focus, the ministry of Zion fully embraced individual participation alongside of the family mobilization and measurement process. I thoroughly analyzed the qualitative and quantitative data on the families and report the results in Part III. Also included is data from families and individuals together, though there was no analysis on the individual data alone. To summarize, TKBF consociation incorporated individuals from Zion's congregation, and the research analysis and report on the project focused on the families and the church family as a whole.

The structure for family-with-family consociation in The TKBF Project consisted of facilitating families and individuals engaging other families and individuals for a period of three months for the purpose of missional mobilization for all as participants, including the facilitators. My wife and I, along with two other leadership couples, served as a support and encouragement to the facilitators while being facilitators ourselves.

We established facilitators for the purpose of relationally supporting the consociation period. As full participants in the initiative, they also completed reflection exercises that were used for measuring missional elements. Facilitators exhibited the gifts necessary to effectively initiate and guide the consociation and reflection process. While facilitators possessed a certain degree of missional understanding at the outset, the training and project experience advanced their own development too.

Thus, the facilitators primarily supported the consociation process with participating families and individuals. Each consociation of facilitators and families was a unique circle of fellowship, characterized by shared contexts, experiences, interests, available service opportunities, and new missional endeavors. A creative tension between pre-existing relationships and newly formed ones enhanced the effectiveness of the intentional relational investment.

The groupings of families shared life together. Scripture study, prayer, fellowship, play, and serving as families was integrated throughout. Times of debriefing, as individual families and with other families, was important for cultivating vision within a family. This was consistent with Umidi's assessment of Jesus' approach of leading His followers through experiences that touched "at the heart or core-value level" to be followed by "transformational conversations around that experience that would change their lives."[43]

Participants' interests and opportunities shaped the reflective, recreational, and missional activities. Facilitator training highlighted the importance of including participants in the planning. This approach encouraged ownership among the participants.

Consociation entailed a variety of normal and special activities that reflected the shared interests of the participants. For example, during this period I led a discussion on the movie *Les Misérables*, which provided a profound experience of reflection on the depth of brokenness in the world while dreaming of redemptive responses rooted in the hope of the gospel. Some of the activities were significant in their commitment of time and resources, like fundraising events for an international adoption effort and a culminating cross-cultural missions experience.

Rodney Clapp's description of the Christian home as a mission base summarizes well the intent of family-with-family fellowship in The TKBF Project:

The Christian home is a mission base when:

- Christians live in intentional community
- Christians who happen to live in the same neighborhood enjoy meals together, share a lawn mower and

---

[43]   Umidi, 27.

tree-trimming tools, or 'exchange' kids for an occasional evening
- We refuse to 'shop' for churches after one church has bored or inconvenienced us
- As in one case I know about, three families covenant that no one family will take jobs and move to another city unless all three families, through prayer and mutual consideration, decide they will go as well
- Members of a church move into the same apartment complex, sponsor Bible studies and organize supervision of the playground
- A family opens its home

. . .The limit, quite literally, is our imagination.[44]

The commitment to lead this initiative began with my family. My wife was in agreement to provide leadership as a family alongside of the other facilitators. As a qualitative research process, my family, with me as the researcher, was instrumental in the project itself, though the facilitators had more direct involvement in the consocation. My family's aforementioned testimony of receiving a revelation of a God-centered life and mission wove into the fabric of the church family as well.

Once the potential facilitators agreed to participate, there was an orientation process to the parameters and purpose of the initiative. The elders designed the process to be an experience where my wife and I along with the other elders and wives coached the facilitators through their training and for the duration of the project. Facilitator preparation consisted of the following:

- An initial meeting to overview the initiative
- Reading an extensive written proposal of the project
- An orientation retreat in which the families gathered together for fellowship, study, prayer, and reflection

---

[44] Clapp, 161-162.

- Engagement of the *Tools for The Think Kingdom – Be Family Project*
- Several follow-up conversations to answer questions, solidify understanding, and encourage planning based upon each facilitator's vision for implementation
- Equipping in coaching conversational principles was conducted in advance of the initiative (I conducted *Real Talk Training* by Lifeforming Leadership Coaching)

The orientation of facilitators was accomplished in about six weeks. The elder team had collaborated on the concept of the project months in advance which led to a fruitful orientation period. During this orientation period, the elders and facilitators introduced the basic framework of the initiative to the congregation and encouraged participation in an invitational and inspirational way. The elders and wives also organized the congregation into consociation rosters linking groups of participants with facilitators. The main pre-requisite for facilitators was a willingness to be a part of the initiative and a desire to grow in a missional understanding and way of living. Though many participants had a similar attitude at the outset, some would develop this desire for missional integration along the way.

A Missional Methodology

The primary research method for The TKBF Project was an ethnographic type of study. This approach examined participating families' narrative reflections, through written questionnaires[45] based upon the concepts detailed below, "to develop a 'thick' description of a cultural or social group," and in this case, the family.[46] Swinton and Mowat confirm that "narrative knowledge is perceived to be a legitimate,

[45] Luciano L'Abate, *Family Evaluation: A Psychological Approach* (Thousand Oaks, CA: Sage Publications, Inc., 1994), 93.

[46] Richard R. Osmer, *Practical Theology: An Introduction* (Grand Rapids: William B. Eerdmans Publishing Company, 2008), 51.

rigorous and valid form of knowledge that informs" in the realm of qualitative research.[47] In addition, various "artifacts and symbols that express group identity and history," such as children's drawings,[48] home décor, and other outward expressions of the family's inner values, could be avenues for reflections. Accordingly, a family's reflection focused on "observable patterns of behavior, customs, and way of life over an extended period of time."[49] Richard Osmer expresses that "the goal of ethnographic research" can be "the creation of a cultural portrait."[50] The TKBF Project aimed to create a missional family portrait.

I developed two conceptual frameworks for measuring a missional family through this initiative: *Missional Family Wholeness* and *Missional Family Characteristics*. My prayerful synthesis of these missional elements was informed by research on the biblical theology of family, family discipleship, family social theory, family history, and missional theory. These serve as theoretical frameworks to guide, clarify, encourage, and confirm an understanding of what it means to be a missional family.

Juliet Corbin and Anselm Strauss acknowledge that "theoretical frameworks can be useful." The instances they cite apply to this research project. First, there are elements "being discovered in the researcher's present study" of literature and pastoral experience that will be used "to complement, extend, and verify the findings" of this project.[51] They caution that it is important to be "open to new ideas and concepts" that develop or aspects of the framework that "do not fit the data." Also, "a theoretical framework can help the researcher determine

---

[47] Swinton, 38.

[48] Jane F. Gilgun, eds., et al., *Qualitative Methods In Family Research* (Newbury Park, CA: Sage Publications, Inc., 1992), 154.

[49] Osmer, 51.

[50] Ibid.

[51] Juliet Corbin and Anselm Strauss, *Basics of Qualitative Research: Techniques and Procedures for Developing Grounded Theory*, 3d ed. (Los Angeles: SAGE Publications, 2008), 39.

the methodology to be used."[52] These reasons connect to this project's context of "practical theological reflection," which involved addressing a current situation from a theological basis in order to create "revised forms of faithful practice."[53]

Grounded theory undergirds The TKBF Project in that the accuracy of these elements and the efficacy of this approach derive from the data collected. Susan Murphy asserts that "grounded theory methodology is well suited to studies of groups and ideally suited to questions where differing family meanings and interactions need to be addressed conceptually."[54] Hence, I applied a theoretical framework for the elements of a missional family to Zion Church's initiative to effectively mobilize its families.

I based participant reflection upon the theoretical framework of *Missional Family Wholeness* and *Missional Family Characteristics*. In particular, families and individuals responded to questionnaires at the outset and conclusion of the project. As a pre-test and post-test, these tools explored the connection of missional elements to the consociation period. This process helped participants articulate the story of God's work in their being and through their doing.

In addition to deriving thick descriptions through such an ethnographic assessment, families were given the opportunity to indicate elemental growth, or lack thereof, by utilizing rating scales[55] in the form of a Likert item for each missional characteristic. This data was then collected to form Likert scales quantifying the families' characteristics from the reflective exercises. Mark Rank advocates for the value in combining qualitative and quantitative methods in family research because of their "complementary nature, additional

---

[52]   Corbin, 40.

[53]   Swinton, 95.

[54]   Gilgun, eds., et al., 149.

[55]   L'Abate, 93.

insights, increased validity," and for "pushing the research further."[56]

The concept of *Missional Family Wholeness* consists of the following developmental dynamics that characterize missional thinking and application: *revelation, awareness, motivation, intuition,* and *integration.* These components parallel the meaning of the phases for "moving adults toward asset-building lifestyles" detailed by Peter Benson: receptivity, awareness, mobilization, action, and continuity.[57]

Each family's development is unique, even within the same dynamic of wholeness. These developmental realms are cyclical in nature as they overlap and continue even as new ones commence. Basically, these spheres provide a framework orienting a family to its missional development. "Wholeness" is preferred over "stages" or "phases" to express that a family does not simply move from one stage to another in a linear way. A better description is that each area flows together through a missional family, or builds upon the next as depicted in the following *Missional Family Wholeness* graphic.

Figure 1.

Missional Family Wholeness

---

56   Gilgun, eds., et al., 295-297.

57   Peter L. Benson, *All Kids Are Our Kids: What Communities Must Do to Raise Caring and Responsible Children and Adolescents* (San Francisco: Jossey-Bass, 2006), 233-237.

Revelation is the work of God in revealing Himself and His mission to the family. This is a revelation of hope in His kingdom. It includes biblical theological insight on the story of God as well as general insight gleaned from creation itself. The family's personal experience of brokenness and God's grace is a major formative context through which God reveals His heart in them. When God reveals His heart, there is often a sense of conviction in areas of pride, materialism, and self-absorption. A clear vision of mission can emerge for families receiving this revelation with repentance.

A growing *awareness* accompanies revelation that leads toward repentance. While the family's broadened perspective does not necessarily yield immediate and sustainable behavioral change, the family can no longer claim ignorance to the needs of those around them. This is because they have seen firsthand their own need for God's grace as illumined by His Spirit.

Motivation is the process through which awareness turns into desire. This dynamic represents the bridge from being into doing. Without the presence of Godly motivation, good works can simply be rote and legalistic. However, through revelation and the establishment of a missional conscious, God's Spirit begins to cultivate His desires in the hearts of His people.

Missional endeavors naturally flowing out of a family in the *intuition* realm. Days begin with thoughts of blessing others, continue with actual follow-through, and close with reflection and celebration of God at work through the family. The family begins to anticipate and expect missional encounters as part of their daily routine.

Finally, *integration* is when a family sees a missional lifestyle, according to the elements of the profile below, established in its delights and disciplines. There is maturity. The family initiates seeking to be equipped for missional ends according to its unique design. The family takes initiative in responding to the needs around them. Calling is not only expressed individually, but there is a collective sense of calling for the whole family. Others in the congregation or close to the family can attest to the sustained changes evident in the family at this point.

It is worth noting that throughout this process, various family members, due to age and their own experiences, may be at different points. The point of this tool is not to label individuals as much as to understand them and provide a sense of family identity during the growth process. The family in its individual members can be in different places, and as a whole the family can understand how they need to grow according to their unique design for being a blessing to others.

Alan Hirsch is helpful for understanding the nature of a group of people developing around mission. In the context of the middle-class values of safety and security combined with consumerist values of comfort and convenience, Alan Hirsch explains dynamics of missional group growth using the concepts of "communitas" and "liminality:"

> So the related ideas of liminality and communitas describe the dynamics of the Christian community inspired to overcome their instincts to 'huddle and cuddle' and to instead form themselves around a common mission that calls them into a dangerous journey to unknown places – a mission that calls the church to shake off its collective securities and to plunge into the world of action, where its members will experience disorientation and marginalization but also where they encounter God and one another in a new way. Communitas is therefore always linked with experience of liminality. It involves adventure and movement, and it describes that unique experience of togetherness that only really happens among a group of people inspired by the vision of a better world who actually attempt to do something about it. . .It is here where the safe, middle-class, consumerist

captivity of the church is so very problematic. And it is here where the adaptive challenge of the twenty-first century could be God's invitation to the church to rediscover itself as a missional communitas.[58]

Whereas *Missional Family Wholeness* is a tool for families to trace their development as a group in the way that Hirsch describes, *Missional Family Characteristics* provides a detailed template for contemplation of the reality of a family's being and doing. It gives practical avenues through which a family can discern their response to God in time, space, and matter. N.T. Wright comments on the big perspective which undergirds application in these spheres: "Jesus saw his own work, his own public career, his own very person, as the reality to which Temple [space], Sabbath [time], and creation [matter] itself were pointing.[59] This profile will allow a family to self-assess the impact of God's kingdom in the space of fellowship with God and others, in the redemption of time for His purposes, and the proper stewardship of things.

Missional Family Characteristics expresses how the core of a family's "being" compels their disciplines of "doing" in the following graphic.

Figure 2.

58 Alan Hirsch, *The Forgotten Ways: reactivating the missional church* (Grand Rapids: Brazos Press, 2006), 219, 221-222.

59 N.T. Wright, *Simply Jesus: A New Vision of Who He Was, What He Did, And Why He Matters* (New York: HarperOne, 2011), 148.

Gratitude is the overall posture of receiving God's grace accompanied with a thankful response. Such an orientation is evident in a family's hope, joy, and worship. Contrary to a grateful orientation is an atmosphere of complaint, negativity, and criticism. It is worth noting that gratitude appears as a culminating quality in Paul's exhortation to the Colossians as they live out the indwelling life of Christ in their midst (Col 1:12; 2:7 – "overflowing with gratitude;" 3:15-17; 4:2). Of Newbigin's six characteristics of a mission-oriented community, praise and thanksgiving are first in focus, because "it is of the essence of the matter that this concern for the neighbor is the overflow of a great gift of grace and not, primarily, the expression of commitment to a moral crusade."[60]

Brueggemann warns of the erosive impact of "consumerism ideology" on grateful praise and subsequent mission: "In that world where jingles replace doxology, God is not free and the people know no justice or compassion."[61] Consumerism is a loss of perspective. The perspective of gratitude thrives when families have margin to reflect, relate, recreate, and refresh. This margin is fundamentally implicit to the next profile category of rest.

Rest is the integration of sabbath reality into the lifestyle of the family. Measurement of this reality includes assessing the meaningful reflection the family does together. The Christian historical practice of examen, which ends the day in prayer and reflection, is something families can do together. Other prayerful spiritual disciplines are included in this sphere, such as contemplation, silence, and fasting. A family that spends time outside together may find that this nurtures their rest and reflection. Rest can undergird a family's healthy response to conflict, thus creating an overall sense of peace in the home. Proper nutrition, exercise, and sleep can also be examined within this category.

---

[60]   Newbigin, 228.

[61]   Brueggemann, 17.

An opposing reality here is busyness. Peterson attributes busyness to laziness and vanity, and his sobering comment about pastors can also apply to families:

> . . .busy is the symptom not of commitment but of betrayal. . .not devotion but defection. The adjective busy set as a modifier to pastor should sound to our ears like adulterous to characterize a wife or embezzling to describe a banker. It is an outrageous scandal, a blasphemous affront.[62]

Busy families are fragmented families. Missional families are fueled by sabbath rest. They have a quality of peacefully being together in the midst of the activity.

Again, Clapp provides clear and confirming analysis [italics added]:

> For what a tired, frenetic world needs to know and see as much as anything is that an integral feature of Christian mission is rest and celebration. Of course there are times when families simply need to rest. But remember that we live in a society that esteems autonomy as one of its highest goods. In our society the individual is independent, ideally depending on no one and nothing. And individuals who depend only on themselves must always be on guard. They can never rest. Thus we live in a world that might be characterized above all else as restless. Yet Jews and Christians are peculiar people *who celebrate the sabbath rest and understand that rest as one of the most crucial aspects of our witness.* Unlike others in our society, we claim that there is a Creator who trusts the goodness of his creation enough even to rest himself on the seventh day! How better can we show that the world and its

---

[62]   Peterson, *The Contemplative Pastor*, 17–18.

welfare do not depend on us and our efforts
than to rest regularly and boldly? How better to
show that the world is good enough to believe
in than to let it be one day a week?[63]

Freedom manifests in a family's delight. Families of delight
play together. To connect with the previous comment, Peterson
sees play as a sabbath activity.[64] Play and delight also connect
to wisdom, which is community-oriented in the Hebraic
culture. Consider how wisdom is personified as the object of
God's delight with the activity of playing and having delight
in people: ". . .I [wisdom][65] was daily His delight, rejoicing
[or playing][66] always before Him, rejoicing [or playing] in the
world, His earth, and having my delight in the sons of men."
One indicator of a family's freedom is the presence of laughter
in the home. Families burdened by unresolved conflict and
unforgiveness are hindered in their freedom. Freedom flows
from gratitude and rest.

Generosity is the first discipline on the doing side of the
profile. This area of a family can be measured by the presence
of hospitality in terms of opening their home to others both
in welcoming and reaching out. Attitudes toward possessions
will be examined as part of this category. A family financial
review will also be in order. *Familia Dei*, a missional family
website, spotlights how the development of a missional vision
as a family impacts financial commitments and planning.[67]

Faithfulness is the next doing category. Current contexts of
home, work, play, and neighborhood are the focus of faithfulness as understood throughout this book and particularly

---

[63] Clapp, 164-165.

[64] Eugene H. Peterson, *Working the Angles: The Shape of Pastoral Integrity*
(Grand Rapids: Eerdmans Publishing Co., 1987), 52.

[65] NASB marginal note.

[66] Ibid.

[67] Familia Dei: Missional Family In The Life Of The Trinity, *Budgeting for
Missional Family*, October 11, 2011. Online: http://jamogck.wordpress.
com/2011/10/20/budgeting-for-missional-family/ [28 July 2012].

informed by James Davison Hunter. Missional families serve as testimonies of converting current contexts to opportunities for missional faithfulness. Clapp agrees, "the Christian family is about faithfully witnessing to the love and power of God in its time and place."[68] With a relational mindset, missional families redemptively engage their investment in hobbies, entertainment, and recreation. Regarding entertainment as "popular artworks," William Romanowski believes that "we need to act as people of faith discerning perspective in these representations of life in God's world."[69]

The last doing category is *going*. While the faithfulness section focuses on current contexts of the family's involvement, the going category explores new contexts for the family. This will be the family's own initiative based on their sense of calling, their relational opportunities through church and others, and the dreams of the family. With the last two categories, the missional family's impact spans from their neighborhood to the nations.

This theoretical framework of *Missional Family Wholeness* and *Missional Family Characteristics* provides a gauge and road map for missional families. As tools for assessment, they overlap for cross-reference as an integrated survey of a family's being and doing. The being characteristics of *gratitude*, *rest*, and *freedom* correspond to the wholeness dynamics of *revelation*, *awareness*, and *motivation*. The doing characteristics of *generosity*, *faithfulness*, and *going* correspond to the wholeness dynamics of *motivation*, *intuition*, and *integration*. The *motivation* aspect of wholeness is like a bridge from being to doing.

As practical theological and qualitative methodology, The TKBF Project was "action research," as Swinton and Mowat conclude:

> For the practical theologian, action is not merely pragmatic or problem-solving, although it may

---

[68]   Clapp, 21.

[69]   William D. Romanowski, *Eyes Wide Open: Looking For God In Popular Culture* (Grand Rapids: Brazos Press, 2007), 18.

contain elements of this. For the practical-theo-
logical action always has the goal of interacting
with situations and challenging practices in
order that individuals and communities can be
enabled to remain faithful to God and to participate faithfully in God's continuing mission to
the world.[70]

Impact of The TKBF Project

The hope of the leadership at Zion Church was that The
Think Kingdom–Be Family Initiative would bless others outside the church, thus glorifying God. The goal was to mobilize
its church family in the *missio Dei*. There are orphans waiting
for families, neighbors in need of wisdom, businesses looking
for trustworthy employees, elderly longing for relationships,
sick children desperate for medicine, indigenous missionaries
ready for training, prisoners hoping for a visitor, students
desiring a teacher, and the list goes on. Truly, Zion's mission
can be as multi-faceted as each family in the congregation
responding to these and other needs as they follow Jesus.

This initiative measured holistic growth for Zion's families.
Subsequently, gratitude, rest, and freedom were cultivated
within the home; and generosity, faithfulness, and going into
new contexts flowed out of the family. This project does more
than tell the story of Zion's ministry. It compels and collects
a chapter in each family's story, and it continues through
further chapters of storied living in God's story.

By identifying elements with measures of missional
families and a paradigm for effectively mobilizing them, this
project can contribute to the missional conversation among
other churches, ministries, families, and individuals. There
is potential to inform Christian schools that are practicing
meaningful partnership with families. Higher education
programs focused on missional training may glean from the
study as well.

---

[70] Swinton, 257.

The Great Commission is an extension of God's own mission. If the church's programs can accomplish the mission, then the power of God is implicitly marginalized as unnecessary. However, if the mission far exceeds the reach of programs alone, then God's presence and power are essential to its fulfillment. As David Platt confesses, "I am part of a system that has created a whole host of means and methods, plans and strategies for doing church that require little if any power from God."[71] TKBF was a dream only possible in the presence and power of the Holy Spirit through the life of the church.

Lastly, I trust that this process can result in sustained missional wholeness for my own family, as we seek our own mobilization to serve "the least of these" (Matt 25:45).

Evaluation of The TKBF Project

The plan for evaluating The TKBF Project involved consulting with at least two people connected with Zion's leadership but outside of the congregation in the preparation and design of the project. One is the church's identified accountability support partner. Another is a spiritual father to my dad and spiritual grandfather to me. Their feedback was valuable because of their knowledge of the congregation. An extended visit with our accountability support partner, where he also spent time with the congregation laying a foundation for the project, was a critical piece in shaping implementation. Dialogue with these individuals, as well as other leaders in the congregation and additional people I consulted with, established a solid foundation and also widened the impact of TKBF to others who might be interested.

The reflections at the beginning and end of the initiative represented a collection of mostly ethnographic and some quantitative data for each participating family and individual. Participants submitted their reflections in paper or electronic format. In addition to this raw data generated by

---

[71]   David Platt, *Radical: Taking Back Your Faith from the American Dream* (Colorado Springs: Multnomah Books, 2010), 48-49.

the participating families, the field notes from facilitators provided further information for synthesis and evaluation. This included observations on the families based upon interviews and interaction. There were also numerous comments from participants in their reflections, in writing, through testimonies before the congregation, and in conversations with facilitators that provided evaluative feedback. At the completion of the project, I collected, correlated, analyzed, and prepared the data as an ethnographic assessment of the elements of a missional family with verification of how the initiative worked to mobilize the families according to these elements. Read further and rejoice with us in our testimony of thinking kingdom and being family.

Part I

The Redemptive Family

―――∽∞∾―――

Overview

P art One surveys the literature undergirding theories, principles, paradigms, models, and outcomes related to family studies, the missional family concept, such a family's being and doing, and missional family wholeness. It also gathers insights that I have gathered from missional-minded families. The potential for identifying elements of missional families and a model for mobilizing them in The Think Kingdom–Be Family Project (TKBF) is based upon the principles and paradigms of a family's being and doing, and the process of developing families in missional wholeness.

This present summary of literature and insight from families with a missional mindset begins with family social theory, a realm of research that is continuously evolving. Perspectives vary on the definition, function, and future of the family. Through these perspectives, there are lines of thought that can be traced toward the development of a redemptive vision for family.

Part One's focus is primarily a sociological context for connecting family studies to the missional family, and Part Two's context is primarily a biblical, practical theological, and historical one. Together, there is a progression from general revelation to special revelation, tracing truth from family social theory to scripture in order to conceptualize the redemptive family.

This redemptive vision, rooted in the hope of the kingdom of God, is an all-encompassing way of living in God's family and engaging the world. The heart of being missional is sharing fellowship with God in His mission. As families embrace their brokenness on a path toward redemption and wholeness, they can become instrumental testimonies of redemption for others. Thus, an outcome for Part One is to position TKBF as a redemptive family initiative.

Chapter 1

Survey of Family Studies

———— ✐✐✐ ————

Family theory is a pursuit that is shaped by a goal to advance or establish understanding. James M. White and David M. Klein, in *Family Theories*, describe its two trajectories:

> The issue is whether emancipation is the central aim of a theory (ideology) or whether the central aim is the production of knowledge (science). If the central role of theory is knowledge, then clearly knowledge claims must be judged by a set of criteria that is universally and equally applied to all such claims. . .The fear of scientists is that if claims support the ideology, then they will be judged true because they are consistent with the ideology. One of the basic canons of science is that mere consistency of a finding with previous beliefs is insufficient to justify a claim. If such were the case, then findings would only need to support the prevailing ideology or 'common sense'. . .In brief, knowledge may be emancipatory, but one of the criteria of knowledge should not be whether or not it is emancipatory.[72]

---

[72] James M. White and David M. Klein, *Family Theories*, 3rd ed. (Los Angeles: Sage, 2008), 202.

41

As already stated, more than a scientific finding or an ideological polemic, mobilizing the missional family has a redemptive aim. In one sense, there is hope for families (emancipation), and in another sense, there is understanding to be established (knowledge). In a greater sense, there is a mission in view that begins with God, who shares it with His creation, including families. This chapter reviews aspects of the body of knowledge within family social theory. Such knowledge can be an asset to families participating in the mission of God. It aims at convergence for the family rather than a mere intellectual or ideological pursuit.

One initial challenge encountered in seeking to mobilize a missional family is defining a missional family. There is ongoing dialogue among family social science theorists as they strive for a definition of family. Seeking to define a missional family must refrain from being arbitrary and overly simplistic, while at the same time settling on a certain degree of understanding in order to move forward without being consumed by a circuitous debate. Sufficient engagement and participation with the discussion can both inform and establish such understanding. Regarding a definition of family, one must reckon with the vastness of human experience, both good and bad. Otherwise, any attempt to focus on a missional family runs the risk of being irrelevant for those on the outside of an unintentional but implicitly narrow definition.

To this end, a basic review of current thought from family studies is itself daunting. There are multiple perspectives and varying opinions. White and Klein summarize three philosophical frameworks to approaching the family as the positivist, interpretive, and critical views.[73] A positivist view seeks to explain and predict "family phenomena and events;" an interpretive view seeks understanding and empathy; a critical view aims for "emancipation and empowerment of oppressed social groups."[74] In positivism, the accepted methods are the keys for separating more and less "adequate

---

[73]   White, 4.

[74]   Ibid.

claims about families." The interpretive view is more "relativistic and reflexive," depending on the meanings assigned by family members, taking into account their particular contexts. The critical philosophy examines how those in power shape understanding for their own purposes.[75]

With positivism, "most current formulations argue a less absolute position in terms of truth and objectivity." For the interpretive view, "'truth' is relative" to the specific family member's understanding. In the critical view, "theories that acquire 'truth' status are those that support and maintain the prevailing power system."[76]

White and Klein's survey of current family social theories reveals ambiguity in the field. They examine each theory's strengths and weaknesses, and they make no attempt to refute or validate any particular theory. They advance the discussion by "bringing together elements of each" theory, depending on what perspective is needed or approach called for. In their view, this "connectedness" is actually one of the "functions of theory."[77] There is a sense that family social theory is driven, like communities themselves according to the critical view, by those who hold the power within this scientific system.

With that said, the multiple theories reveal important avenues for analysis and reflection. Similarly, the hope for a redemptive approach to family can utilize various perspectives to serve and strengthen families. This redemptive approach advocates from a perspective of design and purpose, avoiding a sole basis of methodology, subjective meanings, or human power. The goal is restoration to this design and purpose. Still, it is vital that this redemptive approach benefit from the wisdom present in current family studies.

The perspectives on defining family are a good place to begin. For White and Klein, there are four distinctive

---

[75]   White, 4.

[76]   Ibid.

[77]   Ibid., 15.

characteristics of family as a group compared to other types of groups:

1. Families last for a considerably longer period of time than do most other social groups.
2. Families are intergenerational.
3. Families contain both biological and affinal (e.g., legal, common law) relationships between members.
4. The biological (and affinal) aspect of families links them to a larger kinship organization.[78]

They further note the basis of "methodological individualism" in critiquing microsocial exchange theories. This refers to "the assumption that the individual is the appropriate unit to study to gain an understanding of the family. . .there has never been a definition of the family as simply an aggregation of individuals."[79] The caution is that a hyper-individual focus in defining the nature of a family can treat families like other groups, but the aforementioned distinctives serve to dissuade such an analytical combination.[80] In addition to family social theorists seeking to define the family, this caution related to an over-focus on individuals applies to a missional way of being family as explained in later sections.

The characteristics provided by White and Klein are represented and emphasized to varying degrees through the perspectives compiled by editor Barbara Settles and company in *Concepts and Definitions of Family for the 21st Century*.[81] James Holstein and Jay Gubrium take a "social constructionist approach," where the goal for "the objective truth" is deferred to "a social process by which 'family,' as a social form, is

---

[78] White, 17-18.

[79] Ibid., 88.

[80] Ibid.

[81] Barbara Settles, eds., et al., *Concepts and Definitions of Family for the 21st Century* (New York: The Haworth Press, Inc.).

brought into being as a matter of social practice."[82] In drawing a line between objective truth and social reality, the aim of a social constructionist approach establishes "an interpretive vocabulary, a set of conceptual resources for *accomplishing* the meaning of social bonds. Concretely. . .making family an interactional achievement."[83] This perspective discovers family "in the way family is *used,* not in conventional or idealized social forms," emphasizing "interaction as mediating family meaning and domestic reality."[84] In the context of the debate over definition, their conclusion is that "the constructionist view, in effect, levels the playing field, but without necessarily taking sides."[85]

The social constructionist approach diffuses some tension by choosing function over form. It also provides a helpful focus on the action, or *doing* of family in the context of its relationships. By design, it takes intellectual engagement to interface with all sorts of realities of family. In a society where the only family norm is diversity in experience, this flexibility is helpful. For a widely diverse collection of families looking for a common goal to move toward, this approach may be found lacking.

A goal might be thought of as what people mean when they indicate their desire for a family. Certainly, an initial perception of many declaring such intent would include marriage and children. Yet there are those in the debate that question this common understanding of family.

Whether thought of as an objective institution or viewed through subjective constructionist lenses, nobody can deny that the concept of family is as ancient a reality that humankind has ever known. It is ironic that such an enduring

---

[82]   James A. Holstein and Jay Gubrium, "What Is Family? Further Thoughts on A Social Constructionist Approach," in *Concepts and Definitions of Family for the 21st Century,* eds. Barbara Settles, et al. [New York: The Haworth Press, Inc., 1999], 3-4.

[83]   Settles et al., 5.

[84]   Ibid., 7.

[85]   Ibid., 17.

relationship remains elusive for those seeking a consensus of definition. Shlomo Sharlin comments that the flexibility in "the absence of a clear definition" in the midst of "our struggle to understand it. . .might help us account for the survival of the oldest institution on earth."[86] Flexibility is more than a default dynamic that ensures survival; it can reflect the strength of the design and redemptive potential for the family in the face of brokenness.

For some, the reality of brokenness is reason enough to dismiss a traditional definition of family. John F. Peters cites family dysfunction as one reason for turning away from previous definitions. The other reasons he cites include the dispelling of myths rooted in North American family culture; the radical change in family authority structures; experiences with family that have changed; the development of gender perception; including the co-laboring of men and women in workplaces outside the home; changes in law, and the focus on the individual over the collective whole.[87] This evidence is so compelling to Peters that he advocates abandoning the term "family" altogether.[88]

Peters offers the following criteria for establishing a new definition of family: "self-perception," "public perception," "law," and "history and tradition," which at a minimum is to include "recent history."[89] The subjective and localized nature of such criteria is striking. It is not surprising that the best hope Peters can anticipate in forging into new territory is "ambiguity" and the possibility for a better definition "at some point in the future."[90] Additionally, in his deconstructive

---

[86] Shlomo A. Sharlin, "The Family in Jewish Tradition," in *Concepts and Definitions of Family for the 21ˢᵗ Century*, eds. Barbara Settles, et al. [New York: The Haworth Press, Inc., 1999], 53.

[87] John F. Peters, "Redefining Western Families," in *Concepts and Definitions of Family for the 21ˢᵗ Century*, eds. Barbara Settles, et al. [New York: The Haworth Press, Inc.], 60-61.

[88] Settles et al., 61.

[89] Ibid., 64.

[90] Ibid., 65.

approach, the absence of function in terms of the benefits a family offers to itself and others seems noteworthy. A brief survey indicates the existence of such definitions that focus on the support a family can offer to itself; however, the family as a unique community for exercising benevolence to those outside remains out of view in the discussion.[91]

Jon Bernardes goes further than Peters in arguing that sociologists must refrain altogether from defining "The Family," because in doing so "they act upon society."[92] Such action carries the weight of understanding of roles and expectations of differing views for family actualization and function. This is why he declines usage of "The Nuclear Family," and instead believes "a family" or "family" itself is a safer rendering of the term for discussion.[93]

Bernardes acknowledges that some scholars choose the alternative "concept of "household," which reflects more of an extended and functional grouping of people.[94] Sociologists are not alone in seeing family as an extended grouping of individuals. Marvin R. Wilson offers biblical historical background in his book, *Our Father Abraham: Jewish Roots of the Christian Faith.* By looking at the ancient Hebraic community, he indicates a broader expression, in both form and function, than the immediate family (or nuclear family). A self-contained lifestyle in housing and activity typically characterizes the perceived North American experience of family.

Relating to the form, Marvin Wilson explains that the term for family in Hebrew, מִשְׁפָּחָה (*mishpahah*), "does not include only the nuclear family of mother, father, and children, but implied

---

91   Ruth Flexman, Debra Berke, and Barbara Settles, "Negotiating Family: The Interface Between Family and Support Groups," in *Concepts and Definitions of Family for the 21st Century*, eds. Barbara Settles, et al. [New York: The Haworth Press, Inc., 1999], 176.

92   Jon Bernardes, "We Must Not Define 'The Family'!," in *Concepts and Definitions of Family for the 21st Century*, eds. Barbara Settles, et al. [New York: The Haworth Press, Inc., 1999], 22.

93   Settles et al., 22-23.

94   Ibid., 31.

an extended family or clan. It often refers to a whole social unit including parents, children, grandparents, aunts, uncles, and cousins."[95] Sharlin further notes that the Hebrew term בַּיִת (*bayit*), which is translated as "house," is descriptive of a "subdivision of '*mishpahah*;'" and the extension of understanding does not only go in a smaller direction, because "the 'house of Israel' was considered to be an extension of the family. In fact, the root of the word '*mishpahah*' means to incorporate or to bind together, and, as such, the concept of family was rather loosely defined."[96]

As another example to broaden understanding of the family, the Chinese culture echoes the extended nature and sense of identity that the individual has through their family as a community. This is noted by Philip Brown, who explains that until recent times, "the ideal family in China has included several children and at least three generations under one roof, as well as a collateral kin webbed together in a network of mutual support.[97] Individual identity went in the order of "family member first, a community member second, and an individual only third."[98]

Regarding established definitions of family in the minds of people, Settles acknowledges that sociological scholarship is "doomed to failure to communicate a new understanding of families outside our modest group unless we deal with these prior meanings."[99] She offers interdisciplinary collaboration as a possibility in study and scholarship that will be helpful in refining definition.[100] Along these lines, collaboration between

---

[95]   Wilson, 210.

[96]   Settles et al., 44.

[97]   Philip M. Brown and John S. Shalett, *Cross-Cultural Practice With Couples and Families* (New York: The Haworth Press, Inc., 1997), 36.

[98]   Brown, 36.

[99]   Barbara H. Settles, "Definitions of the Family: Professional and Personal Issues," in *Concepts and Definitions of Family for the 21st Century*, eds. Barbara Settles, et al. [New York: The Haworth Press, Inc., 1999], 220.

[100] Settles et al., 220.

sociological and biblical theological scholarship can be helpful. The latter can establish paradigms and principles that are not subject to the frantic and rapid rate of change in the 21st Century. The former restrains theologians from articulating views that do not reckon with the brokenness and changes society as a whole is experiencing. Collaboration rather than resistance to one another might also allow for both to consider the untapped discussion of how families of all sorts have the unique possibility of serving others.

Paul Hiebert's work is an illustration of such collaboration with a missional thrust. With the backdrop of a biblical world-view, he sees "biblical anthropological theology" as the result of collaboratively answering "questions about God's purpose, design, and intention. . .in which observations about humans and their societies illumine how we understand Scripture."[101] Both synchronistic theory, which is reflected in anthropology and systematic theology as they examine "the structure and function of reality," and diachronic theory, which is reflected in biblical theology that focuses on "the story and end of particular realities," are essential to the task. Hiebert asserts that "more meaning is found in diachronic than in synchronic understandings of reality."[102]

Sociology and a synchronic approach to theology together study the structure and function of family in order to ascertain reality. Perhaps this is why there is so much conflict in drawing reductive and definitive lines around the family. In contrast, there is significant potential for the contribution to be made between a sociological collaboration with a diachronic approach to theology. In short, the study of family as a story informs and redemptively expands understanding and application of both the structure and function of family.

Hiebert acknowledges systematic theological reaction to liberalism and notes that "in doing so they have been forced into an idealist epistemology that absolutizes ideas over

---

[101] Paul G. Hiebert, *Anthropological Reflections on Missiological Issues* (Grand Rapids: Baker Books, 1994), 11-12.

[102] Hiebert, 12.

historical realities."[103] This does not mean that biblical and systematic theologians are in disagreement. They may, "in fact, agree on the contents of theological truth but disagree on the epistemological nature of theology."[104] Hiebert then gives the following admonition, which is essential for unity that leads to mission:

> As evangelicals, we need to distinguish episte-
> mological issues from theological ones so that
> we do not waste our energies and so that we
> can work toward a resolution of our differences
> without misguidedly attacking a brother or
> sister. We need to guard against heresy. We also
> need to carry out the mission Christ has given
> us in this lost and broken world.[105]

Perhaps a more effective way to guard the truth is to carry out the mission of the Truth. The tension that this requires may bring about the proper fullness of both. Such a combination may move the family out of a neglected state into a redemptive one.

A Redemptive Family

In closing this section, it is helpful to envision the family in light of the Creator's design, primarily through a diachronic theological understanding, while reckoning with the vast work and opinion represented in family social theory. Conceptualizing the redemptive family advances the discussion accordingly. The redemptive family is a definition of family that is both based in and fulfilled in its origin – unified

---

[103] Hiebert, 31.

[104] Ibid., 32.

[105] Ibid., 34.

with their Creator and one another, reflecting His image and carrying out His mission on the earth.[106]

This redemptive process is one that must be flexible because of the reality of sin, which began following the creation narrative and continues to ravage the cohesiveness of relational unity and purpose for families today. A redemptive theory embraces approaches from family theories that are helpful for connecting to particular circumstances for families. A redemptive theory also proceeds beyond engagement with the family toward wholeness, in which mission is integrated as a lifestyle. This development in wholeness and sense of mission is uniquely shaped by the brokenness experienced by families. Yet even greater is the grace experienced by God to bring healing from the brokenness.

A redemptive theory provides a definition for family that is rooted in design, though now distorted, but with a vision for once again reflecting that design. Jack and Judith Balswick identify the design as a reflection of the Creator; thus trinitarian relationality is the foundation for their "integrated model of family relationships:"[107]

> Foundational to all interactions, regardless of the family structure, are the biblical relationship principles of covenant (establishing trust, belonging, and security); grace (living in a constant state of acceptance and forgiveness); empowerment (building one another up to reach God-given potential); mutual interdependence (differentiated unity); and intimacy

---

[106] From the Introduction and reiterated in Part Two, this understanding is extended to families from the broader contexts of the people of God in the Old Testament and the church in the New Testament.

[107] Jack O. Balswick and Judith K. Balswick, *The Family: A Christian Perspective on the Contemporary Home*, 3d ed. (Grand Rapids: Baker Academic, 2007), 11.

(communicating in ways that establish deep connections and intimate sharing among members).[108]

Note the important qualification, "regardless of the family structure," making this appeal to design flexible for the fractured condition of the family. A redemptive vision at once has its footing in the design for family while extending its hand into the contemporary reality of family. Therefore, a redemptive theory embraces the necessary processes, described and detailed in family theory study, that support a redemptive definition and purpose for family.

For the Balswicks, this necessarily includes "family-systems theory because it views family life not merely as the sum total of the actions of all the individual members but rather as the interactions of all family member operating as a unit of interrelated parts." This offers a valuable approach in a culture where ministry to families often focuses on its individual members. "It considers individuals in the context of their relationships."[109]

The family systems framework has aided family therapy, communication, and interaction.[110] A redemptive vision for families through this framework initially depends on the family "system that operates on a morphogenetic level," which means the family "is capable of generating or creating new ways of responding to the situation."[111] Limitations to such change include systems that are "overly rigid" or "chaotically structured with few rules or boundaries."[112] Ultimately, redemptive fulfillment for a family depends on "the highest level" of "reorientation," where "the family changes its entire

---

[108] Balswick, 320.

[109] Ibid., 37.

[110] White, 175.

[111] Balswick, 41.

[112] Ibid.

goal."[113] Hence, a developmental and redemptive process toward wholeness for families as missional units emerges in the convergence of these levels: "In morphogenesis new ways of responding are generated, whereas in reorientation the goals themselves are changed. Reorientation involves a dramatic change in family life in which the entire system is converted to new ways of thinking and behaving."[114]

The other theory that factors into the Balswicks' work is "family-development theory, which views the family as developing over time through natural life-cycle stages.[115] For instance, the focus on family "as a 'group' of interactive individuals and organized by social norms" makes family development theory useful in a redemptive approach. This process is particularly helpful due to its unique emphasis on time and change.[116] Studying the family through time is "multi-dimensional" regarding the various moments, seasons, and life experiences, which "are commonly understood 'markers' on the family life course calendar because they happen to most families over time."[117] Family development theory can support a family discerning its redemptive story, because "the family process dimension of time is critical to understanding and explaining family change because it provides the marker events. . .for analyses."[118]

The Balswicks integrate both the systems and developmental theories in order to derive four areas that are characteristic of strong families: "cohesion, adaptability, communication, and role structure."[119] "Cohesion refers to the degree of emotional closeness existing in a family. . .a strong

---

[113]   Balswick, 43.

[114]   Ibid.

[115]   White, 175.

[116]   Ibid., 122-123.

[117]   Ibid., 128.

[118]   Ibid.

[119]   Balswick, 46-47.

sense of belonging."[120] Adaptability consists of "flexibility and stability," which "mark the orderly family."[121] In communication, the Balswicks identify the foundation as "clarity of perception and clarity of expression."[122] The last of their four inter-related concepts is boundaries in roles that are "clear but permeable."[123] A redemptive family is moving toward wholeness from brokenness, so it follows that these four characteristics develop in their being and doing.

Another relevant theory in family studies is found in the conflict framework, which deals with the self-interest, inevitability, and management of conflict within families.[124] Conflict certainly characterizes not only the broken condition of family, but it also is present as families begin to move toward wholeness, leaving behind broken patterns and conditions to embrace redemption. As "class consciousness and conflict is a necessary and inevitable part of the process of extinguishing class conflict itself,"[125] so conflict is a part of the process for redemptive families.

Marriage is "the foundation of family life."[126] A variety of fractured realities in family life can be traced back to a breakdown in this union. Within a redemptive theory for families, there is hope both for families finding a way forward where a healthy marriage is missing and where one is present.

Again, marriage originates in a design that reflects the nature of the Creator. As the Balswicks explain, "The *relationality* between the distinct human beings (male and female) reflects the *imago Dei*–the image of God."[127] This image-bearing leads to an expression of purpose as "both spouses. . .become

---

[120]   Balswick, 47.

[121]   Ibid., 50.

[122]   Ibid., 51.

[123]   Ibid., 52.

[124]   White, 184.

[125]   Ibid., 202.

[126]   Balswick, 55.

[127]   Ibid., 80.

something bigger in their union. . .both distinct (male and female differentiation) and equal (directed to be fruitful and have dominion) in their created purpose."[128]

Marriage is a place for this expression along with other human relationships. A redemptive approach to family seeks to restore a reflection of God's image within the family as relationality compels purpose. Thus, missional reality depends upon relationality, which ultimately rests in the reality of God Himself. Because redemption is possible through the identity and mission of God, there is hope for broken families of all kinds.

In returning to the tension referenced at the outset between the aim of theory being ideology (emancipation) or science (knowledge), a redemptive approach ushers in a perspective that raises the aim from the way a family exists to why the family lives. Truth (knowledge) brings freedom (emancipation) when Truth is the Creator, not merely an ideology. Both knowledge and emancipation are means to the end in the way of this redemptive purpose.

---

[128] Balswick, 81.

Chapter 2

Missional Family Theory

———— ∞∞∞ ————

A metaphorical framework for understanding the missional family as a social system is provided by Alan and Debra Hirsch in their book, *Untamed: Reactivating a Missional Form of Discipleship*. Drawing from a contrast in farming practices, they note two approaches for gathering livestock. One way is to build fences. When the territory is too large for fencing, another approach is to dig a well. In the latter case, "it is assumed that. . .as long as there is a supply of clean water, the livestock will remain close by."[129] It follows that there are churches and families that can be established by fences, "the bounded set," or by a well, "the centered set." The former "has clearly delineated boundaries but no strong ideological center. It is therefore hard at the edges and soft at the center."[130] The latter has "a very clear ideology and vision at the center, but have no real boundaries that people have to cross to in order to join. . .hard at the center and soft at the edges."[131]

By comparing this approach to Jesus' ministry, which "was a rich intersection of relationships, with some nearer the center and others farther away, but all were openly invited to

---

[129] Alan Hirsch and Debra Hirsch, *Untamed: Reactivating a Missional Form of Discipleship* (Grand Rapids: Baker Books, 2010), 152.

[130] Hirsch 152.

[131] Ibid., 153.

join in the kingdom-building enterprise" . . .there is a "sense of belonging before believing."[132] Put another way, a missional family's Christ-centered fellowship can be magnetic toward outsiders, embracing them where they are while introducing them to the well of "living water" (John 4:10).

A healthy family reaches beyond its boundaries. More pointedly to the nature of the family's life as a whole (both inward and outward), the Balswicks argue that "the greatest evidence of strong family spirituality can be seen in the way families reach out to minister to the needs of others."[133] Reggie McNeal concurs that holistic maturity in family life develops "through service."[134] This dynamic integrated into a family, from goals in raising children to a general lifestyle of reaching out to others, is articulated in what it means to be missional.

Missional theory is a "kingdom missiology."[135] The interaction between family theory and missiological understanding is synthesized in the perspective of "the kingdom of God."[136] The mission is God's, and it is a process of engaging people in their "beliefs and lives" and to "gently lead them to truth and righteousness."[137] "Fruitful mission" is as basic as "good neighborliness" and "being a blessing."[138]

What makes the engagement gentle is an understanding of God's presence at work in a broad approach to discipleship. Alan and Debra Hirsch explain that from a missional perspective all believers have discipleship responsibility; and discipleship activity is broader than Christian circles or religious activities, including "pre-conversion disciples on the

---

[132]   Hirsch, 154.

[133]   Balswick, 155.

[134]   Reggie McNeal, *Missional Renaissance: Changing the Scorecard for the Church* (San Francisco: Jossey-Bass, 2009), 100, 105-106.

[135]   S. Karotemprel, eds., et al., *Following Christ in Mission* (Boston: Pauline Books & Media, 1996), 100.

[136]   Hiebert, 14.

[137]   Ibid., 14.

[138]   David W. Shenk, *God's Call To Mission* (Scottdale, PA: Herald Press, 1994), 31.

journey."[139] Missional discipleship focuses on leading people to become more like Jesus from where they are, whether it is a small or large step toward Christ. The work of conversion is God's, which frees believers "to disciple everyone who comes into our orbit of influence–it's that simple."[140]

Again, it is important to guard against striving by focusing on discipleship that flows from being into doing. It is worth noting that the doing of missional activity aims first at redeeming the being of those in need. Steve Corbett and Brian Fikkert explain that helping those impoverished must first address their "poverty of being." [141]

Dualism is an indicator that missional performance based upon human strength has supplanted missional being based on God's presence. When a family compartmentalizes their life, not only can a sacred and secular dichotomy develop, but a handful of disconnected areas become symptomatic. For instance, there may be a recreation compartment, which does not really connect to the church sphere, which is also separate from involvement in education. Then the work responsibilities for the parents and older children can burden all of these areas. When friends are factored in, there are school friends, church friends, neighborhood friends, and of course, family, but the overlap is minimal if at all. Adding volunteering or works of charity to the picture is one more ball among many that a family must attempt to juggle. As a result, balls are dropped. Understandably, the family becomes weary, an effect of idolatry.

In response to this weariness, families attempt to preserve their fragile sense of togetherness in such a fragmented world. The Hirsches note how this "highly protective" fortress mentality as a reaction to "cultural pressure and stress,"

---

[139]   Hirsch, 151-152.

[140]   Ibid., 147.

[141]   Steve Corbett and Brian Fikkert, *When Helping Hurts: How To Alleviate Poverty Without Hurting The Poor And Yourself* (Chicago: Moody Publishers, 2012), 61.

has "effectively become a pernicious idol."[142] One expression of what can ensue is an apparent virtuous stand on behalf of the family, both privately in a family's isolated lifestyle and publicly in the church's political allegiance to the family. The Hirsches caution against a misdirected loyalty:

> . . .the problem is that we find ourselves defending a non-biblical ideal of family. . .our homes should be places where people can experience a foretaste of heaven, when the church is rightly viewed as a community of the redeemed from all walks of life (Revelation 21). Instead, our fears restrict us from letting go of the control and safety we have spent years cultivating. . .This culture of fear is totally inconsistent with Jesus' redemptive vision of the kingdom of God.[143]

In contrast, "the word *missional* should describe the normal mode of the believer's life, living like a *missionary* at all times."[144] Being missional is a unifying vision that is infused into each compartment of a family's life. Rather than defaulting to idolatry through disjointed living or a fearful retreat, a missional family actually deepens their experience of worship through all the activities and relationships that define their life.

Stetzer and Nation focus on the household of God as a key to missional theory:

> . . .the household image sets the stage for both our intimate relation to the Father and the continuation of His sovereign work on earth as we are heirs of His kingdom. This helps us understand the divine mission within the

---

[142]   Hirsch, 166-167.

[143]   Ibid., 167-168.

[144]   Stetzer, 91.

relationships we have with one another as a family. . .As modern believers delve into what it means to be members of God's household, the responsibility to fulfill the Father's desires becomes clear.[145]

The Hirsches summarize: "While *missionally* we need to live incarnationally among a distinctive group of people, *theologically* we need to see the church as a very big, massively extended family. These two aspects ought to be held in creative tension."[146] Out of this tension, the church family's being and doing takes shape. Rather than being ensnared with "defending truths" that are objectively and collectively held, in which the church could "miss Truth–just like the Pharisees," there is another way. It's all about how we *inhabit* our beliefs and how we allow the power of our beliefs to inhabit or mold us."[147]

A family's integration of a missional lifestyle within the context of the family of God is like a type of thread that can go through multiple sizes and types of garments. The thread itself may be used in different patterns, but its make-up is consistent no matter where it is applied. Missional family living can be lived out in as many different ways as there are families, but the heart of God consistently compels all the expressions.

Jan Johnson focuses on the integration of this missional thread into raising children: "Our challenge is to teach children to be *process-oriented* not *product-oriented*."[148] Helen Lee, in *The Missional Mom*, casts parenthood into a bigger perspective by describing "missional motherhood:" "we invest in our children to help them see the big picture, the greater purpose

---

[145]   Stetzer, 128.

[146]   Hirsch, 171.

[147]   Ibid., 223.

[148]   Jan Johnson, *Growing Compassionate Kids: Helping Kids See Beyond Their Backyard* (Nashville: Upper Room Books®, 2011), 8.

to which God is calling our sons and daughters."[149] To this end Johnson encourages parents to incorporate compassion into routine conversations: "When compassion is woven into mundane moments of life, kids don't become adults who find being compassionate odd outside the walls of the church."[150]

A process-orientation can instill in children a trust in God for the sake of others rather than for their own sakes alone. Johnson explains, "Not knowing the outcomes of our actions enhances the nature of service as a spiritual discipline–we learn to trust God for the results."[151] The others in view provide a vivid reminder, for parents and children alike, for why mission is necessary. For example, the thousands of children who die daily from preventable diseases come from families–"at heart, it's a family issue. Each of those kids has a brokenhearted parent or two."[152]

Maturity in children "entails the capacity to contribute in a positive and constructive way to the good of others."[153] A parent-child relationship can become inward-focused as parents simply wish to maintain closeness to their children. From a missional perspective, the parent-child relationship is a formational one that benefits others. Lee explains, "Missional churches understand that when children serve with their parents, these children begin to embrace missional values at a young age."[154]

The Balswicks connect maturity for children to a biblical pattern, which underscores that an outward focus for the parent-child relationship actually enhances that relationship:

---

[149]   Helen Lee, *The Missional Mom: Living With Purpose At Home & In The World* (Chicago: Moody Publishers, 2011), 26.

[150]   Johnson, 62.

[151]   Ibid., 9.

[152]   Ibid.

[153]   Balswick, 104.

[154]   Lee, 172.

Parenting that empowers children to maturity is conceptually similar to the New Testament depiction of discipleship. Jesus gathered and trained disciples, empowering them in turn to. . .'make disciples'. . .Parenting follows a similar course. The ultimate reward for parents and children is a relationship that grows into maturity so that when children have been empowered, they will in turn empower others.[155]

The missional family is more than a theological construct and a process-oriented way of living. It is connecting with God as a family, through the family of God, and loving others as He does. The mission is to restore, rescue, and enlighten through the Word of God, which offers hope to "voiceless people."[156] As parents empower their children and churches empower their families, this reflects the pattern of Jesus. He "routinely put ordinary, voiceless people in power-up positions."[157] In other words, He served them. Missional families walk with God in serving others.

---

[155] Balswick, 121.

[156] Johnson, 27.

[157] Ibid.

Chapter 3

Missional Family Portraits

⸺ ∞∞∞ ⸺

A traditional family portrait is taken from a point in time. The peripheral activity and noise before and after the photograph are left for the imagination. The focus is on the impression and togetherness of a moment in the family story. The portraits of missional families in this chapter are of a different sort. The peripheral processes of a family's life are the focus rather than a staged moment at any given time. Missional families seek storied living more than to portray an image.

This section is the result of an ongoing dialogue with missional-minded families.[158] The "pictures" in these family albums embody the missional family concept from the previous chapters. The stories begin and end in God's story rather than the family. As such, these are partial portraits of families to help paint a broader picture of the varied and unified expression of what it means to be a missional family.

From the perspectives of these families, three foundational components emerge: the proper flow from being to doing, an incarnational reality to relationships and experiences, and a culture of grace that fosters having hope and seeking to bless others out of their own brokenness. These components

---

[158] Some names have been changed for confidentiality. Months are used instead of exact dates when interaction has been more ongoing. All interviews and names are used by permission.

are understood within the unique expression of the following families.

Consider the Weber family. Ed Weber synthesizes his family life through three interconnected elements:

> There are three elements to living a gospel-centric family life: Identity, Mission, and Rhythms. These are linked and flow naturally in progression. First, we need to understand our gospel identity. . .We are loved by the Father, forgiven by the Son, and empowered by the Holy Spirit. This gospel identity must lead us to mission. And the mission, in its simplest terms, is spreading that gospel identity to those around us.[159]

Within this description of a "gospel-centric family life," it is evident that doing flows from being, originating with God's own being. The Weber family's being is expressed as their identity. The doing of mission for them is essentially sharing with others their family's being.

Dave Witmer distills the following principle from his family's missional experience: "Make a *family sacrifice together* for God, not a *sacrifice of the family* for God."[160] The former reflects a reality of a family being in mission before God. The latter serves as a warning to be heeded: families that get lost in doing, even missional doing, can lose their family and the very fellowship from which the blessing itself flows.

In a Father's Day sermon where the two grown Witmer daughters reflect on what a dad can give them, Jenni offers the following encouragement to dads: "Rather than focusing on what you can do with your daughter, ask, what can I be for her."[161] All of this resonates with the understanding of the

---

[159] Ed Weber, interview by author, September – October, 2012.

[160] Dave Witmer, interview by author, September – October, 2012.

[161] Witmer, interview.

Weber family that their identity in Christ is what they actually share as a blessing to others.

Sadly, the tales of families sacrificed on the altar of doing abound. One of these stories belongs to Ronald Parker, whose missional family has been shaped, ironically, from the brokenness he experienced growing up internationally in a missionary family. Ronald's dad was consumed with the busyness of mission work. In the void left at home, the family suffered. His mom battled depression and debilitating loneliness, which left her susceptible to deep struggles related to her identity as a wife, mother, and woman. Ronald's siblings faced significant struggles, and one of them to this day resists God's faithfulness. Ronald himself turned to the pornography he first discovered from a friend at the missionary children's school. This began a journey that ensnared him for many years into his adulthood and his own marriage.

Ronald and his wife then spent years with their own children on the foreign field. Under the pressures of the mission work, they discovered a culture of grace when the "worst aspects of themselves" surfaced. They received help from others that helped them embrace the brokenness, and it has brought a freedom to their identity that actually frees them to enter a missional life of being and doing as a family. Ronald now continues to serve God while holding out a vision for families to be missional.[162]

Missional family life is organic and integrated around a collective sense of vision, purpose, and core values. Families may articulate their vision and values when sharing their story with others. Whether or not they verbally communicate their collective mission, missional families display their vision and values through their lifestyles. It is good for families to regularly reflect upon their purpose in age-specific terminology.

Such reflection about purpose requires time. Missional families value their stewardship of time. They live intentionally, which differs from those victimized by the fast-paced, early-to-rise-late-to-bed, non-stop society that surrounds

---

[162] Ronald Parker, interview by author, October 4, 2012.

them. Rather than seeking balance in life, Dave Witmer proposes a mindset that seeks fullness.[163] Missional families may have very full schedules, but if the energy output is to flow from being, then there will also be intentional rest, reflection, and renewal within their schedules.

Kevin Strite believes that "families are not operating with discernment to make decisions on schedule based upon a missional mindset. This is a major scheme of the enemy."[164] His family's mission includes the adoption of a child from China as well as a child with special needs. They planted a church with a vision to restore "biblical families," which Kevin further describes as "reclaiming family and empowering households to change the world."[165]

One of the core values of their church, which is another core directive reflected in missional families, is intergenerational relationships.[166] This is a value that reflects the paradigm of the incarnational reality in families. The mission itself has depth because of the synergy of intergenerational relationships. The energy of the young combines with the wisdom of the aged.

Another core directive for missional families is the motivation for educating their children. Educational choices for missional families value others through the discipleship of their children. The Witmer family chose public education because of the opportunity to influence others with the light of Jesus. Both of the Witmer daughters grew to know and love God, initiating fellowship and ministry along the way while being schooled in a secular context. Dave Witmer, a pastor and church planter, reflects that "the years of church planting in public school auditoriums had taught our girls that spiritual life could be established anywhere, not just in religious buildings." He also remembers his daughter, Jenni, giving her

---

[163] Dave Witmer, interview.

[164] Kevin Strite, interview by author, October 15, 2012.

[165] Kevin Strite, interview.

[166] Ibid.

testimony of following Jesus in her salutatorian address in her public school.[167]

The Myer family has homeschooled, and they now engage a model of education that combines traditional and home education.[168] The Strite family also homeschools. Kevin Strite and his family chose this route once he came to the realization that his "primary role as a father was to bring his children up in a vibrant, real, and passionate faith."[169] At the same time, he cautions that in his church of mostly homeschooling families, they face hurdles with their families having tendencies toward inwardness, over-emphasizing a particular methodology of schooling, and focusing on the outward behaviors and standards.

The missional-minded families interviewed include those that engage homeschooling, public schooling, or traditional Christian schooling. The families are aware of the challenges that each approach presents, and they face those relationally with their children. While their exact choices of form do not unite these families, their motivation for mission as families and a sense of responsibility to watch over the education of their children, is consistent throughout these families.

The stewardship of time, intergenerational relationships, and motivations for education are examples of core directives in missional families. There are more. Families do not begin by writing these down in order to live them out. Missional families are incarnational before they are institutional. However, when it comes to synthesizing the values of their lifestyles, the family leaders participating in these interviews clearly expressed the ideas evident from their experiences.

Another core directive featured is how missional families engage church. They are all active in a local church. Yet within their stories of missional living, they hope that the church will equip them but not overrun their schedules. The families are

---

[167]   Dave Witmer, interview.

[168]   Allan Myer, interview by author, September 20, 2012.

[169]   Kevin Strite, interview.

not dependent upon church for contexts of ministry, but they do look to the teaching and fellowship with other families to be a compelling influence in their family's mission. In this it appears that churches seeking to be relational and less programmatic associate with the strength of missional families, while highly programmed and age-segregated ministry forms can hinder families from being missional. This can keep families busy doing what appears good while sacrificing their family, and subsequently, the blessing of others.

Communication dynamics within these mission-focused families resonate with the characteristics of coaching. Conversations that cultivate creativity, collaboration, vulnerability, and encouragement bring a freedom to grow rather than perform. Dave Witmer believes their family's communication was blessed by observing the following principles:

- Talk often about the why of mission decisions parents make
- Include children in decisions of carrying out mission, not necessarily the decision to do mission
- Nurture your kids' self-esteem, that according to God's view of their value they can be world changers
- Discipline your comments about what they are doing right on a 7:1 ratio to comments about what they're doing wrong[170]

Dave's daughters reflect that humility in conversation between children and their father cultivates "personal sacrifice that communicates worth, concern that demonstrates love, [and] support that builds trust."[171]

Ronald Parker believes that mission flows from brokenness; thus it is essential that families be honest about their struggles and shortcomings.[172] Often such failures emerge

---

[170]   Dave Witmer, interview.

[171]   Ibid.

[172]   Ronald Parker, interview.

in the midst of the mission itself. The Myer family left to be missionaries on another continent, but they returned abruptly. The communication between the parents began to break down. Allen Myer admitted that driving this fractured relationship was his own idolatry. In this case, Allen made an idol of being a missionary. The doing displaced the being in their family, and they returned from the field broken. Now several years later, they are healed and continuing to engage missions out of their being as a family. This journey toward wholeness began with Allan and his wife.

Not every weakness is a failure. Sometimes a weakness is simply an area of struggle or vulnerability. Karen Bailey and her family are an example of this. Karen and her family were also on the mission field internationally. During their time, specific learning needs surfaced with a couple of their children. When the time came for the family to return home, Karen began to work with her neighbors' children as she worked with her own. Out of this vulnerability and grace, Karen is now opening a school that will minister to students with specific learning needs. When these needs surfaced in her children, God's grace became an abundant source of ministry not only to their family, but for the blessing of others. Karen reflects the attitude undergirding their family's vision:

> We had 'lost' what we thought was going to be our life-long career and calling as tribal missionaries. . .We never considered a "normal" American life of a job, a house, a pet, church, and kids. For us, the only option was to serve as missionaries wherever God placed us. Our children, as well, desired nothing else but to serve God as missionaries. . .Is living a missional life easy? NO!!! It takes much sacrifice, much intentionality and much prayer! Is it worth it? YES!!!! Even one life led to Christ is worth the sacrifice![173]

---

[173]   Karen Bailey, interview by author, September — December, 2012.

Prayer as families for others and by the parents for their children is a commitment that marks the communication of redemptive families. This commitment includes but expands beyond mealtimes and bedtime. It is a prayer life that is expressed in both word and deed. Families connect with others they pray for, when possible. They also invest their resources according to their prayers.

Missional-minded families enjoy being together. Dave Witmer comments "Have a blast as a family; have fun! Laugh a lot. Take God seriously but yourselves lightly."[174] As children join other children in play, so missional families at play are magnetic to others.

Missional families intentionally convert their current contexts of work, rest, and play for missional ends. The families in this dialogue exemplify generosity in their routine interactions within and beyond their home. Such faithfulness leads to a greater awareness of others in the midst of daily chores, shopping trips, and conversations with neighbors. As Ed Weber reflects, "The way our gospel identity becomes gospel mission is through rhythms - daily patterns of living in the everyday. This does not mean a series of events or activities, but rather a re-orientation of the way we are and live that is centered on the gospel."[175] Their "rhythms" form incarnational means through which they minister hope.

Missional families also seek to open up new territory. They reckon with the "going" that is embedded in the ministry and commissions of Jesus. The Beverly family's missional response included adopting a couple of children. However, as God continued to stir their hearts, they walked through a new door to adopt many more children out of foster care. Like the Beverly family, missional families do not "settle" into faithfulness. These families seek to be more and do more, as God leads and empowers. They dream missional dreams. They make the most of the present moment while pressing ahead. They understand that their stories are chapters of God's story.

---

[174]   Dave Witmer, interview.

[175]   Ed Weber, interview.

Chapter 4

Principles of Being for a Redemptive Family

⸺⊶⊷⸺

Redemptive families exemplify the following: gratitude, rest, and freedom. These characteristics resonate in the core of being for families. They are woven into the fabric of a familial identity in Christ.

Gratitude

One principle of a missional family is the embrace of the redemptive opportunity afforded through brokenness. The grace received in this process results in gratitude. It is a posture that pervades a family's being relationally and attitudinally, even in the midst of stress.

All families face stress. Regarding stress, Dolores Curran notes that effective family responses to stress include understanding its temporal nature, growing in communication by working through it, developing new standards and priorities, and expecting the struggle while avoiding an overwhelming sense of failure.[176] These healthy responses indicate an acceptance of struggle with a view toward growth and maturity.

---

[176] Dolores Curran, *Stress and the Healthy Family: How Healthy Families Control the Ten Most Common Stresses* (Minneapolis: Winston Press, 1985), 12.

Gratitude would be expected from a family with such a perspective.

The opposite dynamics occur in families that do not handle stress well. These traits include an overriding sense of guilt with blame passed onto one another. The overwhelmed families give up hope for overcoming problems, and their problems become the focus rather than their strengths. They "feel weaker rather than stronger after experiencing normal stress," and they end up disliking life together as a family as the stress builds up.[177] These descriptions are the antithesis of gratitude.

Based upon these initial impressions, Curran goes on to "define family dis-stress as a condition that exists when family life gets out of control."[178] There is a significant difference between a redemptive family embracing brokenness and developing a greater sense of purpose and a family that simply embraces stress as a constant characteristic. Curran describes the latter families in the following terms:

> . . .a constant sense of urgency and hurry; no time to release and relax, tension that underlies and causes sharp words. . .a mania to escape. . .a feeling that time is passing too quickly; children are growing up too fast, a nagging desire for a simpler life. . .little 'me' or couple time, a pervasive sense of guilt for not being and doing everything to and for all the people in one's life.[179]

There is no rest for a family consistently succumbing to such stress.

---

[177] Curran, *Stress and the Healthy Family*, 12.
[178] Ibid., 13.
[179] Ibid.

Rest

This relates closely to another principle of being a redemptive family–the stewardship of time. Curran notes that one of the traits of healthy family is "service to others," and this "is self-evident in its reliance on available time."[180] An integrated reality of sabbath is lacking when families take on a lifestyle of being stressed-out. Sabbath is an integrated sense of rest in God, observed in practical ways, which profoundly secures a family's *being* and compels a family's *doing*. Richard Foster believes that "we are too busy only because we want to be too busy."[181] Sabbath constantly calls families to re-order their stewardship of time. This involves repentance, especially at the level of motivation for control and familial-actualization through busy activity.

Perhaps a different perspective on time would be helpful for the integration of sabbath. North American culture has a "monochronic view," which "sees time as a limited and valuable resource. Time can be lost or saved. Good stewardship means getting the most out of every minute."[182] A contrasting perspective is found in the "polychronic view," which sees time as an "unlimited resource. . .tasks typically take a back-seat to forming and deepening relationships. . .people in such cultures often have a deeper sense of community and belonging."[183]

According to Peterson, sabbath is a time for prayer and play.[184] Curran confirms that healthy families avoid the stress of time by playing together.[185] She elaborates on the unifying impact of playful togetherness, "There's something about

---

[180] Delores Curran, *Traits Of A Healthy Family* (New York: HarperSanFrancisco, 1983), 119.

[181] Richard J. Foster, *Freedom of Simplicity: Finding Harmony In A Complex World* (New York: HarperPaperbacks, 1981), 116.

[182] Corbett, 152-153.

[183] Ibid., 153.

[184] Peterson, *Working The Angles*, 52.

[185] Curran, *Stress and the Healthy Family*, 160.

playing and laughing together that says to a family, 'We're a unit. We share a history and a future.'"[186]

Missional families can add that they share a story and a mission. A family's awareness and priority of its play and how it is passed from parents to children is something Curran also includes in her work of surveying characteristics found in healthy families.[187] Being missional flows from a genuine sense of joy. Not only does it begin with joy, it also "ends in joy."[188] Missionary writer David Shenk affirms, "Joy that produces praise is vital to fruitful mission. . ."[189]

Such play and joy can help families guard against the tendency toward perfectionism expressed through neatness and order. There is a fluid reality to a missional family's flexibility. Hiebert explains, "Creative chaos is inherent in genuine relationships. . .Our Western need for order and control works against true communication and fellowship, because it is the passage through chaos that forms the basis for real communication and community."[190] What is in order for out-of-control busy families is repentance that, in turning from the shallowness of busyness, embraces the fullness of shalom.

More than a peaceful atmosphere that resonates from rest in God, shalom indicates a reorientation of a family around a focus beyond itself. According to Hiebert's definition, "shalom means to be for the other, rather than for one's self and to commit one's self to the other, regardless of the other's response."[191] Families find fulfillment elusive when they focus on themselves, and they try to cover-up the void through busyness. Yet families' true needs are met when they rest from such self-striving and shift their focus to others. Redemptive family lifestyles are oriented around blessing others, and

---

[186]   Curran, *Stress and the Healthy Family*, 183.

[187]   Curran, *Traits Of A Healthy Family*, 125-127.

[188]   Stetzer, 30.

[189]   Shenk, 155.

[190]   Hiebert, 210.

[191]   Ibid., 210.

along the way, the redemptive family itself experiences blessing. This reflects the image of God.

International speaker, Ellis Potter, elaborates on the relationality of the Godhead and then humans as image-bearers, which focuses on others while also leading to relational fulfillment:

> Such is the Bible's depiction of absolute reality: a totally other-centered God. This other-centeredness is the source of God's energy, for as each of the persons of God empties Himself once, he is filled twice by the others. This energy increases exponentially. It became so great that God could say *Let there be light!* and a universe was born. The Bible gives a name to this energy when it says *God is love.* It is an other-centered emptying and filling, a perpetual building up of energy. It is the energy of life. It is the foundation of all reality. . .Love is the total reality of what God is. Just as God is fully other-centered, we too were meant to be this way.[192]

Shenk summarizes the point succinctly in view of the image-bearing quality of human relationships: "Trinity means that we should love each other."[193]

In this loving orientation around others, there is a dimension of adventure in being missional. Intimacy is a core ingredient for healthy integration of mission. As just referenced, the mission of God begins with God Himself in the intimacy of the Trinity.[194]

---

[192] Ellis Potter, *3 Theories Of Everything*, (Destinée Media, 2012), 60-61.

[193] Shenk, 69.

[194] Karotemprel et al., 51.

Curran asserts that "intimacy is built upon risk."[195] She also links commitment and intimacy.[196] There are many ways to express and strengthen this commitment. Here it is important to once again visit the importance of being in commitment above always doing commitment. It can be as simple as a couple that will "just relax together in the backyard with the understanding that being together is enough."[197]

Through an interview with a pediatrician, Curran gleans perspective about families focused on serving rather than pursuing wealth and success: "they're more relaxed about life, and they seem to like it more. They live a simpler life. . .they have something else. For want of a better phrase, I'd call it contentment."[198] Contentment is linked to rest. It also connects to gratitude.

Freedom

Flowing from gratitude and rest, missional families are free to live a lifestyle characterized by service to others. From surveying the literature herself, Curran builds on the pediatrician's perspective with her own description of service-oriented families:

> What he called 'contentment' goes under many names in the literature that described these families: simplicity-seeking, detached, altruistic, caring, empathetic, and even counter-culture. In contrast to those families are those who are addicted to the pursuit of wealth.[199]

---

[195] Curran, *Stress and the Healthy Family*, 33.

[196] Ibid., 169.

[197] Ibid., 171.

[198] Curran, *Traits Of A Healthy Family*, 243.

[199] Ibid.

Service motivated by guilt simply becomes another pursuit of success, albeit a virtuous one on the surface. Philip Slater says the result for families whose striving for success leads to "an addiction to wealth" is "the isolation this pursuit generates."[200] This same isolation can be expected for families striving to serve as another form of success. If not rooted in gratitude and shalom, a more likely motivation is guilt. Curran even warns that such wrongly motivated "commitment to others can become toxic."[201] Thus, she concludes from her own findings:

> This deep desire many families feel to simplify
> their life is quite apart from guilt for consuming
> so much while others are in need (though they
> may feel that, too). This desire speaks more to a
> human need for *freedom from things*.[202]

Out of this freedom, redemptive families are marked by generosity, which is an observed trait of service-oriented families.[203]

To describe the pursuit of wealth includes a view toward being possessed by things, otherwise called materialism. In contrast, a missional family's being is characterized by gratitude, rest, and freedom. It is from this integrated reality in relationship with God, whose own relationality is so characterized, that other-centeredness and service to others is sustained.

Though well-intentioned, many families spend their primary effort trying to prevent or repair brokenness within their home. Churches are highly invested through staffing and programs in the ministry to disorderly families. Church families themselves follow this pattern of giving priority to

---

[200] Curran, *Traits Of A Healthy Family*, 243.

[201] Ibid., 255.

[202] Ibid., 244.

[203] Ibid., 253.

their own tension and conflict. Speaking of church families, Stetzer and Nation acknowledge that "we are a dysfunctional family as we are still on this earth. Most of the dysfunction comes as family members assert their rights and want their preferences, rather than keeping their eyes on the field that is 'ready for harvest' (John 4:35)."[204]

Therefore, an important principle is in view. Brokenness in the family does not displace the priority of mission to others. As stated throughout, a redemptive response to brokenness can actually fuel mission. Indirectly, much of the dysfunction in a church family or within a home may dissipate or at least come into proper perspective when processed through redemptive living. Leslie Allen notes "that personal suffering can create a deep reservoir of comfort and strength from which others may draw and find new life."[205] He sharpens the focus on healing in contrast to merely trying to fix someone's brokenness, and its relation to mission is evident: "But when both sides are available, healer calls to healer in the other; wound identifies with wound. Empathy results, compassion connects, and hope is transmitted."[206]

The biblical story of Jonah is a good example of how the prophet's brokenness became an opportunity for discovering the freedom to obey the mission before him. For Eugene Peterson, it is a story that subversively convicts and compels:

> Parable and prayer are subversive. The Jonah story is subversive. It insinuates itself indirectly by comedy and exaggeration into our culture-sanctioned career idolatries, and while we are amused and laughing, our defenses down, it captures our imaginations and sets us on the way to the recovery of our vocational holiness. Caught by parable, caught by prayer–caught

---

[204] Stetzer, 129.

[205] Leslie C. Allen, *A Liturgy of Grief: A Pastoral Commentary on Lamentations* (Grand Rapids: Baker Academic, 2011), 85.

[206] Allen, 86.

hesitating at the edge of the abyss–we are led gently into the depths where we can develop a spirituality adequate to our calling.[207]

In looking at Jonah's example, Peterson sees a contrast between "a Tarshish career" and "a Nineveh vocation." The former "is dominated by the social-economic mind-set of Darwinism: market-orientation, competitiveness, survival of the fittest. . .It is work at which we gain mastery, position, power, and daily check on our image in the mirror." In contrast, consider the freedom in Peterson's description of "a Nineveh vocation" where the shaping influence is "the biblical mind-set of Jesus: worship orientation, a servant life, sacrifice." There is a liberating shift "from ego-addictions to grace-freedoms. . .at which we give up control, fail and forgive, watch God work."[208]

---

[207] Eugene H. Peterson, *Under the Unpredictable Plant: An Exploration in Vocational Holiness* (Grand Rapids: William B. Eerdmans Publishing Co., 1992), 7-8.

[208] Peterson, *Under the Unpredictable Plant*, 176.

Chapter 5

Paradigms of Doing for a Redemptive Family

—⊗⊗⊗—

Redemptive families display actions that include the following: generosity, faithfulness in current contexts, and going into new contexts. These missional disciplines flow from desires inherent to a redemptive vision. They are behaviors of the heart for families abiding in Christ.

Generosity

Looking to the family's lifestyle, "rabbis considered hospitality one of the most important functions of the home. . .the home was to be open to all classes and kinds of people."[209] Hiebert links hospitality to mission by referencing the home as "probably the most important neutral territory for evangelism."[210] When a family embraces a broad range of outsiders, the family is taking shape with a redemptive emphasis. God's kingdom is expressed through such communities.

This hospitality is to be directed inward as well as outward. "Domestic harmony was an ideal toward which Jewish families strove. The guidelines for achieving this harmony were

---

[209] Wilson, 219.

[210] Hiebert, 182.

clearly outlined: 'A man should spend less than his means on food, up to his means on clothes, and beyond his means in honoring wife and children because they are dependent on him.'"[211]

Hence, relational generosity within the family is at the foundation of a mission reaching beyond the family. Relationships, in societies outside of the West, "are often ends in themselves."[212] Hiebert elaborates:

> Christians in other lands are often confused by Western obsession with order and lack of relational skills. Westerners rarely open our homes spontaneously to visitors. We are more interested in keeping our possessions than sharing them. . .We are too busy doing things to take time to just sit and visit. For Christians in many non-Western societies, the central issue in Christianity is not order but right relationships. The gospel to them is good news because it speaks of *shalom* – of human dignity, equality, justice, love, peace, and concern for the lost and the marginalized.[213]

Children raised in hospitable homes have the opportunity to see that following Jesus truly influences a family's lifestyle. As Lee puts it, "The more that children can participate with their parents in fulfilling God's mission in the world, the more likely they will grasp that Christianity actually makes a difference in a believer's life."[214] Lee specifies the commitments necessary from mothers in the home, and these can be applied to both parents and any leader of a family. One aspect is an overall resistance to the materialism embedded in the

---

[211]   Settles et al., 47.

[212]   Hiebert, 141.

[213]   Ibid., 144.

[214]   Lee, 133.

surrounding culture.[215] This highlights how families need to discipline their daily choices and attitudes so that they rise above the distraction of materialism.

This is where Lee's next suggestion comes into focus: "Missional moms constantly find ways to demonstrate generosity. There is no better antidote to materialism than to be generous and to encourage our children to give freely."[216] Generosity includes attitudes and actions related to resources such as possessions, money, talents, and time. Relational generosity expresses kindness and mercy in word and deed. Hospitality is a characteristic action of missional families, including "radical expressions. . .such as adoption."[217] In all its forms, hospitality is a consistent thread in the fabric of a redemptive family's lifestyle.

Faithfulness in Current Contexts

As with hospitality, a basic level of consideration for a missional family is the place they occupy.[218] Where they live shapes their missional calling. In Lee's words, "Sometimes, we get stuck trying to figure out what we are supposed to do with our lives, when all we have to do is pursue God's mission with intentionality right where we already are. . .One way to adopt a missional perspective is to think of. . .our homes as 'missional outposts.'"[219]

Making the place of a family's dwelling an origin of outreach is counter-cultural. Lee explains, "With a cultural norm of increasingly privatized lives. . .people are so busy and stressed that they have a hard time making or welcoming opportunities for interactions with others. Reaching out

---

[215]   Lee, 133.

[216]   Ibid., 135.

[217]   Ibid., 138, 140.

[218]   Stetzer, 101.

[219]   Lee, 25.

despite our tendency to 'cocoon' has become much harder."[220] Reaching out may enhance what a family is actually seeking through "cocooning."

Families that serve together have been found to volunteer more frequently than individuals. This is because their level of enjoyment is higher due to the shared fellowship.[221] Children benefit significantly. According to Johnson, "Volunteering within the context of their family gives kids the security they need to reach out to others."[222] An implicit benefit is the security from connection to one another.

As noted previously, there is a lot of attention given to the "battle" to keep the family intact in today's society. At the ground level in many homes, this battle is being lost as families splinter. At a societal level, perceptions of family continue to evolve along the lines of the cultural narrative. This struggle is one that can be understood as spiritual in nature, and its basis is all the way back at the beginning of the biblical narrative where the role of the serpent was prominent in the fall of the first family. At the same time, a redemptive response to a spiritual struggle does not need to be complicated by over-combativeness.

To this point, Hiebert provides a helpful insight on spiritual warfare: "the central issue in biblical warfare is not power but faithfulness."[223] Seeking to be faithful in the place that a family lives, works, and relates is powerful and strategic not only for that particular family, but for all of those who know them. Such a legacy is in God's hands for His purposes and victory.

---

[220]   Lee, 90.

[221]   Johnson, 93.

[222]   Ibid.

[223]   Hiebert, 208.

Going Into New Contexts

The principles reviewed in the previous chapter focus on a family's freedom. This freedom is then a foundation upon which redemptive exploration into new areas can occur. Freedom shapes this venture. Indeed, freedom should not be thought of as the absence of form. Rather, as Potter puts it, "freedom cannot really be valuable or life-giving unless it is accompanied by form. . .their relationship is complementary rather than competitive."[224] As such, the principles of a missional family's being (freedom) are complementary to the paradigms for a missional family's doing (form).

As evident thus far, a family's home life is central to their overall lifestyle and the exploration of new expressions. Another indicator of the home's impact is apparent through its lasting influence in a child's life, which echoes the experiences of families within Old Testament Hebraic communities.[225] The influence of the home establishes a formative context that consists of relationships, values, and experiences.

A childhood perception of home endures throughout a lifetime. Reflecting on the impact on children raised in bi-cultural settings, Hiebert states that "the cultural imprint of their childhood can never be erased."[226] One paradigm shift for redemptive family living is to embrace the service opportunities that are already available in daily life while seeking to cultivate new ones. This redemptive vision builds a bridge between the formative context of the home and the neighboring mission fields.

Hiebert advocates for an incarnational strategy in crossing this bridge: "If success of missions depends largely upon the quality of the relationships between missionaries and the people to whom they go. . .The biblical model is that of

---

[224] Potter, 48-49.

[225] Wilson, 280-281.

[226] Hiebert, 157.

incarnation."[227] Effective mission depends on a relational context more than accomplishing tasks and passing on information. For parents, this missional approach takes priority in their own home as well as their neighborhood. With a view toward mission, Stetzer and Nation support a relational approach to parenting: "The *content* of parenting often doesn't seem so important until we see it in the long-term *context* of parenting."[228] Hence, consociation forms a bridge for making disciples inside and outside the home.

An over-reliance upon content, or right beliefs, apart from an incarnational expression inside and outside the home, creates an enduring disconnect inside and outside the family. Stetzer and Nation further comment: "Christian experts tell us how to raise our kids, how to handle our finances, what music to buy, what movies to see, and which books to read. The bubble is complete. But God is on a mission outside that bubble."[229]

The redemptive family is an incarnational community suited to explore new opportunities "outside the bubble." The flexibility of family can facilitate a healthy and holistic connection with others locally or internationally. Families oriented to the importance of the redemptive context seek to expand their circle of relational influence. "God purposely goes to those who are from Him (that's us). . .God seeks the lost, and we–in our missional assignment–are to do the same."[230] Missional families incarnationally reach into new contexts because they have been reached, and they are now free to do so.

Sight and Sound Theatres®, in their production of *Jonah*, present to the audience a catching experience along the lines of Peterson's description noted previously. In it they explore the storyline with a view toward Jonah's personal brokenness and how it may have both hindered the mission and released

---

[227] Hiebert, 158.

[228] Stetzer, 28.

[229] Ibid., 29-30.

[230] Ibid., 30.

him into the mission, depending on his trust in God. The final lines sung in the musical illustrate the relationship between freedom and mission: "Bless Your name. And as far as the east is from the west. You alone are the difference in me. For now we're free. . .Free to arise and go!. . ."[231]

---

[231] Sight & Sound Theatres®, *Jonah: Original Soundtrack Recording, Finale,* Don Harper, orchestrated by Jim Dellas, CD, 2012.

Chapter 6

Redemptive Family Wholeness

———∞∞∞———

I t would be an understandable tendency to measure a family in mission according to what it does. After all, mission brings to mind the actions of mission *work*. However, if the flow undergirding this project is to be adhered to, then a family's being must be considered as the source from which its doing emanates. Curran notes, "In the healthy family, the individual is affirmed for who he or she is and not for what he or she looks like, has, or does."[232] Measurement begins with this healthy way of life.

According to White and Klein, qualitative methods of research are appropriate when seeking to understanding "how people in specific situations feel, perceive, and experience." Quantitative methods are preferred for seeing "how many people behave in a certain way or what most people do."[233] Thus, qualitative methods are helpful for discerning values, motivations, and areas generally related to "being" a redemptive family. Quantitative methods help trace the growth in the paradigms related to "doing," though qualitative research adds clarity and understanding to this realm.

---

[232] Curran, *Traits Of A Healthy Family*, 62.

[233] White, 116.

The concept of redemptive families is undergirded by qualitative descriptions. White and Klein repeatedly assert, "theories do have descriptive aspects; a theory that cannot explain is not very useful."[234] What follows is a description of the developmental process of a family growing in a redemptive mindset and implementing a redemptive lifestyle.

Revelation

A foundation for wholeness is found in what God reveals to a family through its unique story. This story is shaped by experiencing God's grace in brokenness. The grace is often known within the fellowship of the family's members. Each member is unique, and so is each family.

Measures of the quality of a family's being can include how well the individual family member's uniqueness is embraced and honored.[235] This affirms the Hebraic tradition of focusing on the individual way of each child. By extension, each family collectively possesses a unique way. A family cultivating respect for family members within the home will generate a broad respect for other groups, including other families, outside of the home.[236]

In the perspective of shared mission, redemptive families have a basis for dealing with brokenness effectively. This includes understanding the pressures of routine life, communicating feelings, resolving conflict, accountability and support structures, and being flexible.[237] It is a misconception to think that a sense of mission will remove conflict from family life. According to Michael Griffin, "Two people who care deeply about what is important to them are bound to come into conflict."[238] A missional family cares deeply about

---

[234]   White, 284.

[235]   Curran, *Traits of A Healthy Family*, 80.

[236]   Ibid., 88, 92.

[237]   Curran, *Stress and the Healthy Family*, 29.

[238]   Ibid., 33.

others and what is not right in the world. It is expected that a close family caring so deeply about others will carry burdens. Such pressure has a tendency to bring conflict to the surface.

One example of such conflict could be money. It is already known that couples often fight about money.[239] Imagine how a push for generosity in finances can yield a new dimension of tension over spending. Further examples of challenges exist in this fallen world. Families need not invent brokenness as there is much already at hand within a family's life and relationships.

Communication represents another area where conflict occurs. A missional outlook does not automatically equate to an ease of communication for a family. This includes hearing from God. What a redemptive family does, however, is give place for conversations and relationships through which the family can hear from God and one another. They cultivate meaningful conversations as a discipline. Table fellowship holds the potential as a context for transformational conversations. Curran notes that healthy families "value the dinner hour as prime communication time."[240]

This is where life coaching training can be helpful for families. Conversations that are content-driven can be kept at a distance by its participants. Coaching conversations that cultivate a relational context have the potential to go deeper and tap into a contemplative quality through which God's wisdom can be discerned. For example, a parent-child conversation over a breakfast outing encourages responsiveness in a different way than asking the same routine questions on the way home from school.

This foundation in revelation is particularly shaped by the family's outlook. All families experience struggles of all sorts. A redemptive family has an outlook that is willing to see how God might work through a particular trial for His kingdom's sake. His work is characterized by a revelation of Himself in and through the life of the family.

---

[239] Curran, *Stress and the Healthy Family*, 63.

[240] Ibid., 131.

Awareness

This phase involves a consciousness that continually forms in the imagination of the family. It builds off of revelation and cultivates empathy toward others that reflects God's heart. Fritz Graebe's life exemplifies factors that raise awareness of a missional heart. He rescued hundreds of Jews during World War II. Based upon Graebe's story, Doug Huneke identifies ten characteristics that influence the formation of empathetic adults, some of which are adapted from Perry London's research on altruism exhibited by holocaust rescuers.[241] Jan Johnson views these factors in relation to a growing missional awareness in families; thus she summarizes Huneke's conclusions on these ten characteristics as follows:

1. Adventuresome
2. Identification with a morally strong parent
3. An experience of marginalization of being left out or undervalued
4. Empathetic imagination – the ability to place oneself in the actual situation or role of another person
5. Ability to present oneself, speak up, and be persuasive, often through public performance while growing up
6. Skilled at cooperating and being responsible to promote the well-being of others
7. Exposed to suffering at an early age
8. Ability to examine their own prejudices
9. Belonging to a community or group who valued compassion, so there was not a sense of being in a struggle alone
10. A home where hospitality was of high value. (Hospitality included the act of taking time to talk to

---

[241] Douglas K. Huneke, *The Moses Of Rovno: The Stirring Story of Fritz Graebe, a German Christian Who Risked His Life to Lead Hundreds of Jews to Safety During the Holocaust* (Tiburon, CA: Compassion House, 1985), 177-187.

people who needed to talk. Their homes weren't castles to keep the world out).[242]

This list reads like a list describing a missional family based upon the many thoughts already summarized. Redemptive families are empathetic families. As God reveals Himself to the family, there is a new awareness of others that ensues. Families begin to see their life differently, and they see the needs of others with greater clarity. As this awareness characterizes a family's being, it eventually begins to impact their motivation for action.

Motivation

Motivation is an important bridge from being to doing for missional families. Dreams are good indicators of the nature of a family's being and the desires for doing. Parents with a missional perspective have others-centered dreams for their children. Jan Johnson shares her own dream for her children in *Growing Compassionate Kids*:

> Part of the dreaming picture I have for my children is that God's love will shape them into compassionate people in a culture that is self-absorbed. I long for them to be individuals who like to offer cups of cold water to the thirsty, who dare to whisper words of life to the unreached, who want to love all peoples the way God does, who strive to set aside the pull of materialism and spend their resources on worthwhile purposes.[243]

Motivation is a key to implementing a redemptive lifestyle. For Johnson, focusing on family is not enough. Instead, she asks, "What are you focusing on your family *for*? Is having a

---

[242] Johnson, 36-37.

[243] Ibid., 3.

happy, intact family the goal or a means to an end – advancing knowledge of God's mercy and justice on earth?"[244] Missional motivation is a means to kingdom ends. There are many motivations among families that are noble and accepted in the church as normative for the godly family. These include financial security, safety, unity, good communication, intimacy, fun, and responsibility. However, viewing these through a missional lens discerns whether these are goals ending in the family itself or means to something greater in God's mission.

Intuition

As the motivation toward redemptive living takes root within a family, a missional intuition develops. Whereas in the awareness phase, a family's default mindset might still revert to previous patterns of thought and behavior, it is in this stage when a family's default setting changes. As they consistently initiate missional commitments, they find themselves naturally leaning toward missional thought and activity. It is becoming a normal part of their everyday life. When the family has free time, they may go visit the neighbors, help someone, or do something fun that will place them in the community, where they can show kindness to others. They do this out of delight more than duty.

Families remain intentional during this phase. Lee offers three suggestions that relate to developing a missional instinct as a family. First, she suggests that families "maximize shared interests for missional purposes."[245] If a family loves music, the outdoors, food, learning new skills, how can this be employed alongside blessing others? Second, Lee reminds parents to "keep pointing your kids toward the primary calling."[246] One way this can be accomplished is through meaningful reflection at the end of the day. This relates to the third

---

[244] Johnson, 5.

[245] Lee, 28.

[246] Ibid.

suggestion, "remind yourself often of the 'big picture' of what God is doing."[247] Taking time to prayerfully and conversationally reflect can yield connections of smaller occurrences and opportunities with the broad workings of God's kingdom. Over time, carrying out these ideas strengthen a missional intuition in the heart of a family.

Integration

A key factor for integrating the missional thread into the fabric of a family is the combination of working and playing.[248] Families that work constantly find that play is elusive. A family that plays excessively finds that they do not get to the work. Work and play need not be competing realities. In fact, they can relate synergistically to one another. Work feeds the play, and play helps the work. When they occur simultaneously, the impact inside and outside a family is significant. The integration of mission into a family is similar to this example.

Integration is a focal point of a family's redemptive wholeness. It is built upon the previous spheres already mentioned. It is the sum of a family's relationships and activities. Families that are holistically redemptive do not focus on striving to be missional; it is simply who they are and what they do. It becomes that simple.

This simplicity is due to the function of being, which compels doing. It is characterized by relationships before tasks. As Johnson says, "The simple life is relational."[249] So it is with the family integrated around mission. Therefore, based upon the principles, paradigms, and wholeness of missional families, it is now helpful to conceive a relational model for mobilizing such families.

---

[247] Lee, 28.

[248] Johnson, 49.

[249] Ibid., 137.

Chapter 7

Mobilizing a
Redemptive Family

———∞∞∞———

M issional mobilization is a function of fellowship. Individual identity, more than simply the components of body, soul, and spirit, is understood through relationships.[250] A primary community for an individual is family. In creation, "the image of God was not complete until it was *we* or *us* rather than *I* or *me*."[251] Just as individual identity is understood within relationships, so a family's identity and purpose can become clear through relationships with others.

The Balswicks believe that a family "will never thrive without a supportive community."[252] The basis of trinitarian relationality for family life extends to congregational life.[253] Basically, what is principally true about a small community, such as a family, holds even as the community is broadened.

In a family, "differentiation makes interiority and interdependency possible." When members absorb into one another and lose a sense of distinction, "spiritual enmeshment" occurs. On the other side, when there is little mutuality between

---

[250] Potter, 53-54.

[251] Ibid., 54.

[252] Balswick, 154.

[253] Ibid.

members, there is "spiritual disengagement."[254] The Balswicks explain, "What is needed is neither spiritual *independence* nor spiritual *dependence* but rather *interdependence*."[255] Thus their depiction of the possibility for a congregational family: "Secure identity in Christ at the congregational level means there is a healthy degree of *connectedness* as well as a healthy degree of *separation*."[256] "The church, then, is to be a family to families and a source of identity and support for isolated nuclear families."[257] Therefore, it is vital that church be a place where families can experience togetherness that also prepares them for the unique outward expression of their mission. "We shall know that *shalom* is present when social structures empower the family."[258] Likewise, the church family itself benefits from such empowerment.

Missional-minded families discipling other families serves as a relational structural approach that turns families outward. Families raising up and releasing other families parallels the organic dynamic of a church planting another church. In a natural sense, families beget families. Paul Vadakumpadan explains this essential characteristic as it relates to churches in his essay, *Ecclesiological Foundation of Mission*: ". . .the Church must always be missionary. She manifests her spiritual fecundity in giving birth to new churches."[259]

From a perspective of impacting youth, Peter Benson cautions against the trends of "how cities and towns are now structured – however unintentionally or benignly – to work *against* young people's healthy development." Some of the evidence he cites from his research includes:

---

254 Balswick, 150.

255 Ibid., 151.

256 Ibid., 154.

257 Ibid., 365.

258 Ibid., 367.

259 Karotemprel et al., 106.

- Age segregation that separates adults from the lives of children and vice versa
- Mistrust that undermines relationships between youth and adults, adults and other adults. . .
- Fragmented, ill-equipped, and isolated socializing systems
- A normative climate that emphasizes privacy and civic disengagement rather than a shared vision and commitment
- Isolation of families[260]

The church in North America seems to reflect its cities and towns. Benson's research leads him to propose the trajectory of becoming "asset-building communities." He defines these as "relational and intergenerational places emphasizing support, empowerment, boundaries, and opportunities." His term, "Developmental Assets," refers to "the language of the common good," and it involves a pursuit that is "visible, long-term, and inclusive."[261]

Benson laments that the society has abdicated responsibility for children by turning to professionals. He advocates for a shift "from program focus to relational focus."[262] This shift is needed within the church as part of the society. Benson includes "religious institutions" in his "activate sector" category. As such, it can "mobilize their capacity for intergenerational relationships, educating and supporting parents, structured use of time, values development, and service to the community."[263]

Corbett and Fikkert agree by describing the goal of holistic mission as being sustained by "highly relational, process-focused ministries more than in impersonal, product-focused

---

[260] Benson, 11.

[261] Ibid., 16.

[262] Ibid., 106.

[263] Ibid., 139.

ministries."[264] Discipling families for the mission of God is a highly relational endeavor. It is focused on the process of a family becoming holistically redemptive. This view also agrees with Johnson's previously referenced process-orientation for families.

The process for a model of mobilization consists of one family impacting another family's sense of caring about God's mission. Writing about children, Benson believes that there are two main ways to pass on a sense of caring. With children being in a family setting, it follows that these would apply to passing these values from one family to the next:

> First, caring, like all values, is passed on by *modeling*. It is rooted in the experience of being with people who choose to respond to human need with acts of caring and compassion. . .The second source is *practice, the doing of caring*. . .For caring to become a lasting disposition, the practice of it ought to be in the range of once a week throughout childhood and adolescence. . .Service should be a mainstay of developmental experience, being highly valued and promoted in family, congregation, school, clubs, teams and organizations.[265]

Notice that Benson sees this developing within small communities, with family being first on the list.

Raising up and releasing redemptive families calls for a new model, not for the family, but for mobilization. It involves missional families "planting" new missional families, like churches plant churches. This can happen through family-with-family discipleship. There are ideas within Benson's "Developmental Assets" framework that can be applied to a paradigm of families connecting with other families for the purpose of growing in a missional mindset and

---

[264] Corbett, 77.

[265] Johnson, 38.

lifestyle. For instance, in his "Architecture of Developmental Assets," Benson notes the following dynamics of "human development:"

External Assets

1. Support
2. Empowerment
3. Boundaries and expectations
4. Constructive use of time

Internal Assets

5. Commitment to learning
6. Positive values
7. Social competencies
8. Positive identity[266]

Within these eight categories, Benson details forty assets. Under empowerment, one of the assets is "service to others," which echoes the Balswicks' connection of empowerment and service noted previously, and which he describes in terms of its multi-dimensional impact:

> . . .involvement in service has the potential to contribute to development of many of the other assets as well. For example, serving others can be the catalyst for internalizing values of caring, equality, and social justice. In addition, service activities foster opportunities for constructive use of time. Indeed, if service opportunities are designed carefully, service becomes strategy of reinforcing all eight categories of assets.[267]

---

[266] Benson, 30.

[267] Ibid., 40.

Beyond the youth themselves, these benefits noted by Benson can be reaped by the entire family. Lee comments that "Missional pastors find ways to encourage. . .their whole families to go and serve together."[268] It is for more than using service as means of reaching the children. The children themselves are uniquely suited to bless others. Benson notes that children need the connection with adults in order to be a part of community transformation, and he confirms that they make unique contributions of "new authenticity, energy, hope, and enthusiasm."[269]

This also accomplishes another one of Benson's assets: "time at home." Children need to be home "with parents, reconnecting, resting, relaxing, doing homework, doing chores, being family."[270] Being family is the key. From this time of being together, service can become a natural outflow. In addition, by opening the home up through hospitality, the time and service coincide.

According to Benson, an organization's thinking about families must shift to undergird these realities. One shift is to move away from the thinking that "the purpose of connecting with families is to get more support for the organization's programs and activities." Instead, "the purpose of connection with families is to support and equip them in their primary role as asset builders." Another shift includes seeing "parents' asset-building opportunities and responsibilities [as] just with their own children" to the "many opportunities. . .for other young people." Also, the mentality that "asset building is something families need to add to their already busy lives" can be replaced by thinking of the process as "a tool to help families examine priorities and be more effective."[271] This is integration.

---

268 Lee, 171.

269 Ibid., 224.

270 Ibid., 47.

271 Benson, 224.

It is important that churches in their family ministry equip families according to the real needs of families. Corbett and Fikkert advocate for a three staged pathway to helping the poor: "Relief–Rehabilitation–Development."[272] These same approaches can be helpful to equipping families. Some are in crisis (relief), others are walking through restoration (rehabilitation), and the goal remains to move families into a redemptive lifestyle that can be sustained (development).

How can families be moved toward this integration? Benson reflects on five phases that can be "a helpful tool" in moving families toward asset-building communities that were developed by his colleague, Marc Mannes. These include the following five phases:

1. Receptivity: Cultivating Openness to Change
2. Awareness: Highlighting the Possibility of Change
3. Mobilization: Organizing for Change
4. Action: Making Change Happen
5. Continuity: Ensuring Change Becomes a Way of Life[273]

These stages parallel the aforementioned areas for wholeness of a redemptive family. To review, these five spheres of development toward wholeness include: revelation, awareness, motivation, intuition, and integration. Benson's following comment on the potential value of sharing service through community can support the potential of these phases being developed through an initiative of families influencing families:

> Service to others offers a unique programmatic opportunity for building bridges across sectors, generations, cultures, religious traditions, and ideologies. In the process of taking shared action, people get to know and appreciate each other. Hence an important strategy for

---

[272] Corbett, 100.
[273] Benson, 233-237.

asset-building communities is to weave service to others throughout community life.[274]

Benson's insights on how to impact society coalesce principally with the Balswicks' vision for the church and family also having a positive impact. The latter envision transformation of society that is wrought through the power of God. While much is made in public debate of defending and preserving the family, the Balswicks describe a faithful response, along the lines of Hiebert's previously noted essence of spiritual warfare, through relationship between church and family in mission that can impact the surrounding community while strengthening the family as a result along the way:

> The church can help here by providing a coherent structure of beliefs and values so that the family can achieve a reintegration of consciousness. . .They should have an expanded awareness of and concern for others who might be different in a variety of ways. The nuclear family can develop fictive kin – people who, though they are not blood relatives, are taken in as extended-family members. Church members should seize the opportunity to become world Christians rather than focusing only on the plight of their own group. The church should learn about Christians around the world and respond to them as brothers and sisters in Christ. Wherever there are poor and oppressed people, the Christian community should reach out. . .Only as witnesses to and exemplars of God's love can church family enable their members to resist the alternatives presented by the world. . .Through service and witness to Christ, we have a great hope of reintegrating our lives. . .Contemporary

---

[274] Benson, 291.

society is currently staggering from the blows of modernity and postmodernity. Within this context, the people of God must call for and serve as salt and light. . .Nothing short of radical response will do.[275]

Corbett and Fikkert support a similar approach that they call "asset-based community development (ABCD)."[276] In fact, the four main principles of ABCD can be incorporated into approaching the task of mobilizing the family into missional living: [author's insertions]

- Identify and mobilize the capabilities, skills, and resources of the. . .[family]
- As much as possible, look for resources and solutions to come from within the. . .[family]
- Seek to build and rebuild the relationships among local [spheres]. . .God intended for the various. . .[families]. . .to be interconnected and complementary
- Only bring in outside resources when local [family] resources are insufficient to solve pressing needs[277]

Family to family mobilization is based upon the families sharing life with and encouraging one another. Benson agrees that parents desire input from other parents as well as trusted leaders, including "a religious leader."[278] Lee provides ideas that could be used in small group contexts, applied here to a family-with-family missional mobilization initiative:

- Read works by missional church leaders
- A small group book discussion

---

[275] Balswick, 360-361.

[276] Corbett, 119.

[277] Ibid., 122.

[278] Benson, 225.

- In your groups, take an inventory of gifts and passions represented. Brainstorm about how you can use those gifts and passions collectively to make a difference. Continually ask, 'How is God calling us to help others in our friendships/playgroups/activities/workplaces/communities?'
- Encourage a culture of hospitality. . .as a way to practice more radical expressions later.
- Encourage. . .service projects together, including children if at all possible.
- Make serving and loving the poor and under-resourced a priority. . .
- Create accountability groups. . .in which you are regularly asking each other challenging questions. . .
- . . .have as many people from the group lead other groups to pass along the same ideas. . .[279]

A new model for mobilizing redemptive families can be developed along the ideas represented by the authors referenced in this section. Though proposed for other contexts, it is evident that the principles these authors put forth are portable to a family to family context.

Part One Summary

The Think Kingdom–Be Family Project is a redemptive initiative rooted in the kingdom of God with hope for fruitfulness in and through families connecting with other families. Considering the fragmented state of the family, a sociological quest for definition is elusive and even abandoned by some theorists. Yet it is against this backdrop of the disintegrating family that the redemptive family comes into focus as undergirding both the means and end of restoring families to wholeness.

Wholeness for redemptive families is framed by the missional concept. Such families embody a lifestyle that flows

---

[279] Lee, 174-175.

from being into doing. The redemptive process by which wholeness develops often begins with grace revealed in the midst of brokenness. As families grow in awareness of what the Spirit of God reveals, a new motivational core takes shape. This is evidenced in changing desires that eventually become intuitive and integrated behaviors in the lifestyles of families. Such redemptive family wholeness is characterized by gratitude, rest, and freedom. From this identity within a family's being, the doing of generosity, routine faithfulness, and exploration of increased faithfulness ensue.

A way to mobilize redemptive families is through intentional fellowship with a missional thrust between families. Within the family of God, there is significant potential for missional-minded families connecting and subsequently inspiring other families to live with redemptive purpose. When families are characterized by mission flowing from their home to the local community and to the nations, God is the one at work. It begins with the mission flowing from the fellowship within God Himself. He both shares and receives His own glory when families experience and testify to redemption in the family of God.

Part II

Biblical, Theological, and Historical Foundations

—∞—

Overview

A t Zion Church of Millersville, thinking kingdom and being family fuses belief and behavior into one mission. "Thinking kingdom" is more than a mindset, because it relates to integrating a revelation of God's reign and rule into the essence of the family's being and doing. "Being family" belongs to the context of the biblical narrative of God creating and calling a community of His people to participate in His kingdom. When darkness dawned in creation through the sin of the first family, the relationships changed significantly, but God's mission remained. Now His kingdom's mission carries forward through redemption toward restoration, which employs God's family as both a means and an end.

Part II begins by examining this redemptive biblical narrative. The backdrop of the narrative is God's kingdom, also expressed as His mission, which provides the biblical theological context for understanding the redemptive family. In line with the approach of biblical theology, the narrative establishes thought, form, and function as it relates to family from creation, the fall, redemption, to the hope of new creation.

After establishing a biblical theological framework for the mission of God's kingdom as the context for the redemptive family, the attention shifts to the theological foundation for the missional concept. This focuses on a family's being and doing, which bears the image of God's own being and doing. Trinitarian relationality forms the basis of missional fellowship, because it is sustained through the mutual indwelling between God and His people.

From these biblical and theological foundations, the redemptive family emerges. Mobilizing missional families is an application in the present time that proceeds from previous times. Thus, the historical background for the family both connects and contrasts with what is ancient and contemporary with the modern concept of North American family.

This part gathers contextual threads from God's kingdom of a redemptive biblical narrative for the family, the theology of trinitarian relationality, and the historical expression of family. It then weaves them into the fabric of a vision for cultivating elements of being and doing in missional families. This vision leads to the opportunity for mobilizing families with families in missional wholeness at Zion Church of Millersville.

Chapter 8

Redemptive Family in the Kingdom of God

———⊶∞⊷———

Families have stories to tell that are unique to their members, past experiences, present context, and plans for the future. The presence of an ongoing story is consistent, though forms and functions vary from family to family. Redemptive families understand the meaning of their stories in the broader backdrop of the story of God. To understand the story of God is to understand the kingdom of God. The concept of story is a formative instrument for positioning families within the redemptive narrative of God's kingdom.

James K.A. Smith writes, "It is crucial that the task of Christian education and formation is nested in a story – in the narrative arc of the biblical drama of God's faithfulness to creation and to his people." More than intellectual understanding, it is imperative that "the *story* of God in Christ redeeming the world be the very air we breathe." If families are going to have their core beings "aimed toward God's kingdom, they'll be won over by good storytellers."[280] Accordingly, a redemptive family's being and doing is shaped by the confluence of the biblical story of God and their own. Hence, a family's missional lifestyle flows from this convergence containing those

---

[280] James K.A. Smith, *Imagining the Kingdom: How Worship Works*, Cultural Liturgies, Vol. 2 (Grand Rapids: Baker Academic, 2013), 160-161.

"practices that 'carry' the true Story of the whole world as articulated in the Scriptures, centered on Christ."[281]

God's story begins with Himself. He created human beings, male and female, to be in special relationship with Him by designing them in His image; this relationship enjoined humankind to the mission of God in caring for and advancing the stewardship of His creation (Gen 1:26-28). There was both a sense of identity and mission through this relationship that humans enjoyed with God and one another. A family was formed through the union of the man and woman. When this first family disobeyed God, they compromised their identity and mission. To this day, the sinful condition continues to compromise both identity and mission.

From the beginning of His creation, the Father has designed His people to be in fellowship with Him and to be an increasing presence that reflects His image on the earth. While this is not limited to families, it can apply to them. In the biblical narrative, select families played central roles in God's redemptive work in the face of a sin-ravaged creation, as evidenced through Noah and Abraham's families.

God preserved Noah's family through the flood, thus providing a continuation of His relationship with human beings and the mission that He shares with them. Abram's family inaugurates a special relationship between God and one family from all of the families of the earth, for the sake of all the families of the earth. Whereas the first man and woman were with God in Eden before the fall, commissioned to fill the earth beginning in that place, God's call to Abram in a fallen world begins with the displacement of His family that "all the families of the earth will be blessed" (Gen 12:1-3). Not only is the dawn of God's redemptive story disruptive, it launches God's people as sojourners, finding their purpose and place in His hospitality. This trajectory for Abraham is thus later remembered: "By faith he lived as an alien in the land of promise, as in a foreign land, dwelling in tents. . .for

---

[281] Smith, *Imagining the Kingdom*, 163.

he was looking for the city which has foundations, whose architect and builder is God" (Heb 11:9-10).

Amos Yong explains that "the Abraham narrative is significant not only because of his exemplary hospitality but because his life served as an archetype for ancient Israel's nomadic, national, and exilic experiences." Israel's redemptive position was more "at the bottom half of the social hierarchy than at the top, and the immigrant or migrant status brought with it all of the discriminatory attitudes and behaviors usually displayed;" Yong concludes that "it was precisely for this reason that they were chosen by YHWH."[282]

A potential pitfall for God's people living on the margins is the draw toward self-preservation. Centuries following Abraham, when the prophet Isaiah portrayed the family of Israel as YHWH's servant in exile, God orients them toward blessing. John Levison explains, "Here is a people that has every cause to turn inward. . .Yet from this community arises a servant upon whom God's spirit rests, a light to the nations, for whose teaching the coastlands can scarcely wait."[283] The hope of Israel, consistent with the initial call to their father Abraham, now rests in foreigners becoming a part of the family and belonging to YHWH (Isa 44).[284]

This hope in Isaiah's songs of the servant realizes significant fulfillment in the identity and work of Jesus, the Father's son and faithful servant. In serving the Father, He invited others to follow Him, constituting them as His family and His friends (Matt 12:50; John 15:14-15), and He subsequently sent them to the nations (Matt 28:18-20). Echoing the displacement and establishment of Abram's family in responding to the call of God, Lohfink comments, "Those who follow Jesus, who for the sake of the reign of God leave behind everything they have

---

282 Amos Yong, *Hospitality & The Other: Pentecost, Christian Practices, and the Neighbor* (Maryknoll, NY: Orbis Books, 2008) 109.

283 John R. Levison, *Fresh Air: The Holy Spirit for an Inspired Life* (Brewster, MA: Paraclete Press, 2012), 90.

284 Levison, *Fresh Air*, 83.

had, become a *new family.*"[285] This family is an expression of God's kingdom, because Jesus called His followers "brothers and sisters," which is "itself a sign of the arriving kingdom."[286] Hence, the story of the kingdom of God joins redemptive families to the redemptive family of God.

Redemptive families respond as His followers, His family members who do "the will of God" (Mk 3:35). Lohfink concludes by connecting the new covenant people to the old, that "the will of God can only be the salvific plan which God is now carrying out and which one is called upon to join in ultimate willingness to God to transform one's life," which he further asserts is "the coming of the kingdom and the gathering of the true Israel. . .God's eschatological people."[287]

From the call of Abram to the hope of Isaiah's servant to Jesus' announcement of the kingdom, God's dream is clearly for a family of all nations. Following Jesus' ascension, the coming of the Holy Spirit catalyzes the formation of God's eschatological people. At Pentecost, the Spirit fills the nations represented in Jerusalem (Acts 2). The church becomes the expression of the body of Christ on earth, anointed with the Spirit as He was anointed as the servant of YHWH (Isa 61:1-2; Luke 4:18-19). The anointing of the Spirit of God is empowerment for mission, as is evidenced in the narrative of God's mission through the church recorded in Acts.

James Bowers confirms the point:

> . . .the call to life in the Spirit is a call to mission. Spirit baptism is specifically viewed as a spiritual commissioning into a life of Christian ministry. Believers are empowered by the Spirit for their missionary vocation. The fullness of the Spirit expressed in its sanctifying grace and charismatic enablements finds its ultimate

---

[285] Lohfink, 41.

[286] Ibid., 42.

[287] Ibid., 43.

significance in the missional nature of Christian existence. That is, the fullness of the Spirit is toward realization of God's righteous purpose– the kingdom of God.[288]

To appropriate this connection of the Spirit for redemptive families in a North American context, it is necessary to recover the practices of the Spirit's empowerment for mission. David Moore elaborates:

> Spirit baptism brings believers into the rich experience of God's redeeming love for our world and provides the gift of prophetic insight dispensed by the Spirit to direct the church's mission in diverse and varied contexts. Empowerment and prophetic vision are sorely needed if the church in the U.S. is to carry out God's mission effectively.[289]

In order to interpret and integrate around the role of the Spirit in the church, including redemptive families, a community framework is needed. Unfortunately, much of the North American understanding of the work of the Spirit of God is an individual fascination. Levison concurs, "When we talk about the most mystical and powerful force in the universe, the spirit of God, it is almost always in individual terms."[290]

A redemptive family is one setting for rediscovering the corporate empowerment of the Holy Spirit's presence. Such families belong to the larger family of faith, the church. Even so, there remains the potential for this new family in Christ,

---

[288] James P. Bowers, "A Wesleyan-Pentecostal Approach to Christian Formation," *Journal of Pentecostal Theology* 6 (October 1995), 77.

[289] David Moore, "Empowered for Witness" in *Spirit-Empowered Christianity in the Twenty-First Century: Insights, analysis, and future trends from world-renowned scholars*, ed. Vinson Synan [Orlando: Charisma House, 2011], 526.

[290] Levison, *Fresh Air*, 119.

bonded by faith, to extend to families bonded by natural relation. These families themselves can become communities of
transformed people and agents of the transformational message within the eschatological community of God's people.
Looking to the early church, Lohfink cites the example of
disciples who followed Jesus within their natural families
that stayed together in their commitment to Christ:

> The majority remained with their families. But
> the families of those who remained home were
> transformed. They became more disposable,
> more open. They no longer revolved merely
> around themselves. They offered hospitality to
> Jesus and his messengers. They entered rela-
> tionships with one another.[291]

Within God's kingdom, His people view the mystery of
election according to this changed perspective. Redemptive
families engaged in the *missio Dei* are a part of God's people,
elected for His purposes. On this point with families in view,
it is important that election neither be a burden nor an occa-
sion for a self-preserving existence in the world. After Jesus
clarifies for His disciples that their election and appointment
comes from Him, He indicates its purpose, "that you would
go and bear fruit, and that your fruit would remain." The
ensuing promise for petitioning the Father is understood
within this mission, "so that whatever you ask of the Father
in My name He may give to you" (John 15:16).

From Adam's to Noah's to Abram's to Jesus' family,
election is a call to stewardship regarding the blessing and
mission of God. Leslie Newbigin thus explains this "logic of
election":

> They are chosen not for themselves, not to be
> the exclusive beneficiaries of God's saving
> work, but to be the bearers of the secret of his

---

[291] Lohfink, 44.

saving work for the sake of all. They are chosen to go and bear fruit. To be chosen, to be elect, therefore does not mean that the elect are the saved and the rest are the lost. To be elect in Christ Jesus, and there is no other election, means to be incorporated into his mission to the world, to be the bearer of God's saving purpose for his whole world, to be the sign and the agent and the firstfruit of his blessed kingdom which is for all.[292]

To serve as such an instrument in God's overall redemptive work is a joyful endeavor rather than obligatory obedience. On this point, Newbigin cautions that focusing on obedience to a commandment or mandate for mission work "tends to make mission a burden rather than a joy, to make it part of the law rather than part of the gospel;" in contrast, as exhibited in the New Testament, "mission begins with a kind of explosion of joy."[293] James Davison Hunter emphasizes the point:

As he does not pursue us for instrumental purposes, so we do not pursue him for instrumental purposes. As our creator and redeemer, our highest aim is to be in his presence; worshipping and enjoying him forever. Only by being fully present to God as a worshipping community and as adoring followers can we be faithfully present in the world.[294]

Hence, redemptive families seek to steward election by being "fully present to God" and subsequently "faithfully present in the world." Smith explains that the mission is "to

---

[292] Newbigin, 86-87.

[293] Ibid., 116.

[294] James Davison Hunter, *To Change the World: The Irony, Tragedy, & Possibility of Christianity In The Late Modern World* (Oxford: Oxford University Press, 2010), 244.

pursue their vocations to the glory of God and in ways that are oriented to the shalom of the kingdom."[295] Frank Maachia further details what this shalom looks like in that "the righteousness of the kingdom reaches out especially to the weak and oppressed, to those who cry out for mercy and justice; it is present at that place of utter hopelessness for all. . ."[296]

Smith explains that in order to be "pulled by a different *call*, it is not enough to have a Christian 'perspective' on the world; we need nothing less than a Christian imagination." With a missional perspective only, families will be "convinced but not transformed."[297] Essentially, transformation for families that entails a missional imagination depends on the being and doing of God Himself.

---

[295] Smith, *Imagining the Kingdom*, 157.

[296] Frank D. Maachia, *Justified in the Spirit: Creation, Redemption, and the Triune God* (Grand Rapids: Eerdmans, 2010), 149.

[297] Smith, *Imagining the Kingdom*, 157.

Chapter 9

God's Being and Doing

—⚬⚬⚬—

Trinitarian relationality is the basis of God's being and doing. *Missio Dei* is the mission of God (doing) that flows from the being of God. As Howard Snyder explains, it includes the salvation of people, but it is even more. It is "a divine master plan for the whole creation."[298] Richard Twiss comments on the relationality and mission of God as the true basis for human identity against the false human identity rooted in sin: ". . .the whole creation is part of our human identity. And everything that 'never was,' has ever been, or ever shall be, came first, 'existed,' within the community of the Father, Son and Holy Spirit before it proceeded out from them."[299]

Consider the missional characteristic of hospitality, which originates within God Himself and is shared with humanity created in His image. Commenting from a Lukan theological perspective, Amos Yong articulates this consideration:

---

[298] Snyder, Howard A, *The Community of the King* (Downers Grove: Intervarsity, 1978), 46.

[299] Richard Twiss, "Living in Transition, Embracing Community, and Envisioning God's Mission as Trinitarian Mutuality: Reflections from a Native-American Follower of Jesus," in *Remembering Jamestown: Hard Questions About Christian Mission*, eds. Amos Yong and Barbara Brown Zikmund. [Eugene: Pickwick Publications, 2010], 106.

. . .hospitality reflects the trinitarian character of the hospitable God. The God who invites humanity to experience his redemptive hospitality in Christ by the Holy Spirit is the same God who receives the hospitality of human beings as shown to Christ and as manifest through those who welcome and are inhabited by the Holy Spirit. In this trinitarian framework, Jesus is the normative, decisive, and eschatological revelation of the hospitable God. . ."[300]

Unlike the distortion of humanity because of sin, the unity of God's identity and mission remains, even in the face of a fallen creation. John depicts the oneness that Jesus embodied with the Father throughout his gospel. The gospel begins in the very first verse by noting the with-ness between Jesus and the Father at the creation, "the Word was with God." The Greek word translated "with" in this depiction is πρός (*pros*), and it relates a meaning of nearness and being "in company with" another.[301] The mission of creation is accomplished through the consociation of God and the Word. The rest of John's gospel conveys the relationship of the Father, the Son, and the Spirit as the means through which the new creation is accomplished.

Consider how Jesus' initial invitation to Simon Peter and Andrew, as recorded in Matthew 4:19, was to follow Him, which would yield missional activity: "Follow me, and I will make you fishers of men." Further, Mark notes that Jesus "appointed twelve, so that they would be with Him and that He could send them out to preach" (3:14). The purpose statement as indicated by the phrase, "so that," points to the priority of consociation followed by the commission to ministry.

---

[300] Yong, 105-106.

[301] William F. Arndt, F. Wilbur Gingrich, and Frederick W. Danker, eds., *A Greek-English Lexicon of the New Testament and Other Early Christian Literature*, 3d ed., rev., (Chicago: University of Chicago Press, 2000), 875.

The Greek word translated "with" is μετά (*meta*), and it "denotes the company within which something takes place;" and specifically in this verse it speaks to "close association" between Jesus and His disciples.[302] Jesus uses this same word to declare that His Father "who sent Me is with Me" (John 8:29). Following His resurrection, the same word is employed to assure His followers of His ongoing presence in the going: ". . .and lo, I am with you always, even to the end of the age" (Matt 28:20).

Mission proceeds from the fellowship shared between the Father, Son, and the Spirit. The same missional trajectory results from the community of God with His people. Gerhard Lohfink situates such communities as both the process and fulfillment of the mission Jesus shares with His disciples:

> The apostles, and others as well, founded individual communities from which the church then grew to an ever increasing number of communities–chiefly through the attraction which they exercised on pagan society. So it is not 'teach all nations,' but rather 'make all nations (communities of) disciples.'[303]

Boren's practical theological work connects the relational reality of Jesus and His first followers to fellowship and ministry today. Consider how what he says about the church below also extends to family:

> The relational way is founded upon the God of relationality. Father, Son, and Holy Spirit share life together perfectly, relating in such a way that each is fully available to the others. . .The community shared by the godhead is missional in nature, self-giving in such a way that God invites people to participate in the God life,

---

[302] Arndt, 636.

[303] Lohfink, 136.

sharing in the community in which God exists. As the church enters into this communion with God, sitting at his table with him, the people share community with one another. As the church practices life as community it becomes contagious, sharing life with those who have yet to participate in communion with God. Communion with God, community with one another, and contagion of life overflowing from the nature of the relational God comprise the three aspects of what it means to live as a relational way of being the church.[304]

Boren's reference to God's relational thrust is critical. When Jesus prays for unity shortly before going to the cross, it is clear that His indwelling life in His followers, through the Spirit, compels mission: "I in them and You in Me, that they may be perfected in unity" (John 17:23). A purpose statement completes the verse and expresses His missional aim: "so that the world may know that You sent me, and loved them, even as You loved Me" (John 17:23). The Greek verb γινώσκη (*ginoske*), translated as "may know," indicates "to arrive at a knowledge of someone or something."[305] The subjective tense of the verb, as indicated by the preceding word ἵνα (*hina*), denotes the mood of probability and contingency.[306] Hence, the purpose of the ongoing mission of giving the world a testimony of God's love is contingent on the indwelling of the Son in His followers and the Father in the Son.

Jesus promises the Spirit in assuring His followers of His ongoing presence with them: "I will not leave you as orphans; I will come to you" (John 14:18). This is a relationship based in knowing God, which is Jesus' definition of what it means to live eternally (John 17:3). In the following synthesis from

---

[304] M. Scott Boren, *The Relational Way*, 18.

[305] Arndt, 199-200.

[306] J. Lyle Story and Cullen I. K. Story, *Greek to Me* (J. Lyle Story, 2000), 183.

Seamands, this relational knowledge links heaven and earth for the mission of God: "The ministry into which we have entered is the ministry *of* Jesus Christ, the Son, *to* the Father, *through* the Holy Spirit, for the sake of the church and the world."[307]

Jesus encouraged His disciples to abide in Him and thus bear fruit (John 15:4). To abide comes from the Greek verb, μένω (*meno*), and it describes "someone who does not leave a certain realm or sphere" by remaining, continuing, or abiding in Christ according to this context.[308] Jesus had just used this same word to describe how the Spirit that He would ask the Father to send would "be with you forever" (John 14:16). This broadens the understanding of the indwelling life of Jesus to be a mutual reality, where He and the Spirit are in His followers and they are in Him. It is the presence of the Father, Son, and Spirit in the lives of the disciples that accomplishes His work through them. Therefore, Jesus warned, "apart from Me you can do nothing" (John 15:5).

This context for Jesus' revelation of Himself as the true vine harkened back to Isaiah's judgment spoken over Israel, which was also a vineyard planted by YHWH. However, because of failing to abide in Him, they lacked fruit. What was the specific fruit that YHWH expected from Israel? He was looking for "justice" and "righteousness" (Isa 5:7). These rich terms represent the heart and mission of God (Jer 9:23-24). Surely Jesus places His union with His followers as the catalyst for bearing such fruit.

This theme continues in the Pauline epistles. For example, throughout the letter to the Colossians, Paul emphasizes how the mission of the gospel flows from the presence and pre-eminence of Christ. Seamands notes that "no New Testament writer emphasizes the mutual indwelling" between Christ and the believer like Paul does. "In fact, there is a growing

---

[307] Seamands, 15.

[308] Arndt, 630-631.

consensus among New Testament scholars that *this* doctrine. . .forms the heart of Paul's theology."[309]

The indwelling life of Christ is also prevalent as the church in Acts is filled with and led by the Spirit. The early church's obedience reflects how the promised Holy Spirit from the Father indwells and empowers Jesus' followers as His witnesses throughout the world (Acts 1:8). Seamands asserts "it is the Holy Spirit's mission more than theirs."[310] He adds for emphasis: "Pentecost was more about the apostles joining the Spirit than the Spirit joining them."[311] In light of the "unity of the sanctifying and empowering Spirit," James Bowers cautions against "a separation of 'being' and 'doing' in Christian life. The Spirit who transforms the believer in salvation experiences also empowers him or her for the work of transformation in the world."[312]

Any such dualism is a result of missing the focused nature of Jesus' promised gift of the Holy Spirit to His disciples. He promises "only once prior to the resurrection" that He will send the Spirit; He "promises it only to those who are active in mission. . .only to those who are the objects of official persecution;" and Jesus indicates that the Spirit "will testify to the nations."[313]

In addition, when churches and families overly individualize the experience of the Holy Spirit, there is a lack of understanding the continuity of the *missio Dei* from Jesus through the church. That is, the Holy Spirit continues, through the church, Jesus' kingdom mission He inaugurated through the incarnation. Incarnation relates to the *missio Dei* in its risk and purpose, according to Richard Waldrop and J.L. Corky Alexander Jr.: "The incarnation, then, establishes the pattern for all subsequent missionary activity in various ways. It is

---

[309] Seamands, 147.

[310] Wilson, 166.

[311] Ibid., 168.

[312] Bowers, 64.

[313] Levison, *Fresh Air*, 181-182.

not only opening oneself, but also is the fact of *being sent on mission* for the purpose of the salvation of others."[314]

Smith summarizes the themes reviewed thus far as they can relate to the formative and indwelling nature of God's being and doing in redemptive families as part of the *missio Dei*:

> Christian worship and formation, as practices of *divine* action, culminate in Christian action–being sent as ambassadors of another 'city,' as witnesses to kingdom come, to live and act communally as a people who embody a foretaste of God's shalom. . .Worship and the practices of Christian formation are first and foremost the way the Spirit invites us into union with the Triune God. . .with a sending. . .a co-*mission*-ing accompanied by the promise of the Spirit's presence. . .co-abiding presence and participation.[315]

---

[314] Richard E. Waldrop and J.L. Corky Alexander Jr., "Salvation History and the Mission of God: Implications for the Mission of the Church among Native Americans" in *Remembering Jamestown: Hard Questions About Christian Mission*, eds. Amos Yong and Barbara Brown Zikmund. [Eugene: Pickwick Publications, 2010],117.

[315] Smith, *Imagining the Kingdom*, 152-153.

Chapter 10

Survey of Missional-Related Aspects in the History of Family

---—∞∞∞—---

T he story of God throughout scripture and in the centuries following can be told through the stories of communities, including families. Joseph Hellerman thinks it is important "that we view God's work in human history as primarily group-oriented" so that God "through His people. . .would fully and finally receive the glory that is His due."[316] God's people span both time and the globe, and there are countless local expressions of this community, which also includes natural families.

Claude Lévi-Strauss acknowledges the integral relationship between family and society and its history: "There would be no society without families, but equally there would be no families if society did not already exist."[317] Indeed, for Michael Novak, hope is embedded within the purpose of family, which he states succinctly: "Without it there isn't any future. . .it is

---

[316] Joseph H. Hellerman, *When the Church Was a Family: Recapturing Jesus' Vision for Authentic Christian Community* (Nashville: B&H Academic, 2009), 125.

[317] Claude Lévi-Strauss, "Introduction" in *A History of the Family: Distant Worlds, Ancient Worlds*, Vol. 1, eds. André Burguière et al. [Cambridge, MA: The Belknap Press of Harvard University Press, 1996], 4.

human destiny to be familial."[318] Yet this consistent dependency upon the family for a present and future society does not mean there is consistent expression of family over time and throughout societies. On the contrary, tracing the development of family is an endeavor as diverse as the expressions of family throughout time. Thus, Lévi-Strauss concludes:

> It is no longer possible to believe that the family has taken a unilinear path as it has evolved from ancient forms which we will not see again, moving towards other, distinctive forms that represent progress. On the contrary, it could be that at a very early stage the human mind, in all its inventive power, conceived and laid out on display all the forms assumed by the family. What we regard as a process of evolution would then be nothing more than a series of choices from these possibilities, the result of movements in various directions within the limits of an already defined framework.[319]

Within the framework of redemptive family in the story of God, these possibilities for family are the backdrop for the potential familial responses to God's redemptive call in different times and places. Within each generation, the intention of the Creator is for His people to reflect His image as a joyful and missional fellowship, a community that includes families. Families of this sort are driven by a redemptive thrust in their formation and function.

In terms of what has preceded the contemporary realities of the family, Françoise Zonabend poses the question, "What is the nature of these families which exist everywhere and

---

[318]   Novak, Michael, authors et al., *The Family: America's Hope* (Rockford, Il: Rockford College Institute, 1979), 13-14.

[319]   Burguière, eds. et al., 6.

yet differ from place to place?"[320] The potential for speculative exploration is endless if the scope is a world survey of families within various cultures and societal developments. For the purposes of establishing foundations for The Think Kingdom–Be Family Project, this chapter focuses on family dynamics within the people of God during scriptural history. These redemptive and missional aspects derived from biblical culture are juxtaposed with family life in the contemporary North American context. The aim of this comparative and reflective approach is to build a bridge from the biblical historical context to this contemporary context.

In both form and function, redemptive families in North America provide a broader expression than the nuclear family and its contained lifestyle that generally characterizes the North American ideal of family. This ideal emerged from the mid-nineteenth century, and it departs from realities preceding that time and those that developed following it.

An initial comparison between the Hebrew family from Old Testament times and the North American ideal relates to existential perspective. For Hebrew families at any time, there was in the present both awareness of their connection to the past and cognizance of their future through their legacy. Frank Alvarez-Pereyre and Florence Heymann identify this "genealogical continuity" as the source of "individual and collective identity" for Jewish families.[321] This past, present, and continuous perspective that embraces past, present, and future generations contrasts with the more immediate focus of many isolated nuclear North American families.

---

[320] Françoise Zonabend, "An Anthropological Perspective on Kinship and the Family" in *A History of the Family: Distant Worlds, Ancient Worlds,* Vol. 1, eds. André Burguière et al. [Cambridge, MA: The Belknap Press of Harvard University Press, 1996], 9.

[321] Frank Alvarez-Pereyre and Florence Heymann, "The Desire for Transcendence: the Hebrew Family Model and Jewish Family Practices" in *A History of the Family: Distant Worlds, Ancient Worlds,* Vol. 1, eds. André Burguière et al. [Cambridge, MA: The Belknap Press of Harvard University Press, 1996], 156.

For the broader Hebrew community, "the origins of the family are marked in Genesis by a disruption," where "man has to leave a previous family" to unite with a woman and start a family. Alvarez-Pereyre and Heymann note that "this system of disintegration and integration combines with a temporal continuity, from generation to generation, to create and perpetuate the social organization."[322] Within the redemptive arc of the biblical narrative, there are numerous examples of God's judgment and grace disrupting the pre-existing disruption of sin. These illustrate the integrative and holistic aim for restoration between God and His people.

Consider Noah's family and their preservation through the flood narrative (Gen 6-9). Then there is the call of Abram and the response of His family to leave their land trusting God for the promise of descendants and land (Gen 12-25). The disruptions of judgment and grace leading toward integration continue through the remainder of Genesis in the journeys of Jacob and his sons, especially the story of Joseph taken captive against his will, which in turn preserved his family in the land of Egypt. From Egypt, the intervention of God in the Exodus once again established the Hebrew family in the land of promise before the disruption of exile with later generations. Again, the redemptive narrative illustrates the preservation of God's purposes through His people on earth, through disruption and integration.

Compare this Hebraic context of heritage and continuity, in the midst of discontinuity, with the North American family as it lives out its "freedom." Hervé Varenne questions just how free the North American family is in view of "the 1950s. . .the dream that is a nightmare, a pretext for ideological pronouncements that reveal much about the current situation."[323]

---

[322] Burguière, eds. et al., 167.

[323] Hervé Varenne, "Love and Liberty: the Contemporary American Family" in *A History of the Family: The Impact of Modernity*, Vol. 2, eds. André Burguière et al. [Cambridge, MA: The Belknap Press of Harvard University Press, 1996], 416.

Varenne also notes how the contemporary American family's pursuit of freedom experiences disruption and division:

> Love does not abolish freedom. In marriage one does not really 'give' oneself to the other–as the image may be elsewhere or 'elsewhen' in the Euro-American world. In marriage one 'shares' a self that remains one's own. Love, being about freedom, is also about separation. Marriage is about divorce.[324]

He connects the disruptive trajectory of freedom to parents and children as well: "Parents enjoyed a freedom in the past for which they are now paying with the freedom they must give to their own children."[325]

This progression of the disintegrative nature of freedom in families seeking self-preservation starkly contrasts the integrative nature of freedom in families seeking the kingdom of God. For kingdom-seeking families, the pathway of downward mobility leads to wholeness and the blessing of others. In other words, families receive blessing in lowering themselves to serve others. These families still suffer the disruption of sin, but it yields an opportunity for repentance and redemption. In turning from sin, they experience freedom from the performance trap of "displaying themselves so that they 'look like' the mythical image;"[326] in its place, a healthy family lifestyle emerges based upon identity and work that reflects the being and doing of God Himself.

Varenne laments the optimistic dream of the fifties in his pessimistic assessment of the fleeting nature of the contemporary family's freedom. In his view, the optimism appears problematic because it is neither realized nor realistic. For Stephanie Coontz, the concern is that this hope has not

---

324 Burguière, eds.et al., Vol. 2, 420.

325 Ibid.

326 Ibid., 423.

endured. She sees optimism as the key to what sets the fifties apart in the American conscience:

> The contrast between the perceived hopefulness of the fifties and our own misgivings about the future is key to contemporary nostalgia for the period. Greater optimism *did* exist then, even among many individuals and groups who were in terrible circumstances.[327]

Hope fuels mission, and North American families lack hope. Coontz continues, "As nuclear families moved into the suburbs, they retreated from social activism but entered voluntary relationships with people who had children of the same age."[328] Beyond a mere geographical movement for families, she further notes the accompanying shift in community involvement: "The triumph of private family values discourages us from meeting our emotional needs through mutual aid associations, political and social action groups, or other forms of public life that used to be as important in people's identity as love or family."[329] Coontz implies that families have marginalized themselves by privatizing their lives, and subsequently, the public square is marginalizing the families' values.

Others concur on the shift that has occurred, and they link it to an economic shift as well as a sentimental one. Rodney Clapp adds that this "traditional family, by contrast, has lost the family's earlier function as an economically productive unit. Its main function is sentimental. It serves as an oasis, emotional stabilizer and battery-charger for its members."[330] Beatrice Gottlieb describes it thusly: "The ideology of the

---

[327] Stephanie Coontz, *The Way We Really Are: Coming to Terms with America's Changing Families* (New York: Basic Books, 1997), 34-35.

[328] Coontz, *The Way We Really Are*, 39.

[329] Stephanie Coontz, *The Way We Never Were: American Families and the Nostalgia Trap* (New York: Basic Books, 1992), 120.

[330] Clapp, 13.

family has been completely transformed. 'Family' no longer has anything to do with power and wealth. They are irrelevant to the association of the family with affection, which is equally accessible to all."[331]

Though Gottlieb acknowledges the perception that the family is "being confronted with what looks like insurmountable problems," she likewise holds out the hopeful lesson from history that "many things are possible."[332] While she would not go the route of defending or promoting a return to the ideal of the fifties, her conclusion joins with sociologists, historians, and theologians on dynamics that present an opportunity for the missional family conversation.

Coontz's historical perspective leads her to conclude "that the so-called 'crisis of the family' is a subset of a much larger crisis of social obligation that requires us to look beyond private family relations and rebuild larger social ties." She is aware that some "are very pessimistic about the possibility of extending social reciprocities and interdependencies beyond the family." Yet she holds that in a contemporary culture of "competitive individualism" and its subsequent pressures, "people are deeply dissatisfied with the lack of community and larger purpose in their lives."[333] The opportunity of this moment in time is to rediscover redemptive family within the missional conversation and expression. In fact, the conclusion to her historical study essentially says as much:

> . . .despite all the difficulty of making generalizations about past families, the historical evidence does suggest that families have been most successful wherever they have built meaningful, solid networks and commitments *beyond* their own boundaries. We may discover that the best thing we will ever do for our own families,

---

[331] Beatrice Gottlieb, *The Family in the Western World: From the Black Death to the Industrial Age* (New York: Oxford, 1993), 272.

[332] Ibid., 272.

[333] Coontz, *The Way We Never Were*, 283.

however we define them, is to get involved in community or political action to help others.[334]

Consider this historical family development in light of contemporary church family ministry programming; both suffer from the inward drift and self-preserving nature of homogenous groupings and interactions. Family ministry can easily become sentimental, even with salvific sincerity. Ministry to families within the gospel of the kingdom of God is holistic in its salvation proclamation, inviting all areas of family life–private and public, sacred and secular–into a missional vocation. To this end, gaps exist between the generations in family ministries. As in the society, so it is in the church; there is an isolative trajectory of the nuclear family. However, hope persists for what can be accomplished through families.

This entails a recovery of intergenerational connection and form that characterize the family experience. Regarding how form differs from that which is implicit in the North American ideal of the traditional family, recall Wilson's comment that the Hebrew term for family, מִשְׁפָּחָה (*mishpahah*), "does not include only the nuclear family of mother, father, and children, but implied an extended family or clan. It often refers to a whole social unit including parents, children, grandparents, aunts, uncles, and cousins."[335]

Gottlieb writes that "in the past Western households normally contained nonrelatives."[336] The household concept often considered "coresidence" as "more important in defining a family than blood relationship."[337] In the Hebrew home, hospitality provided an open door to nonrelatives as well. Looking at a Hebrew family's lifestyle, "rabbis considered hospitality one of the most important functions of the home. . .the home was to be open to all classes and kinds of

---

[334] Coontz, *The Way We Never Were*, 287-288.

[335] Wilson, 210.

[336] Gottlieb, 6.

[337] Ibid., 7.

people."[338] With this picture of strangers embraced by a broad group of relatives, family comes into redemptive focus. Such communities express God's kingdom.

In addition to Hebraic and early Western homes, Hellerman draws from the Mediterranean world of Jesus' time and that of the early church. He notes that more than any other social group, "one's family demanded the highest commitment of undivided loyalty, relational solidarity, and personal sacrifice. . .major life decisions were made in the context of the family"[339]–to the point, "the group took priority over the individual."[340] So family featured relationships extending beyond the nuclear family, and the family group was a very influential factor in the life of its members.

The North American understanding of being the family of God is conditioned by its individualist and nuclear-family orientation, but in the New Testament, it is shaped by the perception of "a strong-group person."[341] Whereas North American adults establish their own families, which tend to decentralize sibling relationships, "in Mediterranean antiquity, marriage took a back seat priority-wise to another more important family relationship–the bond between blood brothers and sisters."[342] Therefore, "'Brother' meant immeasurably more. . .it was their most important family relationship." This establishes "brothers and sisters in Christ" in a new light, and it indicates that "there would have been no place in the early Christian church for an individualist."[343] This Mediterranean context emphasizes the expression of sibling loyalty. Regarding the priority of marriage in the present context of North American Christianity, it is helpful to rediscover the loyalty to a spouse as a brother or sister in Christ first and foremost.

---

[338] Clapp, 219.

[339] Hellerman, 31.

[340] Ibid., 32.

[341] Ibid., 36.

[342] Ibid., 35.

[343] Ibid., 50-51.

Hence, the intergenerational and extended relational elements of family life in the Hebrew, Mediterranean, and past Western households are important for cultivating redemptive families with a missional thrust to their lifestyles. As the nuclei for families expand, the gap lessens between private and public life. Both the Old and New Testament homes had public dimensions to their existence, and they serve as an example for families today where the privacy of the home has become separate from public life. Clapp challenges this dichotomy:

> We must be 'just who we are' (that is, persons whose identities are based in and on Christ), in public no less in private. In a real sense, and like the homes of the New Testament church, our homes must go public. Our call is to live not in private havens or retreats, but in mission bases. . .Key to this, of course, is hospitality. . .So welcoming our Christian sisters and brothers is a public act and way of being. It makes Christ publicly available and evident.[344]

Historical realities of families in previous times inform present challenges and opportunities for families today. As this section highlights, a redemptive family embodies key dynamics from family life in biblical times that also connect to aspects from the development of western families. Redemptive families in their form and function redeem values from the past in the present, because the magnitude of the mission requires as much–the *missio Dei*.

---

[344] Clapp, 156-157.

Chapter 11

The Missional Family
of Families

—— ◦◦◦ ——

The Think Kingdom–Be Family Project is an initiative dependent upon missiological integration and ecclesiological fullness. It is designed to encourage, through family-with-family consociation, what Bowers lists as necessary for spiritual formation: "a nurturing fellowship. . .characterized by personal commitment. . .accountability, responsibility, interpersonal intimacy and ethical unity." Indeed, "the shared experience of the Spirit is the spiritual basis for this fellowship and for unity of ethical witness in the world."[345] Kenneth Collins echoes the thought by connecting fulfillment in body life with blessing: "The body of Christ as a living organism must be energetic, engaged in all manner of good works, in order to thrive and be a blessing to others."[346] In short, the church is the missional family consisting of missional families.

The practice of the church as a missional family is expressed in its understanding and practice of hospitality. Yong traces the progression. It begins with the Head of the church, Jesus Christ, who "characterizes the hospitality of God in part as the exemplary recipient of hospitality. . .dependent on the

---

[345] Bowers, 77.

[346] Kenneth J. Collins, *The Theology of John Wesley: Holy Love and the Shape of Grace* (Nashville: Abingdon Press, 2007), 253.

welcome of others. . .it is precisely in his role as guest that Jesus also announces and enacts, through the Holy Spirit, the hospitality of God."[347] Hospitality continues through His followers, who from the first were those "who welcome[d] Jesus into their homes" and became, "in turn, guests of the redemptive hospitality of God." Further, as evidenced in the table fellowship surrounding Jesus, "the most eager recipients of the divine hospitality were not the religious leaders but the poor and the oppressed."[348]

Summing up the progression from Luke-Acts, Yong writes, "The hospitality of God manifest in Jesus the anointed one in Luke is now extended through the early church in Acts by the power of the same Holy Spirit."[349] As a central figure in the gospel going to the Gentiles, the pattern continues through Paul, who "is also both a recipient and conduit of God's hospitality."[350]

Among the poor and oppressed, prisoners for the sake of the gospel were especially dependent upon the hospitality of their church family. Hellerman explains:

> Roman elites did not use their tax dollars to feed their prisoners. They used them to feed them-selves. To survive in a Roman prison, a person had to depend on his family to bring him the necessities of food and clothing, so he could stay alive long enough to face his accusers. For the Christians the church was their family. Believers who were imprisoned and awaiting execution because of their confession of Christ had their needs met by their brothers and sisters in Christ.[351]

---

[347] Yong, 101.

[348] Ibid., 102.

[349] Ibid., 103-104.

[350] Ibid.

[351] Hellerman, 109.

For the church as a missional family, hospitality is an orientation of receptivity of God's blessing as they steward the flow of this blessing to neighbors. The same potential exists for redemptive families expressing the mission of the church. Yong summarizes:

> What is of central import for our purposes both in the life of Jesus and in the ministry of the early church is the themes of household relationships, table fellowship, and journeying and itinerancy. In all of these cases, not only is Christian life and Christian mission mutually intertwined, but we have seen that the roles of guests and hosts are fluid, continuously reversing.[352]

In order for families in North America to cultivate hospitable lifestyles, significant shifts away from self-absorption in thinking and action must occur. Within the contained and isolated existence of nuclear families, priorities of work and recreation often preclude hospitality. Even busyness with church activity needs evaluation. Is church involvement geared for self or others? A customized personal spirituality finds it difficult to embrace the inconvenience of hospitality. Accordingly, Hellerman advocates for this necessary, albeit significant shift away from self-absorption:

> . . .the expression 'personal savior occurs nowhere in the pages of Scripture. . .our radical overemphasis on a personal relationship with God is an American–not a biblical–theological construction. What we find in the Bible, rather, is a God who seems at least as concerned with His group (me in relationship with my brothers and sisters in Christ) as He is with the individual (me in relationship with God).[353]

---

[352] Yong, 105.

[353] Hellerman, 7.

David Platt warns of the peril of focusing on Jesus as "personal Lord and Savior." Doing so leads to "a customized Christianity that revolves around a personal Christ that we create for ourselves...someone with whom we are a little more comfortable." Then he strikes at the heart of what is at stake:

> We dilute what he says about the cost of following him, we disregard what he says about those who choose not to follow him, we practically ignore what he says about materialism, and we functionally miss what he says about mission. We pick and choose what we like and don't like from Jesus' teachings. In the end, we create a nice, non-offensive, politically correct, middle-class, American Jesus who looks just like us and thinks just like us.[354]

Hellerman captures this contrast between the biblical society and North America's "individualist" culture by referring to the former one as "collectivist" or "strong-group."[355] This provides the helpful context for understanding Jesus' challenge to the natural family in several gospel passages. Hellerman warns against a "pro-family theology of the Gospels" that seeks to domesticate Jesus' teaching by deflecting the plain meaning of Jesus' call to distance oneself and deny the natural family relationships.[356]

Jesus challenges identity in issuing the kingdom call within a strong-group society. "The loyalty conflict is not about making a choice between God and people. Rather, it is about choosing between one group of people and another–between our natural family and our eternal family."[357]

---

[354] David Platt, *Follow Me: A Call to Die. A Call to Live.* (Carol Stream, Il: Tyndale House, 2013), 75-76.

[355] Hellerman, 14.

[356] Ibid., 56.

[357] Ibid., 63.

Hellerman elaborates on this important characteristic within the early church, where "the group took priority over the individual. . .a person's most important group was his family. . . .[and] the closest family bond was the bond between siblings."[358] Thus, what Jesus creates in calling His followers after Him is "a surrogate family," which ushered in a "potential conflict of group loyalties;" whereas in a "personal relationship with God" framework, the individual's conflict is resolved in prioritizing the love of God over family. Hellerman challenges that it is "not simply the issue of deciding between love for God and love for family. . .Relationships among God's children were to take priority over blood family ties."[359] This family by faith before blood priority is an important clarification in calling forth and cultivating missional families. They must be contextualized within the family of God first and foremost.

This does not preclude natural families entering the kingdom family, as Hellerman again illustrates: ". . .whenever possible, Jesus encouraged ongoing loyalty to natural family relations on the part of His followers." The priority of belonging to the family of God can actually compel love and loyalty within natural families. "Surrogate family loyalty and natural family loyalty were not necessarily mutually exclusive expressions of relational solidarity for those who belonged to the Jesus movement."[360]

Further, Hellerman notes the possibility of whole families entering the kingdom:

> An ideal and not uncommon situation, we might surmise, would see the conversion of a whole household, with the disciple's natural family embedded in, and serving the mission of, the dominant surrogate family of faith. In

---

[358] Hellerman, 64.

[359] Ibid.

[360] Ibid., 72-73.

this case, there would be no conflict of loyalties. But even here the natural family existed to serve the designs of the family of God, and not vice-versa. The focus was on the church – not on the family. And where conflict between the natural family and God's family did arise, the faith family was to become the primary locus of relational solidarity.[361]

The radical call to follow Jesus in this North American individualist society incorporates a denial of family in order to submit to the family of God as the stronger group. To refuse is to idolize the family. As noted, hope persists that such a submission can be accomplished as a natural family, though this is not always the case. At all times, the family of God in His kingdom must be the collective source of individual and family identity.

Another necessary shift toward a broader understanding of salvation, according to Hellerman, is to pair justification with the concept he terms "familification:"

> Just as we are *justified* with respect to God the Father upon salvation, so also we are *familified* with respect to our brothers and sisters in Christ. And this familification is no less a positional reality than our justification. It would follow from this that just as we need to increasingly actualize the positional reality of our *justification* in the spiritual formation process, so also should we long to increasingly actualize the positional reality of our *familification*, as we grow into the image and likeness of Christ. Indeed, as we have seen throughout our discussion, we simply cannot separate the two. To be sold out to God (and thereby actualize our *justification*) is to be sold out to God's group (and thereby

---

[361] Hellerman, 73.

actualize our *familification*). We need to cultivate both the vertical and horizontal dimensions of what happened to us at salvation, as we seek to mature in the Lord.[362]

Hence, for the church as a missional family, its hospitality is an integrative reality of salvation by God's grace through justification, and God's love through familification. This community of image-bearers proclaims the mission of salvation to the lost by inviting them into "God's household," οἰϰεῖος (*oikeios*; Eph 2:19).[363]

Carrying out Christ's mission in this way is rooted in the very identity of the church. Stanley Hauerwas and William H. Willimon explain: "In saying, 'The church doesn't have a social strategy, the church *is* a social strategy,' we are attempting to indicate an alternative way of looking at the political, social significance of the church."[364] This is what Lohfink sees as "the decisive task of the church. . .[is] to build itself up as a society in contrast to the world, as the realm of Christ's rule in which fraternal love is the law of life."[365] The concepts of community and family and the subversive mission of redemption converge in this summation from Hauerwas and Willimon: "We serve the world by showing it something that it is not, namely, a place where God is forming a family out of strangers."[366]

Families can join "missional communities" that positively "order their lives around communion, caring, and celebration."[367] James Davison Hunter elaborates on the nature of such communities, describing them as "alternative to the 'defense against,' 'relevance to,' and 'purity from'" reactionary camps

---

[362] Hellerman, 132.

[363] Snyder, 46.

[364] Stanley Hauerwas and William H. Willimon, *Resident Aliens: Life in the Christian Colony* (Nashville: Abington Press, 1989), 43.

[365] Lohfink, 145.

[366] Hauerwas, 83.

[367] McNeal, 179.

on the outside; he locates these positive communities by characterizing their existence as a "faithful presence within."[368] Rather than shouldering a complicated and unrealistic burden of changing the world, families join communities of faithful presence where the aim is enjoying God and responding with Him to their surroundings.[369]

Eugene Peterson echoes Hunter's message of faithfulness within culture in contrast to the overstated sentiment of changing the world:

> . . .the mentality of the subversive. . .works quietly and hiddenly, patiently. He has committed himself to Christ's victory over culture and is willing to do those small things. No subversive ever does anything big. He is always carrying secret messages, planting suspicion that there is something beyond what the culture says is final.[370]

Subversive faithfulness is helpful because it characterizes a prophetic lifestyle for the church. Luke Timothy Johnson clarifies how more than spoken words, prophecy is "a way of being in the world; it brings God's will into human history through the words, yes, but also the deeds and character of the prophet."[371] From the perspective of Luke's gospel, Johnson sees a prophetic way of being for the church that is "total dedication to responding to the call of God in every circumstance, more than cultivating institutional self-interest."[372] This approach best expresses the hope of the kingdom of God

---

[368] Hunter, 272.

[369] Ibid., 285-286.

[370] Eugene H. Peterson, *The Contemplative Pastor: Returning to the Art of Spiritual Direction* (Grand Rapids: Eerdmans Publishing Co., 1989), 11.

[371] Luke Timothy Johnson, *Prophetic Jesus, Prophetic Church: The Challenge of Luke-Acts to Contemporary Christians* (Grand Rapids: Eerdmans, 2011), 41.

[372] Luke Timothy Johnson, 70.

through a "people who live by an alternative construction of reality. . .more possible to be realized by small intentional communities than by worldwide administrations."[373]

Walter Brueggemann concurs with Johnson and assigns the cultivation of such "an alternative community" to "the task of prophetic ministry."[374] In addition to the Old Testament prophetic literature, this mindset is present in the writings as evidenced in David's words in Psalm 37:3: "Trust in YHWH and do good; dwell in the land and cultivate faithfulness."

Redemptive families paradoxically establish a hospitable home in the land by sustaining a guest-like mindset. Yong explains: "following the biblical metanarrative, Christians can never be completely at home. Instead, we can always only be exiles in diaspora, always only be 'strangers and foreigners on the earth' (Heb 11:13) who are looking for a homeland in another city."[375] So in the pilgrimage to this new city, "how might we seek the welfare of the cities wherein which Christian exiles find themselves today?" Yong answers, "through the practices of hospitality on the margins;" he expands:

> Hospitality is transformed, in effect taken out of the economy of exchange, when it is associated with hosts who are liminal, marginal, and on the underside of the social order. Hospices, hospitals, and orphanages work most effectively when serviced not by those existing within a system of salary and remuneration, but by hosts who respect their guests and. . .the lines between guests and hosts are blurred, and the conditions for giving and receiving hospitality apply to both sides, even if in (subtly) different respects.[376]

---

[373] Luke Timothy Johnson, 74.

[374] Walter Brueggemann, *The Prophetic Imagination* (Minneapolis: Fortress Press, 2001), 117.

[375] Yong and Zickmund, eds., 167.

[376] Yong, 125-126.

Jesus' incarnation within marginal community summarizes the biblical theological foundation for the idea and practice of a missional family contextualizing the gospel in time and space. Alan Roxburgh and Scott Boren affirm that this was Jesus' way:

> Jesus' way of being a theologian was to embody God in a local setting. . .where people lived in their daily, ordinary stuff. He did not wait for the ideal religious time or setting and then ask people to come to him. He went to them.[377]

Ministry can drift into passivity before the world, waiting for those outside to come in. Luke Timothy Johnson identifies that "one of the invaluable roles that prophets can play within the church is to help it remain in touch with the margins."[378] Stephen Seamands writes about how such an inward perspective in his ministry was challenged by a picture he encountered in his mind of God's outward perspective:

> I pictured myself standing in the United Methodist denominational vineyard in which God had called me to labor. . .Behind me I pictured the risen Christ. Since he has many vineyards in various churches and denominations, he wasn't standing in any particular vineyard. So he was outside the gate. . .Then, turning from the vineyard I had been surveying, I looked at the risen Christ. I thought he would be facing me, but to my surprise, he had his back to me. I thought he would be looking at me and my vineyard, but his tear-filled eyes were focused elsewhere–on the world beyond him. That's

---

[377] Alan Roxburgh and M. Scott Boren, *Introducing The Missional Church: What It Is, Why It Matters, How To Become One* (Grand Rapids: Baker Books, 2009), 94.

[378] Luke Timothy Johnson, 186.

what he seemed most concerned about–not the renewal of my vineyard, or for that matter any of the vineyards, but the redemption of the world.[379]

Seamands reflects how he "had made the renewal of my church and denomination an end in itself."[380] A similar disservice can occur with the family. To present the family as a missional community is a redemptive concept with a restorative thrust. Christ redeems family from its self-absorbed, fractured, and fragmented state and restores it to an outpost of mission within the community of God's people. Further, such a family may serve to engage others, even other families, in the context of God's redemptive purposes and practices.

Rodney Clapp offers the following synthesis as confirmation for the themes detailed in this chapter:

> Kingdom mission and Christian hospitality and community are not instrumental. They are not undertaken *in order* to strengthen and make families happy. The strengthened happiness of families is an important thing. But it is a byproduct of service to a kingdom larger than the family, not the object of the service to that kingdom. To be healthy, the family needs a mission or purpose beyond itself.[381]

---

[379] Seamands, 174.

[380] Ibid., 175.

[381] Clapp, 163.

Chapter 12

Missional Family Wholeness

——— ∞∞∞ ———

Framed within the church as the redemptive family of God, a family can develop a missional vision and practice, alongside of others. In a culture of isolative and fragmented family patterns, this developmental process for missional families is a part of formation that James K.A. Smith describes as "a counter-liturgy." It is "an intentionally decentering practice. . .calling us out of ourselves into the life of the Triune God. . .invited into a Story where we are *hidden* with Christ in God. . .to love neighbors and enemies, widows and orphans." This counter-cultural development must be developed from the inside-out in a family's being and doing. Yet, what might seem paradoxical at first is simply a demonstration of wholeness at work. Smith concludes his thought, "If such a Story is really going to capture our imaginations, it needs to get into our gut–it needs to be written on our hearts."[382] Getting it into a family's being involves doing that is rooted in grace rather than performance. For Smith, this is how students experience formation through Christian education. For The Think Kingdom–Be Family Initiative, families develop wholeness by doing the works that flow from their being.

---

[382] Smith, *Imagining the Kingdom*, 150.

A redemptive family experiences the formation of its desires. Thus, from Smith's perspective, it is a Christian educational endeavor, because the formation of desires is "happening all over the place. . .in homes and at the mall; in football stadiums and at Fourth of July parades; in worship and at work." For families and individuals, "what's at stake" is "nothing less than the formation of radical disciples who desire the kingdom of God."[383]

Smith's "core claim. . .is that liturgies–whether 'sacred' or 'secular'–shape and constitute our identities by forming our most fundamental desires and our basic attunement to the world." "Liturgy" refers to behaviors, patterns, and disciplines of which families are both aware and unaware. "In short, liturgies make us certain kinds of people, and what defines us is what we *love*. . .whose orientation to the world is shaped from the body up more than from the head down."[384]

Steven Garber concurs on the formative centrality of the question, "What do you love?" He explains, "It is in that question and the spiritual dynamics implicit in its answer that belief and behavior are woven together."[385] Through this construct of what families love, an examination and reformation of their outer life begins from their inner life, where their loves originate. As noted, the flow from being (identity) into doing characterizes how families develop missional wholeness. An awareness of the love for God's kingdom and its alternative doing is what begins to change the family's reality of being.

Returning to the broader context of church family, Stephen Macchia reflects on this progression for healthy churches:

---

[383] James K.A. Smith, *Desiring the Kingdom* (Grand Rapids: Baker Academic, 2009), 19.

[384] Ibid., 25.

[385] Steven Garber, *The Fabric of Faithfulness* (Downers Grove: InterVarsity Press, 1996), 35.

> It is God's priority that we understand our 'being,' for it is there that we discover him more intimately. Being in Christ requires that my soul first listens to his still, small voice out of my love and obedience to his Word, his lordship, his revealed truth and will. . .the Latin root for the word *obedience* means 'to listen'. . .'Doing' for Christ means that, out of the inner core of my being in him, I walk and talk and serve and love and live for him.[386]

Macchia's description of living for God focuses on the just actions recited by Jesus in Matthew 25:35-36, 40. These include the following types of caring actions toward "one of the least of these brothers of mine:" feeding the hungry, giving drinks to the thirsty, showing hospitality to the stranger, clothing the naked, taking care of the sick, and visiting the prisoner. Redemptive wholeness for families begins with hearing God and ends with a lifestyle that is responsive to the needs of others.

To further establish aspects of the process of developing wholeness, Macchia identifies "four 'tions' that we dare not shun" if we are "to embrace a season of growth and change:"

1. Reflection – taking the time to hop off the treadmills of our hectic ministry lives and ask ourselves some basic questions about who we are, what we are accomplishing together, where we would like to go in the future, and how we hope to get there.
2. Affirmation – acknowledging the truth about ourselves and our church and affirming the gifts that have been planted in our midst as a result of his work of grace in our lives and in our common kingdom-building service. What are our greatest strengths, our most obvious

---

[386] Stephen A. Macchia, *Becoming a Healthy Church* (Grand Rapids: Baker Books, 1999), 63.

needs, our ability to maximize our strengths, and our openness to change?

3. Evaluation – observing together our relationships, knowledge, skill levels, and the best ways to enhance our ministry initiatives in the days to come. By loving each other enough to be honest with each other, we will be able to give each other permission to fail, restore conflicts as they inevitably occur, and strive for true change in the hearts, minds, and wills of the people in our care.

4. Application – bringing to fruition the changes and growth we anticipate prayerfully as a result of the self-analysis we have completed. Learning how to master the basics and seek improvements over time will lead to a maturing of the body and build far more effective service in unity. In this stage the leadership team is called on to identify the places where we would like to grow and specific direction for how we will get there.[387]

This process correlates to the development of missional wholeness detailed in the first two chapters. Consider the parallels of reflection to revelation, affirmation to awareness, evaluation to motivation/intuition, and application to integration.

Steven Harper reduces the development of missional awareness to a three-fold progression: Insight leads to focus which leads to action. Contemplation is a key part to the insight that brings about focus, and determination is necessary to respond with action.[388] Harper's flow from insight to action parallels revelation to integration in *Missional Family Wholeness*.

What follows are descriptions of the particular dynamics in the process of how families develop missional wholeness. It

---

[387] Stephen Macchia, 219.

[388] Steven Harper, *Embrace the Spirit: An Invitation to Friendship with God* (Wheaton, Il: Victor Books, 1987), 120.

is also prescriptive in the sense that being and doing, though they flow in that order, also contain elements of reciprocity. Smith offers a rationale for the import of intentionality in a being-oriented formational process:

> It's not a matter of choosing between worship *or* mission; nor are we faced with the false dichotomy of church *or* world, cathedral *or* city. To the contrary, we worship *for* mission; we gather *for* sending; we enter ourselves in the practices of the body of Christ *for the sake of* the world; we are reformed in the cathedral to undertake our image-bearing commission to reform the city. So it is precisely an expansive sense of mission that requires formation. It is the missional *telos* of Christian *action* that requires us to be intentional about the formative power of Christian practices.[389]

Revelation

Receiving revelation from God involves content, and it especially involves the context of living a life of following Him. Peter's confession of Jesus' identity was more than an insight of fact; it was a realization in person with Jesus and in the place of Caesarea Philippi (Matt 16:13-19).

For families, reflection is a key formative missional discipline. It requires that families engage in experiences upon which they can reflect. It is not thinking in a vacuum.[390] Rather than viewing reflection and practice separately, the goal in Smith's words is "to foster intentional reflection *on* practice in order to encourage reflective immersion *in* practice."[391]

---

[389] Smith, *Imagining the Kingdom*, 154.

[390] Ibid., 73.

[391] Ibid., 186.

Quite often the revelation of God in the life of a family is realized through the experience of brokenness. C.S. Lewis writes in the story, *The Silver Chair*, "There is nothing like a good shock of pain for dissolving certain kinds of magic."[392] The "magic" that enchants families has already been noted, namely self-absorption and self-preservation couched in an ideal that mixes and customizes Christianity and the American dream. Pain can result in greater persistence toward this end, disillusionment leading to despair and disengagement, or the turning point to a new journey toward a better goal.

This formative context of brokenness is articulated by Paul when he references the development of hope through "tribulations" (Rom 5:3-5), and James who states that "various trials" can lead toward maturity (James 1:2-4). James does not focus on a glorification of brokenness but an understanding that such a context is a place and process to experience surrender and sanctification within the *missio Dei*.

Consider as well Ezekiel's vision of the valley of dry bones, which leads Levison to reflect on the nature of the pivot from death to life: "Yet Eden comes around, re-creation occurs, only in the throes of grief. It is the grieving exiles who hear the promise of a new heart and a new spirit. It is the survivors of catastrophe, the living dead in the valley of the shadow of death, who will receive the spirit and begin, haltingly perhaps, life afresh."[393]

From a secular perspective, Smith points out that even consumerism (as evidenced in the ads at a mall) shapes the desires of people through an implicit message of their brokenness by showing them what they are not. The trap is that this "issues not in confession but in consumption."[394] It is interesting that Coontz notes a similar dynamic at work with the television shows of the 1950s. Families "watched them to see how families were *supposed* to live," which for many

---

[392] C.S. Lewis, *The Silver Chair* (New York: Harper Trophy, 1953), 190.

[393] John R. Levison, *Filled with the Spirit* (Grand Rapids: Eerdmans, 2009), 102.

[394] Smith, *Desiring the Kingdom*, 96.

showed them what they were not. Coontz further comments on how a hopeful inclination was additionally at work in families who watched "to get a little reassurance that they were headed in the right direction."[395] The argument could be made that television in the current decade spotlights what is less than ideal rather than holding forth an ideal, thus providing a false sense of comfort in showing audiences what they are not. Whether watching what is ideal or not, to be compelled by either demonstrates the formative influence of brokenness, though negative, as seen through the deception embedded in the television and the mall.

In view of the mall, and implicitly the idyllic consumption through television, the impact of materialism is that it "tends to focus on *what* is being purchased, rather than calling into question the *gospel* of consumption–the sense that acquisition brings happiness and fulfillment." Herein is the opportunity for the church family to hold out a counter-liturgy; but too often "instead, the evangelical community simply replays the gospel of consumption but with 'Jesus' stuff. . .We even end up reconfiguring 'church' by this strange 'other' gospel where God can be reduced to a commodity."[396]

This commodification of God has to do with the unpleasantness and subsequent escapist tendency in the face of pain, trials, and tribulations. However, Levison notes the work of God in His people through suffering: "[God] works, and works hardest within us, as we lumber through the valley of the shadow of death." Notice the interplay between being and doing as pain applies formational pressure: "Especially when we inhabit the heart of darkness, this spirit-breath pulses, moment by living moment, in every ounce of praise we can muster, in our every struggle to inhabit lives of integrity, in every labored step we take to be faithful."[397]

---

[395] Coontz, 38.

[396] Smith, *Desiring the Kingdom*, 103.

[397] Levison, *Fresh Air*, 35.

Walking through experiences of brokenness form a family's being and doing. Yet this does not necessarily yield wholeness. Brokenness can foster bitterness as it settles into a family's identity in implicit and explicit ways. Still, when God uses brokenness to free a family from the magical enchantment of self, turning them outward, then formation yields a missional family.

Dave Gibbons explains the invitational posture toward others that results from an outward turn through brokenness. According to "the pain principle" in leadership, which also applies to families, "pain in life has a way of deconstructing us to our most genuine, humble, authentic selves." The result of a family in touch with their pain is that others are able to connect to such vulnerability.[398]

Hearing God in the midst of the struggle is the key to transformation. It is not merely experiencing pain. Hearing God reflects an overall posture of receptivity to His leading. Obedience follows. These are the critical dynamics of a family being filled with the Spirit of God. It is living as led by the Spirit. Levison identifies "a love for learning" and "an ear for prophecy" as components for a lifestyle of following the Holy Spirit.[399] The way a family seeks to hear and learn from God about His kingdom, themselves, and their neighbors serves as a catalyst for missional transformation.

In "recovering a missional spirituality," Moore believes the "first priority is discovering a deeper spirituality that emerges from heartfelt prayer and worship as devoted followers of Jesus. Spirit baptism is not an experience that we simply assign a date to and then move on from as if it were merely an historical event. It is an experience in which we continue to live (Eph 5:18)."[400] Indeed, anchoring family life in such prayer and worship instills a counter-liturgy, one that focuses all activities accordingly.

---

[398] Dave Gibbons, *The Monkey and the Fish: Liquid Leadership for a Third-Culture Church* (Grand Rapids: Zondervan, 2009), 43.

[399] Levison, *Fresh Air*, 151-153.

[400] Synan, 537.

This prayerful focus includes an ongoing interaction with scripture. Levison notes how throughout the New Testament, the Holy Spirit "anchors an understanding of Jesus to the Scriptures of Israel." The Holy Spirit's "primary vocation, its principal task, in fact, is to illuminate the person of Jesus by setting his words and actions in the context of Israel's poetry, stories, and prophecies." Such background is essential for understanding scripture as the story of God. Within this narrative families discover "the connections that prove so fruitful, so momentous, so inspired."[401] Families engaged in the story of God discover their own connection to the story of God that continues as the mission of God.

Missional families receive the heart of God while hearing scripture, rather than performing to achieve a "blessing" through scripture study. Bible reading remains a discipline, and its aim is redemptive formation in the mission of God, which may lead to a more uncomfortable life. Levison explains how ". . .regular maintenance can lead to an audacious vision, which, in time, can result in deep, private pain."[402] Even hearing from God itself can lead to a greater brokenness–caring about what breaks God's heart.

Awareness–Motivation –Intuition

During the transformational process of *Missional Family Wholeness*, families develop alertness to the revelation of God's kingdom in a counter-cultural way to the undetected influence of the kingdom of this world. The subtle effects of unawareness are devastating. Smith explains,

> We absorb rival gospels as *habitus*, and thus act 'toward' them, as it were – pulled toward a different *telos* that rivals the coming kingdom of God. . .such deformation often happens under the radar of awareness. . .So we become the *kind*

---

[401] Levison, *Fresh Air*, 210.

[402] Ibid., 87.

of people who are inclined to a sort of low-grade, socially acceptable greed that makes us remarkably tolerant of inequality and the exploitation of the (global) poor; or we take for granted a mobile, commuting way of life that exploits creation's resources rather than stewards them. We might be passionately devoted to ending religious persecution without for a moment considering how our 'normal' way of life exploits children halfway around the globe; or we think it's just 'natural' to turn a blind eye to the suffering of Christians in countries that we bomb in the name of 'freedom.' A way of life becomes habitual for us such that we pursue that way of life–we *act* in that way of life–*without thinking about it* because we've absorbed the *habitus* that is oriented to a corresponding vision of "the good life."[403]

As God reveals His mission to a family, they gradually see with fresh eyes their patterns, or liturgies, that were previously concealed within their lifestyle. Again, Smith highlights how "Rhythms that are 'seemingly innocuous' are, in fact, fundamentally formative; while seeming to demand only the insignificant, in fact they are extorting what is essential."[404] This way of the world deceives many, including Christian families. Smith elaborates on technology as one avenue for this formative deception:

> Cultural phenomena and systems can be laden with an implicit vision of the good life that is inscribed in the very structure. . .of the cultural artifact itself. In that case, not even the best of intentions on the part of users will be able to undo the teleological (dis)order that is built

---

[403] Smith, *Imagining the Kingdom*, 141-142.
[404] Ibid., 97.

into the system. Or at the very least, users can severely underestimate the (de)formative power of cultural artifacts, approaching them with just a little bit too much confidence, assured that they are masters of the technology when it might be the technology that is slowly mastering them.[405]

Interestingly, social media has an intergenerational appeal, engaging grandparents as well as parents and children. Social media itself, Smith warns, "inculcates in us dispositions and inclinations that lean toward a configuration of the social world that revolves around *me*–even if we tell ourselves we're interested in others."[406] Of course, for a family to become missional requires discernment and repentance from this "pedagogy of insignificance."[407] On this point, repentance is easily dismissed as too strong a call for something so inconsequential. Families who are unaware of the influence of what appears harmless remain ignorant of the dangers of what they do not know. Thus, awareness provides critical support to the development of a missional imagination, because "we imagine more than we know."[408]

An awareness of negative influences from such subtle rhythms serves as a first step toward establishing rhythms that have positive influences, which in turn shapes motivation. Smith acknowledges how "actions and behaviors are, in a sense, 'pulled' out of me because of my passional orientation to some *telos*–some vision of the good life and what it means to be human–my love and longing for that 'good life' is itself a signal that I conceive that 'kingdom' as something that attracts me." Thus, with missional development from awareness into motivation, "in some sense, imagination precedes desire;" and Smith's conclusion connects to

---

[405] Smith, *Imagining the Kingdom*, 144.

[406] Ibid., 148.

[407] Ibid.

[408] Ibid., 149.

revelation within the family, "we don't choose desires; they are *birthed* in us."[409]

To reiterate, spiritual disciplines (worship, reflection, scripture reading, prayer, fasting) help a family develop God's heart. Levison explains that this is due to the importance of "the right practices" for a community that will hear from the Spirit.[410] The spiritual disciplines are formative to missional wholeness, because they travel "the way to the heart," which Smith indicates, "is through the body, and the way into the body is through story."[411]

Formation through story as an inductive approach contrasts with deductive and prescriptive methods used to instill a sense of morality, which can become an end in itself. Smith counters, "So generating good, just, virtuous action is not merely a matter of disseminating the relevant rules or principles; it is more fundamentally dependent upon training affect–training people to 'see situations in the right way.'" Helping families grow in discernment with the aim of participating in mission "requires training their *emotions* to be primed to take in and evaluate situations well. Our emotional perception apparatus (which I am linking to 'the imagination') is significantly 'trained' by narrative."[412]

Rituals connect story and action. Out of this connection, a new natural results for families. As Smith describes it: "That is the triumph of ritual: what is learned and acquired becomes so habituated and absorbed. . .that it is taken to be 'natural.'"[413] Therefore, the working out of the revelation of God in families integrates threads of awareness, motivation, and intuition into a fabric of missional wholeness.

---

[409] Smith, *Imagining the Kingdom*, 125.

[410] Levison, *Fresh Air*, 156.

[411] Smith, *Imagining the Kingdom*, 14.

[412] Ibid., 36.

[413] Ibid., 107.

Integration

Levison issues a vision for missional family integration: "Put all these virtues together–a thirst for learning; extreme generosity; an ear for prophecy; and the practices of worship, fasting, and prayer–and you've got the makings of a remarkable community." This community certainly includes the church family, and subsequently the missional family, in which the Holy Spirit "can speak a word that sets mission in motion."[414]

Smith also connects how integration is characterized by a family's being and doing that is ready to receive and respond to their vocation in the *missio Dei*:

> This isn't a matter of simply learning new ideas and content; it is a matter of *tuning*. We are *attuned* to the world by practices that carry an embodied significance. We are conscripted into a Story through those practices that enact and perform and embody a Story about the good life. . .this is how we 'become native:' because 'nativity' is absorbed at the level of affect, on an aesthetic register. This is how worship works.[415]

The fine-tuning of an integrated missional family lifestyle is not a perfectionist ideal. On the contrary, wholeness exposes weakness and allows families to embrace vulnerability and experience God's grace as an abundant source of strength in weakness (2 Cor 12:5-10). His grace can be so abundant for the family in the difficulty, that as with David in Psalm 23, their "cup overflows" (v. 5). Love abounding to others completes the integration phase. Gibbons describes this as chaos leading to love, which illustrates how humility characterizes the condition and culture of missional wholeness in the home:

---

[414] Levison, *Fresh Air*, 164.

[415] Smith, *Imagining the Kingdom*, 137.

At home, we don't like to talk about the chaos, because we want everybody to think that we have it all together, that we are clean, that we have everything in its place. But the truth is sometimes we are struggling to keep up and things aren't all that together. And that's okay; it's part of the third-culture deal. . .movements of God are marked by chaos. They are not systematic and orderly and clean. Why? Because movements of God are fundamentally about love, and there's very little that's predictable and orderly and clean about love.[416]

---

[416] Gibbons, 184-185.

Chapter 13

Missional Family Characteristics

———— ∞∞ ————

B ased in the process of developing missional wholeness, a profile detailing missional family characteristics links a family's being and doing. The characteristics are reciprocal in nature. Smith comments on the influence of this nuance: "We are in the world primarily as *doers*, not thinkers–and even our thinking serves, and grows out of, our doing. We are certainly *more* than our bodies, but we are never *less* than that. . ."[417] Thus, missional family characteristics illustrate the mutual dependence of being and doing.

Though reciprocal and mutually dependent, being as understood and applied to missional families is broader than thinking. It is image-bearing, which necessarily proceeds from the being of God. Therefore, the origin in being and subsequent flow into doing is applied to missional families. Yet in an ongoing way through the family's life, Smith's perspective on the reciprocal nature of being and doing is also true. This echoes the synergistic tension in James between faith and works (James 2:14-26). As Snyder puts it, "the being and the

———————————————

[417] Smith, *Imagining the Kingdom*, 113.

doing go together. The being is fundamental, but the doing is the natural result."[418]

Accordingly, Macchia offers the following summary:

> The being and doing sides of us go hand in glove, both needing proper nurturing along the way. We learn the rhythms of our spirituality, compassion, and action through the disciplines of prayer, study, and practice. If we truly believe that the quality of our relationship with God determines the quality of our vision and ministry, then attending to our souls is a must.[419]

In the characteristic pairings that follow, attention to a family's soul compels its service. Reception leads to response as evidenced in gratitude yielding generosity, rest yielding faithfulness, and freedom leading to going. There is reciprocal potential within and between pairings, as these simply express, in limited terms, the mystery of the character and mission of Christ being formed within a family.

Gratitude → Generosity

Families experiencing the indwelling life of Christ are grateful. As receivers of God's Spirit, their gratitude overflows through generosity. Macchia confirms this as a key point of contact that can be applied to families: "Stewardship and generosity are where the rubber meets the road in our lifestyle as Christians."[420]

As previously explored, generosity expresses itself in hospitality as a characteristic of the missional people of God. Yong confirms the overflow nature and Spirit-filled context of hospitality: "Christian hospitality proceeds from

---

[418] Snyder, 70.

[419] Stephen Macchia, 63-64.

[420] Ibid., 198.

the magnanimous hospitality of God, it is founded on the incarnational and Pentecostal logic of abundance rather than that of human economies of exchange and of scarcity."[421] He continues, ". . .receivers do not return to givers out of any incurred indebtedness dictated by an economy of scarcity; rather, receivers allow the gifts received to overflow through their lives into those of others because of the boundless hospitality of an excessively gracious God."[422]

Levison turns to the church at Antioch as an example of a missional community that embodied "extreme generosity." They were "generous to a fault. . .gave *before* there was a tragedy. . .Their generosity, in other words, came from their sense of well-being, of having enough, even more than enough."[423]

Generosity is distorted if reduced to what is left in a family's bank account, on their schedule, in their emotional reserves, and of the stuff they want to discard. From a missional perspective, generosity flows from a family refusing to possess its own life. The family has their identity in Christ and knows grace through brokenness. They have learned contentment in all circumstances (Phil 4:11-13). What exists within their "home" in God also exists in their family home, where daily life is shared between nearest neighbors. From there, the gratitude extends to neighbors near and far through generosity.

Rest → Faithfulness

Redemptive families exhibit patience that demonstrates trust in the Lord rather than self-striving. This requires rest and faithfulness in the way of the kingdom. Howard Snyder elaborates:

---

[421]   Yong, 118.

[422]   Ibid., 127.

[423]   Levison, *Fresh Air*, 160-161.

The way to work effectively toward the Kingdom today is not primarily through emphasizing evangelism or social justice as things in themselves, but through the rediscovery of the Church as the community of the King. When the Church is the Church biblically understood, it grows and infects the world with an epidemic of health. Kingdom witness and church growth are not a matter of bringing to the Church that which is needed for success in the way of methods, techniques or strategies. Kingdom faithfulness is a matter of removing the hindrances to life and growth.[424]

Families in mission operate from a posture of receptivity to the Spirit's presence and power. Smith compares this dynamic with physical rest: "Sleep is a gift to be received, not a decision to be made. And yet it is a gift that requires a *posture* of reception–a kind of active welcome. What if being filled with the Spirit had the same dynamic?. . .What if we need to first adopt a bodily posture in order to become what we are trying to be?"[425]

The discipline of physical rest is a critical "bodily posture" for missional families. Such discipline is subject to a subtle and often undetected spiritual attack upon the church and its families. Accordingly, Brennan Manning warns: "maybe the most demonic force that is afflicting the church is busyness."[426]

Macchia concurs by determining that the greatest hindrance to "community building is the fast-paced society we live in."[427] He elaborates with examples of time devoted to the

---

[424] Snyder, 191.

[425] Smith, *Imagining the Kingdom*, 65.

[426] Gibbons, 160.

[427] Stephen Macchia, 81.

internet, a focus on individual needs, and "our compulsion to overwork and underplay our lives away."[428]

Rest prepares a family for present action based in future hope. Smith describes an opportunity of faithfulness through "inhabiting the 'not yet' as fields of the Lord that call for both work and play." Rest cultivates a redemptive approach where "problems are now constituted as callings," and God's people of faith "not only inhabit the world differently but inhabit a different world, a world constituted as God's creation."[429] These images of creation, work, and play, are all present in the self-description of wisdom alongside of God in creation: "Then I was beside Him, as a master workman; And I was daily His delight, Rejoicing (*or playing*) always before Him, Rejoicing (*or playing*) in the world, His earth, And having my delight in the sons of men" (Prov 8:30-31).

Redemptive families live in the same way that wisdom existed with God at the creation. Though urgently focused in their obedience, their pace is patient because of their trust and delight in the Father. The Gospel of John depicts Jesus' life of prayerful obedience in this way of wisdom. Contrary to rest, an anxious pace limits perspective and impedes prayer.

Luke Timothy Johnson calls for a re-examination of the church's "prophetic character of its prayer." He notes concern over exclusive trends toward "public worship (the prayer of praise) or of individual request (the prayer of petition)" and private "pleas that what we will be done rather than what God wills."[430] He holds out hope for counter-cultural worship of the community of God's people to "cease from the constant round of commerce and consumption, to resist the manipulation of media that insists that working and possessing defines worth." From this place families can "proclaim with the body language of communal gathering that Jesus, not any other power, is Lord," and to do so "is to enact the politics

---

[428] Stephen Macchia, 82.

[429] Smith, *Imagining the Kingdom*, 167.

[430] Luke Timothy Johnson, 124.

of God's kingdom and to embody the prayer 'your kingdom come.'" Yet Johnson solemnly acknowledges "this prophetic dimension is seldom ever even part of Christian consciousness" in the church or in the home.[431]

Families receive a revelation for faithfulness when they repent of busyness, decrying the popular notion that busy living is worthwhile living. Suffering slows us down and provides an opportunity to hear from God and trust Him. In my life, a lament I offered to God about the laborious breathing endured by my daughter, Victoria Grace, became a testimony of what God revealed about her brief life on earth: "Your very breath is worship to Me."[432] Levison records a similar revelation that ". . .the *spirit* of God is present in every breath I take."[433] Rest reminds families to breathe.

Rest also fosters humility, which keeps families alert to Levison's warning and encouragement that ". . .ambition is the enemy of the spirit and simplicity the spirit's closest friend."[434] Thus, Levison sets forth a goal that applies to missional families "to tend God's spirit-breath with ever-increasing care by living simply and by studying hard, so that this spirit-breath may be a sustainable source of wisdom."[435] Without the rest of God's Spirit and wisdom, the spirit that prevails is the human spirit, which wanes and grows weary in good works (Gal 6:9).

The biblical character, Daniel, embodied faithfulness as the Spirit was faithful to him. As Levison notes, "the only action" the Spirit takes toward Daniel, "which isn't really taking action at all, is to *be* in Daniel. . .So how does Daniel tap into the life of the spirit? Through simple, dogged faithfulness."[436] Rest focuses and sustains families in good works.

---

[431]   Luke Timothy Johnson, 124.

[432]   From the poem printed in Victoria's funeral bulletin on her life from God's perspective, *Victoria Grace Coté,* by Christa McCardell, http://www.victoriasfund.com/victorias-servant-song/.

[433]   Levison, *Fresh Air,* 39.

[434]   Ibid., 61.

[435]   Ibid., 67.

[436]   Ibid., 56-57.

Spirit-empowered faithfulness flows from a family that rests in the Spirit of God. Macchia joins in Hunter's previously noted conviction in calling for faithfulness rather than obsessing and striving over causes that seek "to make a difference in the world, often pursuing the re-Christianization of our land more than pursuing the God of our universe."[437] Accordingly, Macchia depicts how "a church with a healthy missions program" is not "out to conquer the world, but the corner of the planet they have targeted will be well served because of their faithfulness."[438]

After cautioning against a professionalized view of missions, Harper adds his voice to the call for faithfulness flowing from a restful pace in daily life: "When I look at life through that lens, I see how much of my life is missional in nature. If I have time to really see others, and if I have paced myself so as to have time to really see people and their needs, then each day is filled with opportunities for ministry."[439]

Missional families prepare for faithfulness in their current contexts through restful rhythms integrated in their lifestyle. Their eyes are opened in a similar way that Harper experienced. To raise awareness of daily opportunities, Dave Gibbons asks "three questions that become answers:"[440]

1. Where is Nazareth?
2. What is my pain?
3. What is in my hand?[441]

Nazareth identifies those on the margins within a family's community that can benefit from their faithful response. *Pain* is the pathway of the family's brokenness that leads to

---

[437] Stephen Macchia, 82.

[438] Ibid., 152.

[439] Harper, 120.

[440] Gibbons, 109.

[441] Ibid., 114-122.

blessing for others. *What is in my hand* addresses present needs by connecting a family's relationships and resources.

Freedom → Going

Though looking at it from an American framework for cultivating hope and change, James Hitchcock's description of the family as a unique place to experience freedom in a positive sense resonates with certain themes of freedom related to being a missional family:

> All of us seek to find our true selves, to be genuinely free, to achieve our true potential. But these things are attained, and indeed can only be realistically imagined, through the kind of adulthood which involves the voluntary acceptance of responsibility for others, the voluntary giving of ourselves without reservation. For most of us, the family, above all other communities, permits this to be done. In giving we receive. In binding ourselves we are made free. In linking our own personalities with those of others we discover who we truly are.[442]

Redemptive families live with a missional thrust free from the enchantments of the world. These include the ideals ensnared in idolatry, a busy pace that fragments and exhausts, and an identity rooted in performance that never pleases. God's grace redeems families and sets them free in their fellowship with Him (justification) and among His family (familification) to participate in His mission.

For example, the freedom of God's unconditional acceptance releases families to show hospitality to one another and others, and the freedom of God's forgiveness releases families to forgive one another and others. In addition, the freedom from materialism and consumerism releases families

---

[442] James Hitchcock, authors et al., *The Family: America's Hope*, 56.

to be generous, and the freedom from busyness releases families to be faithful. Further, the freedom from citizenship on earth releases families to reach out to neighbors throughout the earth.

Missional families are free to go into new contexts of ministry as they are led by the Holy Spirit. Luke Timothy Johnson traces the foundational element of itinerancy from the New Testament church to its gradual diminishment evident in the institutional church today:

> Precisely because Acts shows us the disciples–as a community–continuing to embody the ideal of itinerancy in imitation of Jesus, it poses a particularly sharp question to the church today. Like the other prophetic values (prayer, poverty, servant leadership), itinerancy requires translation to changing circumstances. Such translation, after all, is an example of the responsiveness and flexible freedom that itinerancy symbolizes. Churches today are not likely to abandon all things and hit the road as did the Twelve and the Seventy and Paul and Barnabas. But they need to ask themselves about the cost of abandoning this form of prophetic abandonment entirely. And they can begin by examining the ways in which their organizational structures actually hamper rather than facilitate obedience to the Holy Spirit.[443]

Missional families experience freedom from justifying their existence with rationale such as, "There are needy people to serve here or there." Justification tends to depict truth as decontextualized platitudes. However, the person of the Holy Spirit leads missional families rather than platitudes. Consequently, God frees redemptive families from saving

---

[443]   Luke Timothy Johnson, 128.

their lives with justifying rationale and releases them to lay down their lives in following His call.

Dave Gibbons' concept of "third-culture" explains the freedom to be missional: "Third culture is the mindset and will to love, learn, and serve in any culture, even in the midst of pain and discomfort."[444] Patricia DeWitt convincingly describes this freedom of third culture that can compel families into new contexts of doing, because it flows from being with God:

> Third culture just brings a whole new face to what missions is. And it takes away that word even–missions–because the word is too small. Instead, it's God who is doing things, and if we open our eyes and ask him, 'Open my eyes. Open the eyes of my heart so I can see what you are doing.' It is not God telling us, 'Go clean your room in Thailand,' or 'Go build something there.' It is 'Hey, I'm making something in the kitchen. Do you want to join me?' That is such freedom![445]

---

[444] Gibbons, 38.

[445] Ibid., 171.

Chapter 14

Mobilizing Missional Families

———— ❧ ————

The Think Kingdom–Be Family Project is a model for mobilizing families through family-with-family consociation. The model parallels key principles detailed in other approaches referenced before and below. For instance, Smith explains that formation is "not primarily a matter of getting the right ideas and doctrines and beliefs into your head in order to guarantee proper behavior; rather, it's a matter of being the kind of person [family] who *loves* rightly–who loves God and neighbor and is oriented to the world by the primacy of that love."[446]

Noteworthy parallels also exist between The TKBF Initiative and the core assumptions in The Convergence Model for education as proposed in the work of James Flynn, Wie Tjiong, and Russell West. Consider their following assumptions as synthesized below to apply to families in the approach modeled in TKBF:

- Holistic Approach – cognitive (factual), experimental (practical), and affective (value-based)
- Formation – transformational spiritual and moral formation for the participants as opposed to the accumulation of knowledge

---

[446] Smith, *Desiring the Kingdom*, 32-33.

- Fluid Structure – can take place anywhere, and is best facilitated in a variety of settings
- Active Participation – involvement in the process using dynamic reflection, communication, and adapted to meet their real and felt needs
- Facilitators – specialize in tying together, through coaching principles, cognitive, experimental, and affective knowledge, rather than merely prescribing a body of knowledge
- Contextualization – to meet the unique needs of culture, tradition, gift-mix, and destiny-mix of the families
- Dynamic Communication – methods appropriate for the culture of the participants and varied in medium, setting, and delivery to best communicate what is being taught
- *Praxis* – structured and deliberate in each learning experience, geared toward application in the family's vocational context and aimed at a process of dynamic reflection that links knowing and doing, leading to spiritual and moral formation. . .it is profitable to do and be in addition to know.[447]

Not all Christian formation in churches, homes, and schools, aims at families' desires through their doing. Much of it focuses on teaching the right concepts and principles, with the application left to the family's own discretion. In Smith's words, the focus is "the dissemination and communication of Christian ideas rather than the formation of a peculiar people." This widespread reality leads him to question if Christian education might be "loaded with all sorts of Christian ideas and information–and yet be offering a formation that runs counter to that vision?"[448] If true, then current discipleship approaches, including those for the family, need to be significantly altered.

---

[447] James T. Flynn, Wie L. Tjiong,, and Russell W. West, *A Well-Furnished Heart: Restoring the Spirit's Place in the Leadership Classroom* (Fairfax, VA: Xulon Press, 2002), 207.

[448] Smith, *Desiring the Kingdom*, 31.

To this end, Macchia asks, "What would happen if your church suspended all of its programs for a season in order to focus on hearing from God and building relationships with one another?. . .Such a 'retreat' from programs and activities will help us see what's most important to reinstate a ministry foci for the future."[449]

TKBF provides such an experience and connects the meaningful discipleship dynamics that occur at a retreat, camp, and mission trip to the families' lifestyles. The disconnect that exists between the Holy Spirit and routine life "is dangerous," according to Levison, who observes that "each and every one of the students with whom I've discussed these ideas" has indicated that in their church experience, the Holy Spirit "has come to be associated with special events rather than daily life: retreats, summer camp, Sunday worship. All of them agree that they don't know how to make the connection between those unique moments and their everyday life."[450]

Lasting formation depends on the continuity of these "retreat-like" rituals. In The TKBF Project, this continuity is sustained in a focused way through the fellowship and missional activity of family-with-family consociation. It is a focused initiative designed to be continued naturally once the momentum is initiated.

As Smith pointedly remarks, "Quite simply, there is no formation without repetition. There is no habituation without being immersed in a practice over and over again." He follows with a warning that unless formation, as worship, "eschews the cult of novelty and embraces the good of faithful repetition, we will constantly be ceding habituation to secular liturgies."[451]

The family-with-family consociation resembles a dynamic in mentoring as exemplified in Elijah and Elisha. Rickie Moore comments: "The success, indeed, the succession of this

---

[449] Stephen Macchia, 83.

[450] Levison, *Fresh Air*, 135.

[451] Smith, *Imagining the Kingdom*, 183.

mentoring relationship is shown to turn not so much on the *doing* of mentoring but rather on simply *being* a mentor and *being with* a mentor."[452]

It is important the consociation of families include the children. The context of such fellowship itself is formative, and the end of formation has already been established as mission. Moore sees this in Isaiah's life:

> The 'Here am I' of chapter 6 is now sharpened to a focus on the new generation: 'Here am I and the children, whom the LORD has given me.' Isaiah, like Moses after the failure of the older generation in the wilderness, is called to be a minister to the youth. Isaiah knows the children are signs, he knows they are significant, and he know his prophetic call is to be their mentor in light of this revelation.[453]

Hence, TKBF joins with Moore in emphasizing "the importance of prophetic insight in recovering and reclaiming a divine revelation of the intrinsic significance of children." Family-with-family consociation recognizes "a profound spiritual dimension to raising up and blessing a new genera-tion."[454] This can certainly include children's discipleship pro-gramming, but it needs to progress further to the formative context of fellowship and mission alongside the generations and the nations.

Moore continues, "It is more about *being* and *being with* someone than knowing what to *do*." This requires "elders to go places beyond themselves where only a vision of God can overcome the *division* between generations." He concludes, "Finally. . .the call of the prophet as mentor is ultimately the

---

[452] Rickie D. Moore, "The Prophet as Mentor: A Crucial Facet of the Biblical Presentations of Moses, Elijah, and Isaiah," *Journal of Pentecostal Theology* 15(2) (SAGE Publications, 2007), 164.

[453] Rickie Moore, 169.

[454] Ibid., 172.

call addressing us all to follow, even to *be*, the suffering servant of the LORD, giving up our lives for our children, indeed seeing the holy seed from the travail of our souls and being satisfied."[455] Missional families raise their children for the sake of God's kingdom. Therefore, children function strategically in church families and families in the *missio Dei*.

Steven Garber's research among college students confirms how consociation supports formation. His summary of liturgies for formation confirms practices embedded within The TKBF Initiative: "A worldview, a mentor, a community–these are the habits of heart that grow and sustain a faithful life, that so nourish a soul that a career can become a calling that gives coherence to the whole of life."[456]

Bowers also summarizes what formation can look like for individuals, which can also be applied to family-with-family consociation:

> Christian formation, therefore, should guide persons in development of a missionary lifestyle. Educational processes and relationships which affirm ministry call and giftedness, opportunities for all ages to participate in corporate mission, and specific small group discipleship structures devoted to development of a missionary and ministry lifestyle can help realize this aim.[457]

Intellectual and content-based approaches to mobilization have limited results. Smith explains: "We might say that an intellectualist model is able to register only discrete sinful *actions* but is unable to account for a sinful *way of life* – the rhythms and habits and routines that disorder a people or a culture in ways that run counter to what God envisions for

---

[455]   Rickie Moore, 172.

[456]   Garber, 21.

[457]   Bowers, 81.

creation," which is a kingdom-based "vision of flourishing and justice."[458] Relational mobilization through TKBF hopes to release families into the communal life in God's kingdom. Accordingly, The TKBF Project embodies "four New Testament family values:"

1. We share our stuff with one another.
2. We share our hearts with one another.
3. We stay, embrace the pain, and grow up with one another.
4. Family is about more than me, the wife, and the kids.[459]

Hellerman conjectures that "Churches of less than 200 members may be able to live out the family model as a single group. Larger churches will need significantly to retool their ministry priorities to facilitate such a social reality." As the former, TKBF seeks to give expression to being family as a single group while still creating smaller pods of consociation. The areas along these lines that need attention from church leaders include "the content of our teaching and the various social contexts in which this teaching takes place."[460]

The content of TKBF includes a small adjustment promoted by Hellerman, like the use of plural pronouns because of understanding how "pronouns are a powerful teaching vehicle where worship is concerned. . .We should take advantage of the power of corporate worship to teach our people that the church is a family."[461] Pronouns implicitly inform social contexts. Indeed, Hellerman concludes "that surrogate sibling relations are better 'caught' than 'taught,' so it is essential to provide for our people the kind of social settings in which church family relations can be experienced firsthand."[462]

---

[458] Smith, *Imagining the Kingdom*, 140.

[459] Hellerman, 145.

[460] Ibid., 176.

[461] Ibid., 177.

[462] Ibid., 178.

Beyond its form and function, the relational dynamic is the heart of formation within The TKBF Project. Macchia comments on relationships as the means for healthy ministry:

> I am convinced that virtually everything we accomplish in ministry is the direct result of the quality of our relationships. Without true community there is limited growth and learning. Without first creating a safe environment for each person in the faith community to be himself or herself, their growth in Christ will be hampered. Therefore, as leaders in the local church, we must consider the needs of the disciple and all who are in the disciple-making process and determine ways to facilitate their development, whether in a classroom setting or in a small group, a ministry context or on the mission field.[463]

Maachia demonstrates the same conviction evidenced in an initiative called "The Sustaining Pastoral Excellence (SPE) Peer Learning Project." In it a collaborative team of eleven researchers conduct a qualitative study of the impact of peer fellowship [consociation] on pastors and their ministries.[464] The findings of this research illustrate among pastors what The Think Kingdom–Be Family Project aims to show among missional families. Particularly, their research indicates that pastors sharing peer fellowship have better balance in their lives and engage more in service along with their congregations. Shared leadership from the pastoral peer fellowship carries into their churches, which are growing congregations.[465]

Families with families in TKBF reflect the following from pastors with pastors in the SPE Peer Learning Project:

---

[463] Stephen Macchia, 84.

[464] Marler, Penny Long, authors et al., *So Much Better: How Thousands of Pastors Help Each Other Thrive* (St. Louis: Chalice Press), 2013.

[465] Marler, et al., 1.

1. Fellowship that is based upon calling.
2. Commitment for "spiritual support, theological challenge, and mutual accountability."
3. "Spend time with one another in prayer, at meals, and through travel."
4. Apply "what (and how) they've learned into their ministries." "In doing so, they replicate a first-century disciple model. This kind of peer learning is sacred practice."[466]

"The Rhythm of Peer Group Life (Covenant–Challenge & Confrontation–Cohesion–Commission)" also has points of contact with the consociation between families and the process of Missional Family Wholeness (Revelation–Awareness–Motivation–Intuition–Integration).[467] Both projects share "a covenant model." This includes a process that is "rooted in the relationships between spirituality and structure. . .an intentional renewal process requires structure. But an adequate structure should be shaped by desired outcomes." The necessary structures in these initiatives for pastors and families facilitate "personal, vocational, and ministry change."[468]

Though speaking of pastors, consider how the following can also apply to families The TKBF Initiative:

> Given the relational nature of discipleship, a covenant context for pastoral formation and renewal is biblically and theologically commended. Spiritually transformative experiences, identification and affirmation of call, and discipleship for ministry leadership have always been functions of faith community or congregational life. The Wesleyan Pentecostal spirituality. . .is essentially covenantal. Scripturally, covenant is

---

[466] Marler, et al., 5.

[467] Ibid., 14.

[468] Ibid., 68.

grounded in God's initiative, involves inward transformation (written on the heart), results in relational intimacy with God and others, and is marked by redemptive integrity.[469]

In sum, the being and doing of God Himself can transform families as they share in this being and doing with one another. It begins with being in the heart of the family and is carried out through mission through the lifestyle of the family. Within the mission of God in His kingdom, there is fulfillment for the people of God, including singles and families. "The kin-dom of God, therefore, is both a place and a state in which persons are valued equally, work and resources are shared equally, and where everyone is safe. We may also conclude that this is a definition of the church and an understanding of what the Body of Christ is intended to be" and do.[470]

Part Two Summary

The biblical theological context for The Think Kingdom–Be Family Project is the kingdom of God. The biblical narrative of creation, fall, redemption, and restoration as carried out by God is His mission, the *missio Dei*.

As understood in the theological context of trinitarian relationality, God invites His people into fellowship with Him and so shares His mission with them. This mission involves His people as a family, expressed throughout the Old Testament in families and communities. In the New Testament, Jesus constitutes anew the family of God by faith before blood. Those faithful to the Father carry out His mission of hospitality as both recipients and vessels of His salvation.

In turning to the North American context, the realities of family life have not aligned with the productivity and extended nature of the household common in both Hebraic and Mediterranean settings, as well as common even in the

---

[469] Marler, et al., 68-69.

[470] Ibid., 178.

history of the Western family. Instead, a sentimental pursuit of an idealistic form and function of the nuclear family has become a flashpoint for defense, offense, justification, and condemnation. Both society and the church reflect the resulting isolative trajectory of the family. Families find themselves fragmented, fractured, and self-absorbed. The concept of the redemptive family holds out hope within the contemporary historical moment for families to rediscover their collective identity in God's family and purpose within His mission.

Upon these biblical, theological, and historical foundations, Garber's three strands synthesize the relationship between revelation, integration, and consociation: "Understanding those who have kept faith over the years–who with substantial integrity have connected belief to behavior, personally as well as publicly – requires the weaving together of these three strands: *convictions*, *character* and *community*."[471]

Convictions connect to missional wholeness development in a family where the missional vision gets into the heart of the family's story from revelation to integration. Character is the maturity in a family's being and doing that reflects missional characteristics. Community is the foundation for the family-with-family consociation model that mobilizes missional families. It is a relational approach through which people "commit themselves to others who have chosen to live their lives embedded in that same worldview, journeying together in truth after the vision of a coherent and meaningful life."[472] In this way, The Think Kingdom–Be Family Project at Zion Church of Millersville is positioned to identify the elements of an effective model for family-with-family consociation that mobilizes its families in mission, beginning among the nearest neighbors in the church family and home, and from there overflowing to neighbors near and far.

---

[471] Garber, 51.

[472] Ibid., 185.

Part III

The Think Kingdom–
Be Family Project

———— ◦⧓◦ ————

Overview

The Think Kingdom–Be Family Initiative at Zion Church of Millersville was a focused time of fellowship, teaching, and reflection around God's call to think kingdom and be family. The goal was to develop a biblically grounded, research-based, and relationally delivered discipleship approach to mobilize missional families through family-with-family consociation. Accordingly, the research identified elements that constitute these redemptive families. The primary research method was an ethnographic type of study with some quantitative aspects to facilitate family assessment.

The description of the project includes the structure of the initiative itself within the life of Zion Church. The project depended on the selection, recruitment, and training of the facilitating families and individuals. This process is detailed, and the roles of facilitators are described from relevant research.

The nature of the focused time was an intentional commitment to form new connections and experiences in fellowship with others. It was also a continuation of values and practices already in motion for many within community life and mission. Thus, the conclusion of the project occasioned both calls for its continuation and expressions of confidence that it would.

The coordinated teaching during The TKBF Project spanned biblical foundations with their practical implications. Seizing contexts both routine and unique, teachers within the congregation established understanding in TKBF wholeness and characteristics while encouraging discerning responses to redemptive opportunities during the initiative. The coordinated teaching involved a strategic outline to undergird the relational context, throughout the focused time, with biblical theological understanding.

This ethnographic type of study utilized questionnaires at the outset and conclusion of the initiative. Initial and follow-up questionnaires were provided to the congregation as tools for reflection on missional wholeness and characteristics. In addition, the worship services during this period of time incorporated opportunities for reflection. Reflection-based activities were ongoing features of the fellowship and teaching.

Throughout, The TKBF Project aimed to provide a response to the Whiteheads' call for "a *portable* method: a reflective process that [families] can carry with them to the daily duties and challenges of their life of faith." In its design for mobilization through consociation supported by teaching and reflection, the TKBF model provides "a *performable* method: a style of discernment that is simple and straightforward enough to lead our reflections toward practical action." The Whiteheads continue, "we need a *communal* method: a shared strategy by which Christian gatherings can face the challenges in their surrounding culture and come to agreement of how to witness to their faith here and now."[473]

Families along with individuals were invited to submit their initial and follow-up reflections in writing, and testimonies offered throughout the project were noted with help from

---

[473] James D. Whitehead and Evelyn Eaton Whitehead, *Method in Ministry: Theological Reflection and Christian Ministry* (Lanham, MD: Sheed and Ward, 1995), 3.

the facilitators. Facilitators also compiled field notes with their observations from their experiences. I recorded these results of the qualitative analysis with substantiating comments from the participants. Many of these reflections consist of the participants' own words, and others are carefully summarized according to their plain meaning.

This supporting data is presented as an outline of *Missional Family Wholeness* and *Missional Family Characteristics*. Hence, the reflective comments progress through the developmental stages of revelation, awareness, motivation, intuition, and integration. Then the reflections supporting the paired characteristics of gratitude–generosity, rest–faithfulness in current contexts, and freedom–going into new contexts are presented. Participant reflections that are better expressed as narratives open the section on *Missional Family Wholeness*.

Along with the qualitative data, I gathered quantitative data comparing the twenty families and eleven individuals' degree of satisfaction in *Missional Family Characteristics* at the beginning and close of the project. Though this is clearly a small sample of the general population, it represents about half of Zion's family units in assessing TKBF's effectiveness as a model for missional family mobilization in this single congregation.

The evaluation of the project is based on facilitator and participant feedback along with reflections from Zion's leaders. These evaluative comments are drawn from formal feedback offered in the facilitators' field notes and informal discussions assessing the project throughout. Outside of Zion's accountability support partner, who helped align the project for implementation, the most helpful feedback came from those closest to the experience.

The results of the research are favorable for establishing elements for *Missional Family Wholeness* and *Missional Family Characteristics*. Though the aim is neither a comprehensive nor exclusive claim regarding these elements of missional wholeness and characteristics, the research does demonstrate their validity and importance. Other potential elements would be worthy explorations for future research.

In addition, TKBF aimed to mobilize families alongside of individuals, as supported by various perspectives in theology and other literature. The results are positive in this model for both families and individuals, and it appears slightly more satisfactory for families. This supports the missional orientation to formation in community, and it also beckons future study focusing on individuals and the differentiating factors that impact missional formation. One could also conduct future studies with enough participants representing different types of families in order to identify the impact of a variety of influences in family life.

In closing, The TKBF Project could contribute to church ministry in North America. Whereas the common programmatic approach segregates families and can limit missional integration into family lifestyles as a whole, this research project tells the story of one congregation that has been changed through a biblically-grounded, research-based, and relationally-delivered discipleship approach to mobilize families for missional living, through family-with-family consociation.

Chapter 15

Facilitator Profile and Preparation

———— ✆✆✆ ————

The facilitators were instrumental in the successful implementation of The TKBF Initiative. The term "facilitator" communicates the function expected of a group of families and individuals selected and trained to support the initiative. The facilitators participated just as much as those they served. The term fit both families and individuals. It also emphasized humility in servant leadership that can at times either be lacking or under-appreciated in a hierarchal structure. Zion's leadership discerned that "facilitator" expressed leadership responsibility with a missional heart.

From the outset, we as church leaders emphasized the heart of the facilitators according to Nouwen's missional understanding of authority: "Compassion must become the core and even the nature of authority," of which a missional leader makes "the compassion of God with man–which is visible in Jesus Christ–credible in his own world."[474] Facilitators had to demonstrate a readiness to grow and handle their responsibility compassionately. In addition, their weaknesses, as humble and compassionate facilitators, connected with those whom they served. Nouwen explains how such

---

[474] Henri J.M. Nouwen, *The Wounded Healer* (New York: Doubleday, 1990), 41.

compassion is authoritative, because it "is the possibility of man to forgive his brother, because forgiveness is only real for him who has discovered the weakness of his friends and the sins of his enemy in his own heart and is willing to call every human being his brother."[475]

The Whiteheads describe such facilitative leadership as follows:

> The word *attendant* captures well this shift in the stance of Christian leadership. Ministry is moving away from a more authoritative and hierarchal style in which a minister is one who molds and rules. The shift is toward a style of servant leadership in which the minister is an attendant–one whose role is to listen for the Lord's presence and to assist other believers in their attentive response to God's movement in their lives.[476]

Based upon their work with The Sustaining Pastoral Excellence (SPE) Peer Learning Project, the researchers discovered that "radical agency facilitators are process, not content, leaders."[477] Accordingly, "Facilitative leadership. . .includes practices that empower the group to achieve its purpose of Spirit-led covenant formation and renewal." However, too often the dynamics in ministry training "and many coaching models. . .are focused on an expert's control of the content and structure of learning."[478]

Hence, the following aspects of the "Facilitator Selection Criteria" of the SPE Peer Learning Project parallel the principles considered by Zion's leadership in selecting facilitators for The TKBF Initiative:

---

[475] Nouwen, *The Wounded Healer*, 41.

[476] Whitehead, 68.

[477] Marler, et al., 35.

[478] Ibid., 70.

- Committed to ministry excellence
- Respected by peers for integrity, wisdom, and spirituality
- Demonstrate a sense of call to peer care
- Willing to learn and improve personal facilitation skills
- Willing to invest time in training and facilitation of a group
- Embrace commitments to diversity, respect, and collegiality
- Endorsed by leadership
- Embrace the core values, model, and process[479]

In short, facilitators needed to be people who could connect relationally and encourage others by their own examples and through their genuine interest in them. As noted by the SPE researchers, "Good facilitators are marked by the capacity for authentic dialogue and are willing to learn the skills for leading a healthy group process. An innate or learned ability to model relational-interactive dynamics is essential."[480] For this reason, TKBF facilitators needed to possess these qualities and also receive the *Real Talk Training* by Lifeforming Leadership Coaching that I provided before the project's launch. Zion's leaders concurred with the research that groups do not thrive "when facilitators see themselves as ministry experts or take a controlling teacher-to-student approach."[481]

Over a period of several weeks, the elder team identified potential facilitators, and we invited these families and individuals to an introductory meeting to learn about the vision and structure for The Think Kingdom–Be Family Initiative. If they decided to participate as facilitators, then we invited them to attend a one-day orientation retreat. My wife and I hosted this retreat in our home in order to contextualize the preparation of facilitators in the setting of consociation that

---

[479] Marler, et al., 75.

[480] Ibid., 76.

[481] Ibid.

would be vital to the initiative. The introductory meeting was primarily informative, and the retreat provided an inspirational and reflective experience that included clarification on the nature and design of the project.[482]

There were eight facilitating couples and three facilitating individuals. Consociation rosters were developed to include the entire congregation. The facilitators would focus on intentionally sharing life and reflecting on their lives of mission with the particular families and individuals on their roster. Here is how we described the role to the facilitators:

- Facilitating families are responsible for leading the consociation process.
- Facilitating individuals serve alongside the facilitating families as part of their team.
- Facilitators form a koinonia connection with each family/single assigned to them.
- Facilitators may connect with those on their roster individually, or in groups, based upon the facilitative team's discretion.[483]

At the introductory meeting, facilitators received an extensive overview of the project very similar to the Introduction of this book. They reviewed it as preparation for discussion at the one-day orientation retreat. By the end of the retreat, the facilitators took ownership of the vision and the unique potential for their involvement with those on their roster. Over the next couple of weeks, facilitators took the initiative to contact those on their rosters to invite them to the Easter breakfast, which would serve to launch the congregation-wide TKBF Initiative in a celebratory context of consociation.

---

[482] See Appendix A for the introductory presentation to potential facilitators. The schedule for the Facilitator Orientation Retreat is Appendix B.

[483] Based on the guidelines from the TKBF Consociations Roster, in author's possession. It is not appended in order to protect confidentiality.

Regarding terminology, though the term "project" is one term used throughout this book, "initiative" was the preferred description for implementation with the congregation. Also, the phrase "Think Kingdom–Be Family" was used more than the term "missional," since the term itself was one with which not everybody was familiar. Therefore, within the initiative itself, we used "TKBF wholeness" and "TKBF characteristics" instead of "missional wholeness" and "missional characteristics."

Overall, the process of selecting and preparing facilitators coincided with revisions to the plan for implementation. Facilitators and other leaders provided feedback that ensured a missional approach to inviting people to participate in the initiative aimed at mobilizing participants in mission. We emphasized simplicity and effectiveness.

Chapter 16

A Focused Time
of Fellowship

———⊗⊗⊗———

Z ion Church, through The TKBF Project, desired to grow in
being a ministering community. The Whiteheads describe
how "a ministering community is challenged simultaneously
on several fronts: to nurture a common vision, to show their
concern for one another in genuinely appropriate ways, to act
together effectively." TKBF embodied a vision, an opportunity to serve one another, and a catalyst for together serving
others. "Community groups take seriously both their tasks
and the quality of their life together." The implicit reality is
that "time demands can be considerable."[484] TKBF attempted
to address this and other challenges through convergence in
the fellowship, teaching, and reflection.

The period of intentional consolation between families,
including individuals, began Easter Sunday and continued
for three months. In the months leading up to The TKBF
Project, its design and implementation were ongoing points
of discussion among the church leaders. Continuous study
and teaching of truth related to God's kingdom mission complemented this discussion. This awareness and anticipation
were critical for an effective six weeks of focused and final

---

[484] Whitehead, 96-97.

preparation. In addition to logistical planning, these six weeks included the selection, recruitment, and orientation of the facilitators detailed in the previous chapter. Also during this period, we consulted with Zion's accountability support partner, John Hobbs. He is an identified leader outside of the church to whom the leaders look for counsel, correction, and confirmation.

This support partner, who serves as a pastor of a church in another region, visited the church for an extended weekend in the midst of the final preparation. During his visit, he met with the elders to discuss implementation, and he provided teaching to undergird the project in multiple congregational gatherings. Alongside of this visit, there was a special Sunday morning observance of the fifth anniversary of Victoria Grace's life and death. A new chapter in her legacy opened when, following this remembrance, we introduced The TKBF Project to the congregation.[485]

Zion Church is a family committed to relating well with one another, and the revelation of God's mission has been turning this fellowship's focus outward in the years preceding this initiative. One individual described coming to Zion as finding "people who just want to follow God and do life together."[486] Another described a similar welcome: "I came to Zion and I felt connected–I felt like family."

Even so, families can easily settle into comfortability in being together. As a common human experience, people can cluster around these relational comfort centers. Those on the periphery can feel isolated. Most often the marginalization that occurs is unintentional. Hence, the intentional nature of fellowship in The TKBF Initiative encouraged further this outward trajectory to the fellowship within the Zion Church family.

---

[485] See Appendix C for the overview presented to the congregation during this Sunday morning service.

[486] Quotations from participants at Zion Church will remain anonymous throughout this chapter and those following to protect confidentiality. All participant feedback is in author's possession.

Participants recognized this intentional dynamic. One person described being involved "as much as possible, and thoroughly enjoyed connecting with people in a more intentional way." Another family was compelled to face the obstacle of time: "The fellowship was worth fighting for in our schedules, and we desired it."

In the preparation period and at the outset of the project, some had concerns of how to avoid a programmed fellowship that would feel forced and unnatural. Freedom was a critical foundation from which to nurture mission based on an intentional yet natural fellowship. This freedom consisted of an ongoing posture of invitation to this initiative from the leadership of the church as well as from the facilitators. Leading up to the initiative, facilitators reached out to invite those on their rosters to come to the congregational Easter breakfast, where they would learn more about the forthcoming special initiative.

Those voicing a programmatic concern cautioned that we not make people feel like projects. One facilitator noted at the conclusion how having relational facilitators avoided this concern. This person also credited the intergenerational dynamics as disarming and helping everyone enter into the fellowship time. This concern motivated our use of accessible terminology throughout the initiative.

In addition to relational facilitators, intergenerational dynamics, and an invitational approach, we empowered facilitators and participants with ownership of the consociation process. The SPE Peer Learning Project researchers describe the potential of such empowerment in andragogical settings:

> Peer learning is energized by radical agency. . .adult learners are trusted to plan transformational learning experiences that will lead them out of their comfort zones, enable them to take risks, and hold them accountable for results. Given this freedom, radical agency peer groups invent exciting new ways of

> studying the subject. Energized by the method, change for the better is dramatic, quick, and observable by congregations, spouses, and clergy themselves.[487]

The intentional fellowship over a three-month period at Zion consisted of a variety of simple and effective activities. Interestingly, the feedback from participants did not focus on "what" occurred in the gathering with others. Simply being together in an intentional way was enough.

One facilitating family progressed from initially finding "it very difficult to be organic" because of being "so plan-driven." In addition, they found themselves wanting "people to be happy and pleased, and I find it hard to get everyone to want to do things." However, this person realized that "this is me putting it on myself." This struggle led to this key realization: "The best way for us to 'be family' is to simply include people in what is genuinely us: baseball games with our children, doggie play dates in our yard, inviting people to bless the elderly at a nursing home while we sing." This family was challenged to "stop thinking of our 'performance goals' and just follow God," which did not always mean a lot would attend, but it always meant ministering to "the *one* that is in need." Thus, this family progressed from uncertain striving to please others to a secure invitation to serve others.

One facilitating family evidenced the free invitation by coordinating "several gatherings like park hangouts, meeting at each other's houses for games and fellowship, having a few meals together. . .Most of what we did ended up being. . .group-oriented rather than just individuals getting together on their own." However, they did not find this to hinder personal engagement, because the times of fellowship were "always very laid back, [and] it seemed like people were able to connect in small groups/conversations in the midst of the fellowship."

---

[487]   Marler, et al., 27.

The invitational approach encourages people to come alongside one another as a rhythm of living life as opposed to scheduling an extra commitment in an already busy one. Missional living transforms normal life along the lines of kingdom purposes. By coming alongside one another, it allows for people to catch the inspiration of the Spirit through fellowship with Him in serving one another. This approach embodies a supportive style of accountability. A principle from the SPE Peer Learning Project confirms it: "Accountability in a peer learning model that gives radical agency cannot be based on 'you must' (law). Rather, it is based on 'you can' (grace)."[488]

A grace-based approach can be unpredictable. One facilitating family discovered that connecting with those on their roster did not proceed as expected: "The ones I thought would be the easiest weren't, and the ones I thought would be harder also weren't." A grace-based invitational approach requires leaders to guard their expectations. Otherwise, it is grace-based on the surface only. Others will sense the pressure and obligation if it is not sincere.

We also encouraged freedom in fellowship through routine conversations. As conversations occurred daily, people developed alertness to those around them. This conversational alertness was a theme in participant reflections. With TKBF in mind, one person intentionally had conversations in and out of the church and in and out of the country. Another person noted, "Fellowship has definitely grown. . .there is more vulnerability and depth in our conversations." The benefit of pre-initiative *Real Talk Training*, which many in the church received, was both directly and indirectly evident in the participants' reflections on their experiences with TKBF.

Two important perspectives for the invitational freedom of the initiative came from a new family to the congregation and a participant living in a foreign country. The new family arrived at the congregation on a Sunday morning at the beginning of the initiative, based on a recommendation from

---

[488] Marler, et al., 32.

one of their family members who knew of the church. So they entered the church without having previous connections, and they themselves had moved into the area. This family responded to the invitation to share fellowship with others, and at the end of the three months, one of them offered their reflections: "It was a great point for us to enter the congregation. . .it was not only very interesting and an important aspect of church life, but it was also a really important part of my transition here, i.e. it 'got me through.'" This family found it similar to the church community they were a part of in their previous hometown.

Not only was the TKBF experience open to this family entering the church, it extended to a member serving on the foreign mission field. This individual participated remotely, "by listening to the teaching and sermons and living as family with the missionary community. . .Even though I was somewhere else, I was struck by how my 'family'" in another country "and 'family' in Zion is all one family focused on God's kingdom."

Table fellowship was a common context for consociation among Jesus and His disciples, and TKBF participants utilized this context as well. We launched the initiative around congregation-wide table fellowship in keeping with this living tradition of God's people:

> Food is a central metaphor and substance of hospitality. Communion, the Lord's Supper, the Eucharist is central to Christian worship. Behind this practice are Jesus' acts of gathering people around a table for a common meal. In his meal practice, Jesus enacted an ancient Hebrew tradition in which every meal was a sacrifice to God. A fundamental characteristic of these ancient meals was hospitality. Jesus extended this hospitality as a host at his table. His open invitation to meals was an affront to the cultural

practices that used meals to separate people by rank, status, and purity.[489]

One facilitator discussed how their two initial dinners "were great times of fellowship." This person connected with a couple of others for the first time: "I'm quite confident I never talked to either of them before." The facilitator further reported that another couple "shared how they loved just being able to spend time with people; they even rearranged their schedule to come to one of our picnics. Time together mattered to them."

Another facilitating family commented on the meaningful impact of their table fellowship:

> We were also reminded of the importance to hear others' hearts and perspectives within our church body. People expressed being so excited about these get-togethers and longing for more fellowship. We were struck by how many people long for deeper fellowship, but don't know how to access it whether it's a busy schedule, shy personality, insecurities, or something else. There were a few who were very "shy" in our group. One woman shared how hesitant she was to come, but then after, how elated and encouraged she was that she did come. One night of meaningful fellowship meant more to her than 50 Sunday mornings in her pew.

The intergenerational dynamic encouraged the quality and accessibility of table fellowship. The participant feedback confirmed how this intergenerational fellowship strengthened consociation and the exploration of mission. Children have a way of nullifying a performance orientation. The facilitating family just referenced came to a deeper realization of their responsibility to support fellowship through their children:

---

[489] Marler, et al., 147.

> We've also come to see the importance of giving children that place to relate to others. They have a *huge* role in leading fellowship and connecting in ways we may not be able to. Many of our connections with people during this time were led by one of my children. Having. . .young children in our church, we actually feel a responsibility to bring them into fellowship, not just for their sakes, but for all those around them!

How quick the church is to sideline its children through age-specific programming. Children could be the keys to unlocking the hearts of others, which in turn can unlock their own. These particular children were orphans adopted from another land, which is a special ministry they have within the church of turning hearts toward the mission of God.

Overall, each participating family experienced a unique time of fellowship even as some aspects were common to many. One family described their involvement in broad-ranging terms. Their descriptive terms express the fruit and foundation of fellowship built upon freedom: "fellowship, rest, intentional, focus, purposed, thought-provoking, relational, natural, organic, ongoing."

The SPE Peer Learning Project researchers concluded that "sharing meals, conversation, worship experiences, personal stories, and developmental goals over a three-day period has an amazingly transformative effect."[490] This research strongly suggests the potential for sustained transformation over a longer period by intentionally nurturing the same dynamics.

---

490   Marler, et al., 73.

Chapter 17

A Focused Time of Teaching

—◆◆◆◆—

An integrated missional lifestyle is more than a belief system. Nouwen expresses the concern that ". . .for many people, Christianity has become an ideology."[491] As Smith's comments in the previous chapter indicate, patterns of behavior that express belief cultivate a lifestyle. In other words, within a community on a mission, teaching must embrace both belief and behavior simultaneously.

The TKBF Initiative exemplified the tandem nature of hearing and obeying God's word. As stated earlier, the background of teaching biblical theology with a focus on the kingdom of God and the mission of God established an essential foundation for this initiative. This preceding season of teaching lasted more than a decade and included increased involvement in mission. The process illustrates that "assisting adults to think theologically is neither a quick fix nor low investment educational program."[492]

Further, "assisting theological thinking is most easily done when the members of the group are studying the tradition in some way, whether that be Scripture, church history, or theology."[493] At Zion, the small group gatherings, Sunday School

---

[491] Nouwen, *The Wounded Healer*, 12.

[492] Whitehead, 105.

[493] Ibid., 104-105.

curriculum, and sermons have particularly focused on inductive scriptural study while connecting the themes that span the scriptural story. This approach aligns with the Whiteheads': "The first practical step toward intimacy is getting to know Scripture. . .what is important at this stage is getting to know what Scripture is, how it is put together, and thus how to make proper use of its diverse images and stories in pastoral reflections."[494] Specifically, a basis of biblical knowledge was laid previously at Zion through teaching an inductive Bible study method and curriculum in Sunday School, which included an Old Testament and New Testament survey. Additionally, in order to further establish the narrative context of the biblical story, the church went through a multi-month coordinated study in small groups, Sunday School, and sermon series covering the overarching narrative of scripture in the year prior to this project.

Focused teaching for the purposes of The TKBF Project began with the visit of Zion's accountability support partner one month prior to its start. His five sessions with the congregation included the following highlights in encouraging the mission of thinking kingdom and being family:

- It is about kingdom more than church. . .family more than church, and we will have church if we are family in the kingdom.
- Philippians 2 is what it is to be family.
- Devotional life must focus on hearing God.
- The focus is on being servants.
- The highest place is where the Father puts you right now.
- We must have a heart to simply be with Him.
- It is really wearisome being around miserable people who claim to know Jesus.
- In order to be family, we must detox from busyness; we must want what we're looking at more than what is killing us.

---

[494] Whitehead, 31.

- The particular focus over the next few months at Zion is about taking what happens at 'camp' (a retreat, missions trip, etc.) and implementing it at home ('bringing it back to the house').
- Learn how to be family by seeing how the Father loves us.
- We have the freedom to structure programs but still value people and relationships above the program.
- Structure facilitates mobility and flexibility.
- It is important to be presence-driven (presence of the Father showing us what He is doing).
- Family is messy.
- True fellowship is two or more people having the same nature (of Christ) coming together to hear His word and do it and committing to love each other unconditionally in an atmosphere of faith.
- When Jesus and His disciples did life together, the Father was pleased, and people wanted to join in.[495]

This visit and the reflection that occurred around Hobbs' teaching provided strong support for the initiative in several ways. The leaders consulted with him on matters of implementation. His teaching also stirred anticipation within the congregation for the upcoming initiative. As a trusted consultant to the congregation, his promotion of the project inspired others and added to its invitational quality.

During The TKBF Initiative, we suspended the normal small groups to create the flexibility in schedules for consociation among families. The teaching occurred on Sunday mornings, during Sunday School and in the sermon. Sunday School teachings covered the phases of missional wholeness and the missional characteristics as represented on the initial and follow-up reflective exercises, which are detailed in the next chapter.[496] We informed the congregation that Sunday

---

[495] Author's notes from John Hobbs' teaching sessions, in author's possession.

[496] See Appendix D for an outline of the Sunday School subjects for TKBF.

School would be a time to explore these reflection questions in depth. The letter to the Colossians provided the scriptural text to undergird the application of missional wholeness and characteristics.

The preaching outline for The TKBF Project began in the first month with the foundation of trinitarian relationality for missional wholeness and its characteristics.[497] This essentially linked the being and doing of God Himself with the being and doing of His people. In the second month, "Think kingdom" was the focus with messages that examined various aspects of God's kingdom. The preaching focus for the third month was "Be family," seeing the church as a family. This involved examining the New Testament context for family with application to the contemporary North American family. Part Two thoroughly detailed the content that informed these themes for the sermons in TKBF.

Excursus: Consociation of Christ with the Colossian Community

With the emphasis in this project on trinitarian relationality and the mutual indwelling of Jesus and His followers, Colossians provided an excellent textual foundation. In it Paul focuses on Christ indwelling the Colossian community. Throughout the study, we highlighted the revelation that the indwelling life of God in a community's being fueled the doing of the mission of the gospel. Trinitarian union shared with believers establishes them as a vocational community in the church universal, in their local church family, and in their family.

The following points from Colossians applied to mobilizing missional families. Echoing the relational knowledge and unity with God from Jesus' prayer in John 17, Paul links "every good work and increasing in the knowledge of God" (1:10). This expresses the goal to impart and receive knowledge, which Thomas Groome explains: "Thus for Paul,

---

497   See Appendix D for an outline of the sermons for TKBF.

'knowing God' is grounded in a loving relationship and leads to loving service for others."[498]

The fruit of the Colossians' reception of the gospel is evident in their love (1:4, 8). This love compels Paul's steadfast commitment on their behalf. His commitment manifests itself through unceasing prayer (1:9), "sufferings for your sake" (1:24), "labor" and "striving" (1:29), and "how great a struggle" he endures for their sakes (2:1). Paul's sacrificial work on their behalf connects to their comprehension of the mystery of the gospel, "which is Christ in you, the hope of glory" (1:27). Thus, Paul wishes on their behalf, "that you may be filled with the knowledge of his will in all spiritual wisdom and understanding" (1:9), "that we may present every man complete in Christ" (1:28), and their "attaining to. . .the full assurance of understanding. . .a true knowledge of God's mystery, that is, Christ Himself" (2:2). In fact, Paul explains that for him to "fully carry out the preaching of the word of God" means the revelation of "the mystery. . .which is Christ in you, the hope of glory" (1:25-27).

The indwelling life of Christ in a family provides hope for the glorious fulfillment of resurrection, redemption, and restoration in a new heaven and earth. This is the hope that compels a family's life of service to others. Indeed, George Eldon Ladd indicates the importance of the indwelling life of Christ in establishing this hope: "It is Christ in the believer that assures him or her of the hope of final redemption (Col. 1:27)."[499]

The awe-inspiring mystery of Christ's indwelling presence among God's missional family, which includes the Gentiles, is magnified by Paul's previous statements underscoring Christ's supremacy and prominence (1:15-20; italics added):

- the image of the invisible God
- the *first*born of *all* creation

---

[498] Thomas H. Groome, *Christian Religious Education* (San Francisco: Harper & Row Publishers, 1980), 143.

[499] George Eldon Ladd, Ed. Donald A. Hagner, *A Theology of the New Testament*, Revised Edition (Grand Rapids: Eerdmans, 1993), 530.

- by Him *all* things were created
- *all* things have been created through Him and for Him
- He is before *all* things
- in Him *all* things hold together
- head of the body, the church
- He is the beginning, the *first*born from the dead
- He Himself will come to have *first* place in *everything*
- *all* the fullness to dwell in Him
- through Him to reconcile *all* things to Himself

Paul's exaltation of Jesus continues in ascribing Him as the possessor of "all the treasures of wisdom and knowledge" (2:3). To those who freely received Christ, Paul commands that they "so walk in Him" (2:6). This imperative does not represent a shift to human striving. Rather, their "good discipline and stability" is commendable (2:5) because it occurs through the same posture of surrender that marked their reception of Him. His followers "overflowing with gratitude" indicates the key to obedience rooted in the reality of Christ's indwelling presence (2:7). Gratitude is a foundational missional characteristic.

On the matter of the erroneous influence hovering over the Colossian church, if their lives are fulfilled in Christ, then the commands, traditions, and disciplines of man hold no authority over them (2:16-23). In fact, if man's religion has no authority, then it is powerless to cause righteousness in the flesh (2:23). In short, the striving of man subverts the mystery of the gospel and hinders its mission. Paul confronts this deadly legalism, because it separates the people from "being" in Christ and thus obediently "doing" His work. This flow forms the foundation for missional wholeness and its characteristics.

Paul goes on to elaborate in chapter three on the process of living righteously and justly before God because of the provision of having their "life hidden with Christ in God" (3:2). He immediately applied this principled teaching to household relationships (3:18-4:1). The different relationships noted contain varying degrees of human freedom and limitation, but all who are in Christ have freedom, another vital missional characteristic. Clapp's comments on the heart of Paul's household codes in 1 Corinthians 7:17-24 also relate here:

> Paul can find freedom in the ordinary, nitty-gritty qualities of all these limitations. . .God is able to meet us and enrich us in a variety of circumstances. . .Within the community engendered by the kingdom of God, we can faithfully affirm a variety of calls and 'conditions.' Indeed, it is our very conditions and limitations that turn us from fantasy and self-pity to the genuine freedom to be found in the actual circumstances of our lives.[500]

Then Paul's ministry purpose of preaching the "mystery of Christ" returns to focus with the sobering reminder that Paul is in prison for such mission work (4:3). The Colossians must likewise be mindful of the message of their lives because of the missional opportunity "toward outsiders" (4:5-6).

Though Paul did not know them personally, he fills his closing with personal references and connections, highlighting how they are part of his family of faith engaged in God's mission of the gospel (4:7-17). The cost of Christ's sacrifice throughout the letter undergirds the realization of the indwelling life of Christ. In Paul's farewell, he calls on them to remember the cost of carrying out the mission of the gospel: "Remember my imprisonment" (4:18). Yet this quickly yields to the impetus for proclaiming the message, "Grace be with you" (4:19).

As it is true for the Colossian community and churches today, so it is for families as an extension–only in Christ can the church and its families find hope in the gospel. Only in Him can they participate in His mission of hope as a family.

---

[500] Clapp, 112-113.

Chapter 18

A Focused Time of Reflection

—— ⌘ ——

Integrating family life around the mission of God requires reflection. It bridges God's revelation with sustainable application. Without reflection, we reduce fellowship to socializing and teaching to a theoretical endeavor only. Missional lifestyles are countercultural; thus, intentionality is involved. Reflection fuels this countercultural practice.

Consider Nouwen's comments on the saturation of diversity in modern culture: "One of the most visible phenomena of our time is the tremendous exposure of man to divergent and often contrasting ideas, traditions, religious convictions, and life styles."[501] Postmodern culture has continued this trajectory. Hence, in The TKBF Initiative, reflection was instrumental alongside of the fellowship and teaching, as explained by the Whiteheads':

> Many ideas and insights come during a reflection. . .the idea or insight that might be most significant is likely to be forgotten. . .precisely because it alters one's habitual meaning-making interpretive frameworks. So, if people are going to claim something from a theological reflection, they must do so actively, by writing it down,

---

[501] Nouwen, *The Wounded Healer*, 10.

embodying it. . .to invite support from group members to take a specific action as a first step in living by the new insight.[502]

To this end, we distributed "Initial Reflection Questions" at the congregational Easter breakfast to launch the initiative. Every family or individual present received a copy of the informed consent along with the reflection exercise.[503] These were also sent electronically to the congregation. Participants had two weeks to complete the initial reflections. We distributed the "Follow-up Reflection Questions" in person and electronically two weeks prior to the close of the initiative.[504] Facilitators were asked at the beginning and end to encourage those on their consociation roster to complete the reflections, though nobody was required to do so, which was always communicated. This also continued the invitational quality to the initiative.

During the preparation period, the elder team collectively revised the reflection tools with further revisions completed by the facilitators at their orientation. The open questions on the reflections were designed to require the time and discipline for contemplation. They were not questions that could be answered quickly. One family commented on how the initial reflection ended up leading them into a very thorough process of discernment and discussion. Another person found that the questions were difficult "to think on or express yourself with–especially pinpointing specifics." Others also commented on their challenging nature, but the depth in their responses to these open and penetrating questions are readily apparent.

Many people were encountering trials in life as they worked through the reflections. The potential for such a structured reflection process in the context of struggle, fellowship,

---

[502] Whitehead, 109.

[503] See Appendix E for the informed consent and Appendix F for the "Initial Reflection Questions."

[504] See Appendix G for the "Follow-up Reflection Questions."

and teaching is described by the researches in the SPE Peer Learning Project, who synthesize principles of the process as informed by Walter Brueggemann's work:[505]

> Orientation serves as a reminder of our commonality amid our diversity and speaks to the times in our lives when things are good, steady, and predictable. Moments of disorientation remind us that life is a journey of unexpected twists and turns. With God, an open mind, and peer support, however, we can move beyond these challenges to new levels of knowing, being, and doing–to reorientation. This sometimes means getting up, dusting ourselves off, and going on. At other times it means getting up to integrate aspects of new experiences into our personal and professional lives. Sometimes reorientation means simply finding the serenity to be still and know that God is God.[506]

Reflective exercises such as those utilized in The TKBF Initiative provided opportunities for acknowledgement, realignment, and trust. The reflective nature of TKBF was also integrated into the weekly worship service. We added corporate and responsive prayers to the congregational worship experience to support and sustain reflective prayer. Beyond the service, families and individuals were encouraged to keep their copy of the prayer as well as the weekly prayer requests to use in their personal prayer times. One facilitator wrote a prayer that we used several times during the initiative.[507]

Another practice valued at Zion, which was continued intentionally during TKBF, is public testimonies. Whether in

---

[505] Walter Brueggemann, *The Psalms and the Life of Faith* (Minneapolis, MN: Fortress Press, 1995), 9.

[506] Marler, et al., 90.

[507] See Appendix H for this corporate prayer used several times during TKBF.

small group settings, during Sunday School, or in the service, we encouraged people to share testimonies. The following chapters contain some of the reflections shared in these venues throughout the initiative. Not only do testimonies strengthen reflection while connecting teaching and mission in life, but they also cultivate fellowship:

> One of the most effective ways that group members begin to develop relationships is through the practice of 'sharing testimony'. . .The God of history gives our stories significance in the larger drama of redemption. So sharing testimonies is a way of interpreting our stories in light of God's story.[508]

A dozen of the participants completed their "Follow-up Reflection Questions" while on a missions trip at the conclusion of the initiative, or having been in a foreign missions setting at some point during the reflective process. Accordingly, the following applies to these TKBF participants: "In a distant context, they reflect critically on who they are, where they are, and the meaning of ministry." In addition, "socioeconomic contrasts" contribute to seeing "ministry through a different prism, and such comparisons help them reevaluate the resources required for effective ministry."[509]

The missional contexts are formational components for redemptive wholeness and redemptive characteristics. As the Whiteheads state, "When a reflecting community learns to value experience, it begins to notice the absence of certain voices in the on-going conversation of faith."[510] The missing voices of the marginalized weighed on the minds of the congregation. Another significant aspect to the teaching leading into this initiative was the church's emphasis and ongoing

---

[508] Marler, et al., 69.

[509] Ibid., 99.

[510] Whitehead, 48.

reflection on the theme of God's justice, particularly focusing on the Old Testament prophets and the gospels. Hence, for participants mindful of these marginalized voices locally and in societies around the world, their reflections became redemptive opportunities to give place to the voiceless.

Moreover, this others-centeredness illustrates the method of reflection in The TKBF Initiative. It is not simply an individual endeavor. Reflecting in families and within fellowship, it becomes a way in which a community interacts and nurtures one another. The reflection exercises in TKBF were carried out by families, couples, individuals, siblings, a four-generation household, and in familiar and unfamiliar settings. Such contemplation yields the mindset of being others-centered. Such a reflective community shares a sense of rejoicing and freedom: "When we engage in a corporate reflection on some significant question for Christian life, a discernment which intends to move through clarification and purification toward some practical, graceful action, what are we doing? We want to suggest that what we are doing is playing."[511]

---

[511]   Marler, et al., 143.

Chapter 19

Families Developing
Missional Wholeness

━━━∽≪≫∽━━━

Participant reflections before and after The TKBF Initiative reveal that wholeness is God's work in and through families. No formulaic approach causes families to arrive at wholeness. Participants reflected on *Missional Family Wholeness* as it related to what has been on their hearts recently, and if and how this progressed toward integration with their lifestyles. During the focused time of three months, a broad group of families encountered a range of experiences including births, deaths, relocation, career changes, and various occurrences of stress and celebration. In all, thirty-three participants filled out the initial or follow-up reflection, with most of them completing both. Twenty filled out the reflections as families, and thirteen as individuals.

We live out missional wholeness in a tension of serving others from rest which leads to renewal, as opposed to striving which leads to weariness. One family entered the initiative with "fellowship, hospitality, [and] engaging those around us" on their hearts, while "trying to also keep from becoming weary of doing these good things." They knew it need not be grand, but they found it challenging to routinely share life with others. Even so, they were learning to "trust God for strength as we faithfully do what is in front of us."

This couple faced the challenge of remaining together in their efforts. Sometimes it would be "slightly more of a challenge for one of us than the other." The revelation they were discovering in their being as a family was a peaceful one in the face of weariness, an understanding of identity as "God's son and daughter in every aspect of life:"

> As a son, it has led to taking advantage of the opportunities God sets before him to engage in relationship with friends, co-workers and just generally looking for opportunities to help others. As a daughter, it has helped her realize that it's all about who she belongs to and allows for greater purpose in all the seemingly 'little' tasks done at home with small children. Living this way allows the sonship/daughtership to speak for itself–it's a reality that doesn't depend on our actions.

At the end of the three-month period, the focus on intentionally connecting with others remained, still accompanied by wrestling particularly "with knowing when we should say 'yes' to things and when we say 'no'. . .which at times can be frustrating, but we have found that even in the midst of perhaps feeling tired, we are still connecting and moving forward with those around us."

The TKBF Initiative was not an appeal to remain within the realm of what was comfortable or easy. Rather, it called for church families to intentionally, and in some ways, sacrificially, invest in one another. Those willing to respond with such investment received blessing that would be shared with others. The family in focus described what a reward it was to continually "discover what a treasure community truly is." Further, they also discovered the overflowing nature of how purposefully being family within their consociation "naturally overflowed into how we related to others in our lives" outside of the church. Thus, they could rejoice that they persevered through the challenges, as evidenced in their noted growth in the characteristics, as well as in their conclusion regarding their sense of an integrated missional wholeness:

> It has given us continued purpose in making our home not only a place for us (immediate family) to enjoy one another, but [to] offer it as a place of fellowship for others. Whether that be for small group settings, random hang outs, allowing individuals to stay over. . .meals together. . .not just offering the physical aspect of our home, but also offering our family to others as well. . .having others simply take part in regular life with us has been happening a lot this season.

Another family began the initiative with a desire for "more fellowship and friendship" within the church family. They desired "to give more of self" while "finding rest and knowing when to say yes/no." They also expressed a desire for openness, honesty, and realness. By the end of the initiative, their hearts coalesced around the following focus: "Life is so short. . .Just–go–be–God has gone ahead of you." What they discovered echoes the revelation of *missio Dei*: "When we think we are going to try and bring people to Christ, God has a bigger better plan–just join Him in His plan."

In particular, an extended family member was critically ill, and they desired to minister the hope of the gospel to this loved one. In their words: "When we went to see [him], though our minds were set on. . .offering him to know Jesus. . .when we got [there], we found just how clearly *God had gone before us* [the relative was already reconciled to God; italics added for emphasis]. We set out with a purpose and wanting to be a blessing. . .we left the times. . .being blessed. Knowing that God was God–and that the kingdom is so much closer, heaven is so much closer than we sometimes think." On follow-up visits, they "had *real* talks with him that finally got started here on earth but. . .will continue in heaven. In our last conversation he thanked us for driving those hours for one day together and told us it was special to him – that was 'family.'"

Their experience over a weekend trip to see this sick family member paralleled the revelation and renewal of a meaningful missions experience. Connecting with this family member and ministering to him through their presence continued to be a major focus for this family over the months in which they were also participants in this initiative. It was this relative who "kept telling us life is just so short. Make the most of it."

This focus set in from the outset, when one of the members of their consociation passed away unexpectedly even before they could physically see one another. However, there had been a connection with this person over the phone, and as a result, they "had a few good phone conversations–*real* talk. . .lesson learned–I purposed to call her. I'm glad I did. . .It's such a reminder to be family daily."

Another opportunity also presented itself to this family during this initiative. A close relative has a young infant, and this family felt called by God to help provide the care for this child. Through The TKBF Initiative, this family was mobilized to be responsive to the leading of God in these daily opportunities, to minister to a couple of people as they neared the end of their lives and to care for an infant who was just beginning life.

This family became an incarnational expression of what Nouwen calls "waiting in life" and "waiting in death" with people.[512] On living to lead others toward tomorrow, Nouwen writes: "Let us not diminish the power of waiting by saying that a lifesaving relationship cannot develop in an hour. One eye movement or one handshake can replace years of friendship when man is in agony. Love not only lasts forever, it needs only a second to come about." In being such a ministering presence, one can save another life "by becoming his

---

[512] Nouwen, *The Wounded Healer*, 65, 67.

tomorrow."[513] Even if there is no tomorrow on earth, Nouwen offers this hope that compels a ministry of presence: "One can lead another to tomorrow even when tomorrow is the day of the other's death, because he can wait for him on both sides."[514] This family from Zion was able to wait with their relative in life and death, assuring him that they would be present with him on this side and waiting to be with him on the other side. Even with the church family member who died unexpectedly, this family waited with her through the phone conversations in the midst of her pain and suffering. Now, this family is waiting on a little child in life, offering through their presence the hope of tomorrow.

The family synthesized the vision of TKBF in their reflection: "Thinking kingdom and being family comes down to love." This echoes the musical, *Les Misérables*, where the characters approach the fulfillment of redemption singing "to love another person is to see the face of God."

Incarnating the hope of tomorrow with those who suffer is one way to respond to the cries of those in the world, cries from those longing for tomorrow. Again, this is expressed in *Les Misérables* as sung by the students in the song "One Day More": "One day to a new beginning. . .Every man will be a king. . .There's a new world for the winning. . .Do you hear the people sing?" The whole chorus concludes this song with a soaring statement of hope: "Tomorrow we'll discover what our God in heaven has in store! One more dawn. . ." The fulfillment in this musical storyline points to the scriptural hope of a new heaven and new earth as expressed in the chorus of the "Epilogue:" "Even the darkest night will end and the sun will rise. They will live again in freedom in the garden of the Lord. . .Is there a world you long to see? Do you hear the people sing. . .It is the future that we bring when tomorrow comes! Tomorrow comes! Tomorrow comes!"[515]

---

[513]   Nouwen, *The Wounded Healer*, 67.

[514]   Ibid., 69-70.

[515]   *Les Misérables*, Universal Studios, 2013.

Hope in God fuels incarnational responses from redemptive families. The hope for His tomorrow can encourage wholeness today. Hospitality is such a healing ministry that waits in the present according to the hope found in God for tomorrow. Indeed, Nouwen explained that hospitality is a healing ministry:

> . . .because [hospitality] takes away the false illusion that wholeness can be given by one to another. It is healing because it does not take away the loneliness and the pain of another, but invites him to recognize his loneliness on a level where it can be shared. Many people in this life suffer because they are anxiously searching for the man or woman, the event or encounter, which will take their loneliness away. But when they enter a house with real hospitality they soon see that their own wounds must be understood not as sources of despair and bitterness, but as signs that they have to travel on in obedience to the calling sounds of their own wounds.[516]

As families serve others, this can "prevent people from suffering for the wrong reasons."[517] One family continued to visit a friend in the hospital "hoping that being there will help her to know others care," thus possibly preventing an unnecessary suffering of feeling unloved.

Missional Family Wholeness is about the formation of hope within families, "not because wounds are cured and pains are alleviated, but because wounds and pains become openings or occasions for a new vision. . .the wound, which causes us to suffer now, will be revealed to us later as the place where God intimated his new creation."[518] For families at Zion, TKBF

---

[516] Nouwen, *The Wounded Healer*, 92.

[517] Ibid., 93.

[518] Ibid., 94, 96.

provided an opportunity to walk out the lesson they have been learning that "life after death can only be thought of in terms of life before it, and nobody can dream of a new earth when there is no old earth to hold any promises."[519]

Therefore, revelation from God relates closely to brokenness and hope as it relates to the poor in the world. This has been revealed to the Zion family. The Whiteheads explain the nature of this revelation with its accompanying brokenness and emerging hope:

> What is the revelation here? Is this more than a romanticizing of poverty? What is the special merit of suffering and the longing for justice? Why are such experiences–in the Scriptures and in our lives–so privileged? Perhaps this priority is to counterbalance the human impulse to separate ourselves from other people's suffering and to insulate 'our kind' from responsibility in their plight. Satisfying this impulse, we soon find ourselves imbedded in self-righteousness or mired in boredom. We are safe but, with little thirst for justice, distant from God. . .But experience, come as chance or grace, puts our safe distance in doubt. . .In this gathering of the marginalized–'the lowly' of Hebrew Scriptures and Mary's Magnificat–we hear again the sound of our redemption breaking through our righteousness and boredom. . .Or the revelation arrives as a serious illness or family crisis that ushers us into the house of 'the lowly.' Stricken by some loss, we watch our confidence and our plans fall away. The distress wrenches us open to beliefs we had all but abandoned. Self-sufficiency and self-righteousness are burned away; in their ashes faith stirs again. . .Otherness–in the face of the poor and the sick and the outcast–interjects

---

[519] Nouwen, *The Wounded Healer*, 14.

> tension into our shared life of faith. In these disruptive experiences life becomes more urgent, more charged with meaning. Our discomfort sets us on the journey toward conversion. Religious hope rekindles as we sense the call to live more faithfully, more courageously.[520]

This courage is evident in the testimony of one of the participating families, who in five years has adopted their first three children from another country. The Zion family has walked this journey alongside them. After having a natural child, they have their sights on a fourth international adoption. Clearly, the things on their heart for the past few years and at the beginning of the initiative include "children, orphan care (adoption), honoring life, loving/serving others, abiding, and trust." Abiding and trust represent the foundation of being that fuels such doing.

Much of the brokenness that has opened the eyes of this family has come from entering into the redemptive stories of their adopted children. In their words, "There's been tremendous loss in our children's lives, and out of this brokenness has emerged healing, restoration, and wholeness that we never thought possible. As we yielded and learned to trust and abide, God's literally created our family out of ashes. Pain is real and has taught us to daily trust and abide in Jesus, our only *hope*." They see my daughter Victoria Grace's life, their niece, as a gift through whom the Father has "given us an eternal perspective of belonging to God, period."

Their passion is to train "young children in God's ways." Overall, they entered the initiative with children on their hearts as part of a kingdom-focus and "big picture" perspective. At the end of the consociation period, this family was seeing personally how effective their own children were in blessing others. They were particularly "reminded of how pivotal children are in the kingdom. It's so important that they are given a place. . .not just a place, but a place of honor."

---

[520] Whitehead, 50.

The family's passion was "inspired to continue" through the initiative. It was evident in practical ways what an honorable and effective role children play in the fellowship of the family of God:

> . . .Seeing how much people love our children or just children in general. Our kids were a part of all the events and many people found such great joy in just being around them. In our group, our children really led in some neat ways relationally. They have no fears or preconceived ideas and were able to jump right into things, especially when food was involved! At one event, several middle-aged women started working a puzzle with our five year old. By the end of it, our five year old had moved onto something else, but these three women were left doing a kids' puzzle, laughing along the way, and having a great time getting to know one another better. . .over a puzzle! They just needed a child and a silly thing to bring them together. It led to two of them having a very meaningful conversation. There were many times like this, where the kids made someone feel more comfortable, made them smile, and brought so much joy to the group. Our oldest is especially still connecting relationally based on things/ events that took place these past three months.

For another family on an adoption journey, they have been learning "what God's best is in every area. But His 'best is not an event or a thing; it's who He is and who we are in Him." Hence, it is a revelation in their being and in "living as His sons and daughters because of our identity in Him." Overall, from the formation of the relationships between the husband and wife to the growth of their family through two children and now a third on the way through international adoption, this family has experienced "a waiting, watching, seeking period before His 'best' or even just His grace was revealed." Indeed, this pattern reflects the development of missional wholeness.

In entering the project period, this family had their adoption of their next child not only "on" their hearts, but "tattooed [on their hearts]. . .which is a painful process but a lasting and a good one." During this time, they had been learning "that 'waiting' is simply an act of obedience. Waiting is action, and action takes place during the waiting." During the period of the initiative, this family experienced the presence of family "both close and very distant to serve" them in the waiting. As this has occurred, "those people who have helped us as family have been on our hearts."

As the preparation has continued for the adoption, this family has been struck by the "family" that has come to help. Though these helpers may not seem to be "the most capable," their willingness and ability to serve was something they learned not to take for granted. As the family realized, "If Christ is in them, they are a strong family member with a purpose." This family even sees the strength applying to those who do not speak of following Christ but are willing to help. The process has been humbling "when strangers and 'weak' family are called up to bring your child to your arms." Their testimony is one of God using the marginalized to reach those on the margins: "We asked God to move heaven and earth to make our adoption possible, and it's like He has lined up people all the way to" another country "and back again to pass her to us. We are constantly amazed and humbled at the people in line."

Community is often a gift experienced in the process toward wholeness. Its instrumental role is evident in another family's testimony. They reported a high degree of "work stress and anxiety" leading at times "to the point of wanting to give up." In the midst of this struggle, the parents began to regularly read God's word. One of the parents also viewed a good bit of religious programming. This person reported initially "some progress," but overall still felt overwhelmed. There was no mention of regular fellowship in the initial description of this struggle. In fact, it seemed to be lacking.

In this family's follow-up response, it is noteworthy that regular fellowship characterized their experience during the consociation period. There was an outward focus referenced in a specific and ongoing outreach to another member of the church. Even more, the focus of what was on their heart was still "dealing with work stress," but right after they noted "receiving support from others" accompanied by "being there as others share their trials." Though likely still a part of their life, the religious television programming referenced throughout the initial reflection was absent in the follow-up while fellowship and an awareness of others was more prevalent. Another key focus in the development of this family was processing forgiveness, which was not mentioned in the initial reflection. A transition is also approaching with the beginning of a new career.

A member participating as an individual on the mission field was able to learn "about obeying God, trusting in His timing, and the Godly nature of being communal and family with those around us." At times lonely and facing difficulty, this person learned how daily delight in the midst of another culture expressed the vision of The TKBF Project:

> I simply lived life with the families around me, doing routine activities together and special activities together, such as a ministry trip. I've seen how God refines us as His people within community as well as individually. As we each obey God, we invite others to obey God as well and function as His Kingdom, one Body of Christ. Living as family within the context of serving God's Kingdom gives a picture of God's ultimate redemption and restoration.

This illustrates an important lesson of walking out a life-style of thinking kingdom and being family. Living the vision is not always ideal and pleasurable. Loneliness can often accompany the life of discipleship for a family or individual. It is easy and popular to try and anesthetize people from this reality. Indeed, listen to another person's description of a struggle: "As much as I love the investing element of my life, I get lonely because I'm lacking people to play with and communicate with on a level where I'm not the investor/mentor. Sometimes I just want somebody to laugh with who will listen to me for a change. That's been weighing on me a lot lately and I don't like it. It makes me feel selfish."

One can easily feel the pull to try and fix this struggle for this person. However, Nouwen believes to do so can discard an incredible gift:

> The Christian way of life does not take away our loneliness; it protects and cherishes it as a precious gift. Sometimes it seems as if we do everything possible to avoid the painful confrontation with our basic human loneliness, and allow ourselves to be trapped by false gods promising immediate satisfaction and quick relief. But perhaps the painful awareness of loneliness is an invitation to transcend our limitations and look beyond the boundaries of our existence. The awareness of loneliness reveals to us an inner emptiness that can be destructive when misunderstood, but filled with promise for him who can tolerate its sweet pain."[521]

A kingdom focus redeems and strengthens an individual facing the limits of loneliness. A common theme throughout the reflections, families realized how limits yielded a greater and more fruitful focus in their lives. One family wrote, "The kingdom has gotten *so much bigger* yet our life purpose seems

---

[521] Nouwen, *The Wounded Healer*, 84.

to have gotten much more simple." Another echoed this simplicity: "Really, the past three months simplified things even more for us. Loving God and loving people is at the heart of His kingdom. It was very restful to be reminded of those truths. We just long to live life in a deeper way with those around us and continue to say *yes* as the Lord leads us."

For some, limitation and focus were instrumental for pursuing missional practice. One family had on their hearts "to get rid of the unnecessary things in our lives and focus on what is important and helpful." This sharpened during the consociation period as they prepared for an extended stretch of service in another country. Another person acknowledged limitation and focus in creating space with family and pursuing "a greater connection among others" during this time. In reaching out to others, a different family was already becoming aware that in their desire to serve others, they were learning the limit of not being able to "'fix' others or their problems." Still another individual, facing difficult circumstances, found rest in applying this personally. He offered a grateful testimony of realizing in the midst of his own life's struggles, "we don't have to fix it."

For others, the limit of death created an urgency to relate well to others. As one person saw it, the brevity of life left no room for holding grudges. Regarding the opportunity to reach out, another person commented on a focus on follow through: "I have an *urgency* to spend *time* with people instead of just saying, 'We need to get together' and not following through on it. This is *very* recent based upon the death of a high school classmate of mine who I haven't spoken to in decades." Also in relating to others, one family described a growing conviction that there was "no time or sense to superficiality." Continuing along these lines, grandparents mentioned having "international adoption" on their hearts. They have been learning throughout life "as you go, our life here on earth is temporary."

Limitation and focus also relate to how families view possessions. For one family, a changed focus helped alter their perspective on possessions. They described a growing awareness of focusing "on what we *do* have rather than what we feel we need and *don't* have."

In these examples, a healthy acknowledgement of limits can encourage a focused creativity for engaging missional opportunities. As the Whiteheads put it, "It is precisely in the interplay of possibility and limit that we play out our lives. With no sense of limit we live irresponsible lives. With no sense of mobility – of possibility, of change, of newness – our lives grow stagnant, losing their flexibility and play."[522]

Children do not need perfect circumstances in order to play. In fact, what adults might consider a mess, children tend to see as a potential playground. I was reminded of this in watching my own children play with other children while in Peru for the summer. Heavy rains had washed mud onto the driveway. What adults were ready to shovel away ended up providing weeks of free and creative play for the children in their very own "mud factory." All of this reminds us that missional wholeness may not look whole from a human perspective. It might even be messy. However, it is *redemptive* wholeness, which God has always demonstrated as something His power is able to accomplish in working through the weaknesses of humans. Perhaps one of the hidden hindrances to missional wholeness is the neat and tidy approach to ministry that can characterize a programmed Christianity in North America. God often reveals Himself in messy circumstances.

The narrative reflections to this point offer perspectives relating generally to missional wholeness. The following reflective comments are organized according to the flow of *Missional Family Wholeness*. Often this flow progresses from messy circumstances to a more mature perspective with a missional motivation and ethic. TKBF served as a catalyst for some participants and a confirming experience for others.

---

[522] Whitehead, 148.

Revelation

One family faced difficult circumstances from the "effects of huge changes in our lives." They are "learning to trust God to reveal his plan and timing, which can be difficult – learning this can serve His kingdom but also being torn by discouragement. . .sources of hope remain how faithful God has been, examples of others in our lives, scripture. . .dreams for our family. . ." Another one echoed the common experience of God's faithfulness in trials. This one, who had been "sick and broken," has learned that "God is *always* faithful." This person also has "*hope* because of Him."

One person has confessed to a significant struggle with sin, commenting, "if it were not for TKBF, this issue would have most likely been eventually addressed, but I do not believe that it would have been handled, approached or addressed as comfortably and effectively."

Another person has been burdened by division in the church. The initiative has encouraged him in seeing others as part of his family and rising above the doctrinal differences that so easily divide the church. As part of a neighborhood Bible study, he rejoices that they have been experiencing great fellowship. "By God's grace, we have lovingly accepted differing views and still continue to worship together."

One family acknowledged a preoccupation with finances in terms of their own plans and outlook. Another family noted "financial setbacks" with a change in employment. This changed their perception on the importance of their "stuff," and they realized the priority of sharing their possessions with others. Following The TKBF Initiative, they found that they "continue to be focused on helping others."

Difficult scenarios continued as an individual described bodily torment with physical pain entering the initiative, but acknowledged an unwavering faith in God as an "anchor" and "refuge." TKBF overlapped with "a troubling time of uncertainty," yet this person experienced "inspiration" along the lines of "faith, love, [and] hope." This person also understood the value of "friends and neighbors." TKBF became an opportunity for this individual to re-connect with the church family, acknowledging the church family's "welcome with open arms."

Many families talked about struggles and perspectives within their families. One couple talked about the burden of balancing difficult family dynamics as something weighing on their minds. Another family felt the need to have "more complete openness. . .including sensitive subjects." They desired to have servant-oriented "hearts to one another."

Another family reflected their concern for their extended family. The husband and wife come from broken homes, and they often have the opportunity to bless their families of origin. Someone in their church family encouraged them "to not focus on the feeling of love, but on the action of love." It has helped them focus on showing love even when they do not feel it.

One participating family at the beginning and the end of the initiative had on their hearts "being there for family through difficult times." One person began the initiative burdened for the salvation of family members. In the follow-up reflection, this person had more to share on how God was working in these family relationships.

There was a subtle yet significant shift expressed by several participants. Consider one family who was focused on their "family in general," and they desired to invest "time and energy into family relationships and situations." At the end of the initiative, their focus was now on "family–biological and relational." They were learning "how to relate to everyone through a 'kingdom perspective.'" Another talked about the importance of "learning how to extend family past what people typically categorize as 'immediate family.'" Along with this extended understanding of family has come the comfort of knowing how church is to be a safe place. Still another saw their family focus broaden to include deepening relationships with others, noting that "it has expanded our family."

From the various struggles that participants were facing to the longing to be family for and with others, one family summarized well the priority of consociation in families for looking beyond self and experiencing healing:

> There can be such difficulties and trials within the relationships of marriage, parenting, and family. The support and accountability given through the body are a huge help in navigating through these difficulties. Just the presence of others is a significant reminder that how we live directly impacts others. It lifts our eyes beyond ourselves. Isolation is never a good thing. We were made for relationship, fellowship, community, family, oneness. The old Irish proverb says it well: 'It is in the shelter of each other that people live.'

Participants also applied TKBF wholeness to their places of work. One family member was adjusting to transition at work. At the close of the initiative, this person reported a response of walking out purposeful conversations in the face of the transition. Seeing the missional opportunities at work characterized what others were seeing as well. One person expressed, "My heart has been breaking for friends and families at work in need."

Other participants were facing change, including one transition that spanned family, work, and housing. In their words, "we are walking into a new season that is requiring a great degree of trust in God, especially as sustainer and provider." Indeed, significant changes occurred for this family, which provided opportunity for trust and caring for one another.

For another, the lack of change was frustrating at the beginning of the initiative. This person was facing "discontent and struggle" related to "being single." Yet an understanding persisted in "abiding fellowship. . .allowing His love, His peace, His strength to flow through me instead of relying on my own." This was significant for this individual because of a consistent struggle to "rely on relationships with others over my relationship with the Lord." By turning first to God, this person was discovering the freedom to also relate to others. Such an opportunity to serve others out of the place of singleness was echoed by another who had a vision "to build families and help families grow together."

Another single person began the initiative focusing on a way forward at work and a mindset of mission for all of life. This person concluded the initiative realizing "what it means to be in/live in a community. And it's more than just living close to others, but I've found it to also be an understanding of co-laboring toward the same goal."

For many families in North America, the goal of life is personal fulfillment in relationships and an idealized retirement. Consider how one family experienced a broadened perspective in the midst of an approaching retirement while navigating the developing dynamics in relationships with family members over time. This family experienced a missions trip of one of its members to another country. Now on this person's heart is how this experience should shape all of life. The individual who went on the trip offered this comment at the end of the initiative: "Seeing the world more as potential brothers and sisters in Christ and trying to include them as church family seems more important than ever in the last several months."

Another family shared some parallel thoughts on perspective and its impact on family and mission. Coming into the initiative, they were already seeing their life as "getting simpler and simpler. . .seems to have come into focus around this one truth: everything we are and do is about relationship, loving God and loving others." Through the project, they saw more clearly how their family's fellowship could overflow as a blessing to others. It is important to note the sanctifying nature of a missional outlook as evident in this family's experience:

We have also come to see more clearly that living life loving God and others leaves little room for such things as unforgiveness, offense, pride, and other sins. It is hard to be about serving in God's kingdom and remain in a place of serving sin. So, as a personal testimony, there have been areas of sin in our lives that have been revealed and then seem to lose their hold in light of receiving God's love, loving Him, and loving others.

It seems that a missional flow out of a family hinders sin from flowing into a family.

One person's initial reflection on what God had been revealing was focused on a personal career path and the future. Identity was very much at the center – "identity as a daughter of God." On the follow-up reflection, this person credited the TKBF experience with a realization for "my growing need for grace, patience, and more humility in dealing with others. When I see others as my brothers and sisters, that relationship is no longer 'optional.' This taught me that I truly need to extend grace and forgiveness for those who may seem 'hard to love.'" The realization included seeing "my own pride and need for humility when I realized that I may be that person for someone else." Thus, this person's own reflections shifted through the initiative from a personal focus to an others-focused reality.

Awareness

As God reveals Himself to people through their brokenness, a new perspective develops. Like a child who puts on glasses for the first time and sees the world more clearly than before, the children of God have the opportunity for clearer vision as they receive God's revelation during trials. Participants in The TKBF Initiative describe what this has been like for them.

Some participants reported increased awareness in various aspects of discipleship. One individual described the positive attitudes and broad perspectives that resulted because of God's faithfulness through trials. Another began to discern "stark contrasts–the times when I'm abiding and trusting vs. the times when I am striving and relying on myself." Following "an extremely raw period of brokenness," one individual testifies to "a much more accurate, true perspective on the role of Christ's divine atonement for sin." Another individual's awareness has been helped by the simpler and less materialistic life while being on a short-term missions trip. Relationally, one experienced "the *urgency* to invest in people," and another had a blind spot revealed of seeing "my own need for others."

For some participants, dynamics of being family at home deepened. One family realized that transition "required us to ensure that each step we make is taken in unity with one another." Having a child for this family "changed our perspective in every way. Our understanding of 'family' has been enhanced."

Another family connected how seeing the need to show love to extended family members has heightened the importance of holding "each other accountable in our feelings and actions towards our family and each other." In addition, they see the "need to communicate our frustrations with each other and offer encouragement."

Though natural family relationships were included, multiple reflections echoed a missional awareness of family expanding beyond natural relationships. Consider how this is evident in two members of the same family, who were experiencing some "discouragement" and "disappointment" coming into the project over difficult relational dynamics. Through the TKBF experience, both were encouraged to have a broader approach to relationships. For one member, it was being intentional about conversations and opportunities to serve others. For the other, it was "to stop putting limits on relationships." By relating to others like family, whether they are or not, means it is possible to be more "real" with others than previously thought. But this does "mean giving out continual grace when I seem to think they don't deserve any."

One family put it succinctly, "we have begun to see *everyone* in our life as 'family' in the kingdom of God." Another person described the missional impact of this same outlook: "To recognize all in the family as brothers and sisters has really dissolved the prejudices I've had toward race, gender, and especially helping me to seek God's word by the Spirit on differing views than my own." Still another individual mentioned viewing "my relationships through more of a missional lens," which meant being more 'in the moment' with people."

One family's testimony of growing awareness and ensuing desires had to do with time and relationships: "We are continuing to learn to fully live in each moment - that our time belongs to God. Our days are His to fill. If there is an opportunity to be with someone, we want to do it. More and more, relationships drive who we are and what we do."

Motivation

As families walk in the awareness of the revelation they receive from God, their desires begin to align with God's. Motivation represents a bridge from a family's being into its doing in the development of *Missional Family Wholeness*. Participants in The TKBF Project provided insights on how their desires began to take shape around what they were hearing from God.

Some general discipleship-related comments included one family's claim that "we just want to be happy and please God." This family was particularly trying to walk this out in their financial and family planning. As families grow in missional understanding, financial and family planning can become two areas in which traditional aims come under fresh scrutiny.

One person explained a new desire stemming from awareness growing out of revelation: "I honestly have not had much interest in the Word of God and who He is until I realized how desperate I am for His guidance and grace." Another individual's motivational development was evident in responses to falling "back into old habits." This person now sees these as old habits to fall back into rather than the norm. Further, when experiencing such regression, the person now senses "a hunger and thirst like I've never known."

Within one family, growth was noted in more collective thinking as "their desires were more individually-based" when they got married. "This can be seen in our desires with material things, our jobs, time, finances. . .more and more, our perspective on these desires has changed to be more family-based. Asking the question, 'What is best for me?' is gradually changing to 'What is best for our family?'" During the consociation period, this family noted how "life has taken a more eternal focus and much less temporal."

A theme emerged in the reflections of families developing others-centered motivations. In the words of one, "I think I've just become more aware of others and what goes on in their lives. This awareness has led me to desire things with a less-selfish perspective. This is something I definitely am still understanding and growing in, but God has really opened my eyes to how narrow and self-focused my desires were/are."

Some members of the same family noted that the initiative helped them to be alert to "the kingdom context" and to be fully "present" in conversations with others. One family put it succinctly following the initiative: "We find fellowship sweeter. We desire it. We look for it. We expect it."

One person, who concluded the focused time on the mission field, noted how the whole process encouraged a "purpose to maintain and invest in my relationships/community." This person's initial reflection was lacking the community focus, which became central in the follow-up reflection.

There was also a keen missional trajectory evident in desiring to connect with others in daily life while also being open to new opportunities. Having been through rough times, one person now "looks forward to helping others through rough times." Another described her experience: "I have a better perspective on my own situation in life. I *want* to see people and don't get annoyed about scheduled times together; I no longer view times as obligations to be met, but rather as opportunities to invest, love, and share life and God in me." One family looks "forward to meeting new people." They also find joy in going to work and encountering people in everyday life. One person continues to desire to be a light "in the mission field of life where I now serve." In addition, this person reports, "I have really attained a desire to go on a mission trip."

One family's desire to "care for the least of these," from local daily encounters to international ventures, has brought meaning to everything. Even "going to the library," they discovered, can "become about more than getting books out." They have found that alertness on a daily basis requires rest on their part. Thus, "we play hard and sleep well in our household." Their rest included freedom from sin. In their words, "Many habitual sins have lost their power as we've focused on these things." Following the initiative, in addition to the aforementioned desires continuing to grow, they found themselves looking "forward to Sundays in a different way. There are new relationships that were forged. We also greatly anticipate our fellowship time and realize our great need for that."

In closing, revelation and awareness not only change desires, but behaviors are also altered over time. Families develop a missional intuition. These elements are evident in one family who discovered that their increasing focus on matters regarding mission was diminishing the influence of television and possessions on their family: "We choose activities that would align with our life views and don't have a desire to do things that don't." They further noted the focus of taking "more time to spend with neighbors and making the most of opportunities."

Intuition

As families carry out the newly formed desires of their hearts, which are rooted in their new perspective emerging from God's revelation received in brokenness, new habits and behaviors take shape. New tendencies replace old ones. At the core, families and individuals gradually discover that these new tendencies become intuitive.

Several participants reflected on changed behaviors. Here is one person's testimony:

> I feel that I have eliminated some very destructive, sinful habits. . .I have simply lived life with my focus on Christ. . .In just purposing to view Christ in the forefront of my life, I have found a freedom beyond understanding. This perspective has also affected my immediate reactions, by God having provided me with additional patience, and additional wisdom."

Another person initially reflected on an ongoing struggle with making major decisions. Even so, "one simple joy" prevailed: "God's kingdom rules and reigns and will continue to do so, and I have the privilege of joining in the work if I will take up my cross and follow. . .There's freedom to serve with my whole heart no matter where I am or what I'm doing." After the three-month period, this person confirmed the ongoing freedom: "My immediate reaction might still be the same, but I tend to make final decisions with the reality of God's Kingdom in view." In making decisions, this person developed a confidence that "God would use me for His Kingdom no matter where I served. If I willingly served Him and sought out His heart, I felt assured He'd use me."

In seeking changed behavior, one person in a particular relationship has "been checking my words, tone, and actions *a lot*." The underlying motivation for this person is to lead the other person toward God through the example of godly behavior.

Patterns in communication are evident in another family's embrace of tendencies such as being "slow to speak," "closing my eyes and listening because when my eyes are open I can't see," and also thinking before acting. In the end, this family mentioned the importance of still taking the necessary action.

The cross-cultural and focused context of being on a short-term missions trip has helped another in similar ways to "slow down my reactions and think through situations before responding." The necessary action for this one was made possible by relinquishing control in favor of a mindset of serving "in whatever way is needed." Another major component of these changes in patterns in this person's life was linked to watching less television. Interestingly, this person lacked enough certainty to offer any thoughts on such behavioral changes in the initial reflections.

In seeking to see "natural tendencies shift to a more gracious and loving reaction and response" to others, one person has "been praying this recently. . .That I would be slow to react, get angry, assume, judge, lash out, justify, take offense, speak, and quick to think, love, give the benefit of the doubt, extend grace, see my own faults, forgive, and listen." This aligns with previously noted thoughts from James K.A. Smith calling for liturgical responses in order to form habits of the heart. Another individual's reflections illustrate this important commitment to formation:

> At first I had to be very intentional about establishing new habits–placing scriptures at strategic places, setting aside frequent times during the day to talk to God. Now those things are becoming second nature. My Bible app on my phone is constantly open, and I'm talking to God all day long. My reactions to stressful situations are becoming much less anxious and much more peace-filled.

A holistic missional approach to those outside the home begins in the home. For one family, tension and misunderstanding has been replaced by consideration for one another within their home. Finances were the context in which their individuality would feel "controlled" when trying to plan and discuss in advance. In their growth leading up to this initiative, they noted that they "now feel unified in the effort as we both seek what is best for our family." During the three months, this family realized greater perspective through their own experiences, "which has helped us to 'not sweat the small stuff'. . .teaching us selflessness as we reorient our focus to caring for one another as a family."

One family observed their tendency to overly focus on home, to "close ourselves in" from extended family. Their change in behavior is a discipline that at times runs counter to their emotions and desires to remain isolated, and they are purposefully spending time with and enjoying their extended family.

A family member's expression of needing to be more patient in the initial reflection was confirmed by a commitment to "take a few steps back and wait on God." A comment from the Whiteheads relates here: "The skill of attending begins in active patience. To listen, we must hold ourself still enough to hear."[523] Practically, this includes relying on others in all the broad expressions of family. Within this person's natural family, the patience has taken a focus of allowing others "a greater role in family functions."

Themes of communication and momentum beginning inside the home and extending outside the home combine in the following family reflection. They referenced a couple of times the need to grow in being able "to listen and hear one another. . .we need to hear and search out the heart of each member. . .to hear what is the heart of one another without overshadowing it with our own heart's desires. . ." All of this was directed toward the natural family in the initial reflection. In the follow-up reflection, there was a noteworthy shift

---

[523] Whitehead, 69.

in focus toward the broader church family as "attitudes of distrust in people and not really wanting to invest in relationships has been challenged." Through this new awareness, they referenced "the expanded church family" and "more of a 'family consciousness' to relationships in all areas." The reference included others in the church as well as the community. One spouse noted that "TKBF has given us time to reflect *on others* and our family" (italics added), and the other spouse concurred: "We have been more intentional about including others in our activities."

One family explained: "We had a weaker understanding that 'family was a high priority, but now our vision of who our family is and how their needs take priority is clearer. Our day is more structured around 'family' time which seems to result in less man-made structure."

Structure and stewardship of resources are central to a missional family's intuition. Often the obstacles for a family trying to live outwardly rather than inwardly include a protective posture with their resources. One family has found that their "time and financial resources have been multiplied as we continue to give to others." This in turn has challenged their "natural tendency. . .to 'guard' our resources."

As a general observation on North American family culture, a self-preserving mindset appears common in families when it comes to scheduling evenings. Consider how regularly families complain about losing their evenings to busyness. In contrast, consider the way God redeems time according to this family's experience: "We find that when we 'lose' an evening for another person/people, we walk away having received a fuller gift from the fellowship and love." Indeed, this family takes it further by making the following comment in their closing reflection: "Things look very different in terms of time, money, possessions, etc. when people are living by God's sense of life, love, and economy." They were actually learning coming into the initiative, and it was confirmed within The TKBF Project as well. Here are more of their initial insights that were confirmed during the initiative:

> Loving one another isn't an 'economic' experience. We live much more 'in the moment,' realizing moments pass us by if we do not connect with what is happening. Love will always find the time. So, we try to take the time. We say 'yes.' We read one more book to our kids. We stay late. We change plans. We have another cup of coffee. Also, we have found that, more and more, money is not the governing factor for our decisions, plans, and hopes. It is simply something we try to steward as a part of God's kingdom.

They offer this conclusion: "Life isn't about what is convenient, the least messy, or works. It's about what and who God has put before us."

In addition to being more intentional about time with the family, an individual described a commitment to restructuring her schedule in order to create margins for spending time with others. It is apparent in her reflections that the period of consociation encouraged her to implement practical measures to respond to what God had been revealing about investing time in others. This is also corroborated by another who found TKBF to be "a great way for me to reach out to people I may not have naturally, and it's been a real blessing to me."

Another family discovered increased freedom "to engage in experiences, opportunities, and relationships that may look completely different." Thus, a missional intuition cultivates flexibility within the family's lifestyle that readies them to respond to the leading of the Spirit with the resources God has entrusted to them. In an integrated way, the family together seeks to follow God daily in His mission.

Integration

Ultimately, *Missional Family Wholeness* results in a lifestyle. It is a lifestyle of sustained participation in the *missio Dei*.

It is marked by a normal rhythm of community being and doing. The testimonies at the beginning of this chapter, as well as throughout the phases outlined, reveal momentum from the TKBF consociation, teaching, and reflection toward consistent practice. Though not necessarily confirming a change in lifestyle with just a three-month snapshot, changes are evident to perceptions and trajectories in a family's initial implementation and purposefulness. Also, struggles surface when the goal is integrated action rather than occasional and convenient action.

One family acknowledged a lack of identity and direction. Earlier, this family noted their striving to adjust to new aspects of their life together. They differed in their degree of satisfaction in the missional characteristics. Yet there was noteworthy growth in a global perspective. Understandably, changes to desires and intuition can be a painful process. In the end, this family still noted growth in each of the characteristics following the initiative.

A family's sense of identity anchors its lifestyle. Discerning this identity can also be a struggle. Busyness is one factor, as indicated in the family that referenced the feeling that sports involvement "has taken over our lives at times." Boundaries can also be difficult to maintain. For one family, their "sense of identity is very strongly influenced by our roles as part of an extended family. . .we often lose parts of our identity as parents and spouses."

Some participants gained clarity in their struggles with identity. For one who was struggling with the future but still grasping a personal identity, the concluding reflection synthesized initial ponderings with the changes realized during the initiative:

> I realize my identity is not better or worse than anyone's, as we are all called His beloved sons and daughters. I care less now about 'what' I do in the future, but I know 'how' I want to live–loving always in whatever I do. Being a

daughter in His family, I see it doesn't matter what I do, but it's just important to represent Him as a daughter of His.

Another individual came to a similar place of "trying to be more content with my identity being in Christ rather than the gifts that I have and the roles that I fill."

Others expressed outward implications from clarity with their identity. One entered the initiative having experienced a transformation in life–from being "in a person" to being "in God now." This has also opened doors for this person to help others.

A "deepened sense of family" took root with one family to the point that "in a time of transition, we are somehow feeling more and more settled." A possible explanation they offered is that their "focus has moved off of each other and is gradually shifting to the vision that God is giving us for our family. This has deepened our relationships with other families." A new and deeper focus began to limit their self-focus. At the end of the three months, this family saw "greater depth in our marriage. . .new and added purpose in life and specifically in our home."

One family's initial observation on their lifestyle surfaced through their ongoing experience of serving others in a variety of ways: "The only way it seems, to truly grow as family is to lay down self. Not an easy place to remain, so it's a constant laying down, or a daily laying down."

Coming into The TKBF Initiative, one person was confused by a "blurred" line between family and the church family. The person felt like trying to escape from natural family to the church as a "real family." The initiative helped confirm and bring clarity on the validity of being family in various settings. Rather than a disjointed and confusing outlook based upon relational circumstances, resolution occurred through a vision of an integrated life: "As I recognize the various family units (i.e. nuclear family, church family, neighborhood family, work family, etc.), I realize that I need to stay the same in each setting."

An individual participant also felt "equipped to engage more wherever I'm at no matter the circumstances." This has been especially helpful for adapting and finding "new purpose in this new season." Another commented: "I'm continuing to see my entire life as integrated, not separate events. So I see my family life, school life, mission life as more connected to each other than I did before. I was really challenged by thinking about how my [missions] trip connected to the rest of my life."

One family also explained how they grew in an understanding of an integrated life around family and church family: "We enjoy being with one another and our family. Our church family is very important to us as well. But I think we have realized how important our place is in each one."

One also testified to a desire for a life of sharing "the gospel not only when with the family of God, but to those outside the family." For this person, this includes natural family members who are outside of the church family.

The relational theme continued as participants described a lifestyle more focused on others. In not needing to fix others' problems, a family felt free to focus on sharing God's love, which was more energizing. After The TKBF Initiative, they also noted that they now "seem to 'need' less."

One family "used to try and 'get everything done' first—now we have less busyness by simplifying our activities, and more margin when something comes up." This led to preparedness for relational opportunities. For one family, the initiative facilitated "a new vision and focus to what we already do. However, the vision and focus has helped us to go farther and be more relational."

The revelation that "people matter" has been increasing to the point that one participant is now hoping for a new employment direction that focuses on this passion. One person noted how focusing on service brought about resonance with his place of work, where some vacation days were matched if taken for service trips, and some more were made available unpaid as well.

Participants at different life stages were reflected upon changes in their lifestyle as they have learned more about the mission of God's kingdom. One single person commented: "The direction of my life is much more undefined and much less planned out in the little details (who I'll marry, where I'll work, where I'll live, etc), but my life feels more focused with a greater sense of God's Kingdom and His Community." In a later season of life, grandparents have seen their life impacted by being "more aware of orphans around the world." This in turn "causes us to see how fortunate we are," and they are "more willing to support orphans financially."

That the project met some people who were already flowing with the mission is evident in this family's description of their lifestyle at the outset: "We don't know where we're going exactly, but really that isn't the point. We just want to belong to God and be a family." At the conclusion, the confirmation is evident as well:

> We want to live as children, belonging to God, with all of who we are and what we do surrendered. We want to be a family that lives and glorifies Him, being a "doorway" for others to see and receive an invitation to receive the gift of God's love and grace and His family. May we love each other and our children in a way that brings God's hope to others. And may we live with others as "family" in such a manner. We trust that our lives, every step and day, will be shaped and led by God and His eternal reality of love and life in His kingdom. We want *this* to be the inheritance for our children now and forever.

The integrated vision and the beginnings of practice that emerged during The TKBF Project at Zion Church exemplify the following description from the Whiteheads:

> A ministering community is a group in which *shared values* lead to *common action* undertaken in a spirit of *mutual concern.* In a community. . .they wish to *be something* together as well as *do something* together. Shared values, joint action, and mutual concern are not absent from other pastoral settings. But in a community each of these elements demands *explicit* attention.[524]

---

[524] Whitehead, 96.

Chapter 20

Families Displaying Missional Characteristics

———∞∞∞———

A s families mature in *Missional Family Wholeness*, they also display *Missional Family Characteristics*. Functioning at the core of a family's being are gratitude, rest, and freedom. These yield the doing of generosity, faithfulness in current contexts, and going into new ones. Participants in The TKBF Project had the opportunity to describe the presence of these characteristics in their lives.

Gratitude → Generosity

Gratitude is a receptive posture toward God, and it is a worshipful one. It is thankfulness to God. One family depicted their gratitude "for the place God has brought us as a family." Another found gratitude to be "very natural for my family" and also described the qualities of being "always hopeful" and worshipping always. . ."it's so easy to worship." An integrated life of worship appears to connect to the natural expression of gratitude. Worship is also rooted in hope, as indicated by another participating family: "Life's too short to *complain*! We must be thankful and live with hope!"

Another family wrote of seeing heaven and earth connect by often speaking of those whom they love, both alive on earth and those who live eternally in God's presence. In their words, "This keeps us living 'eyes-up,' which is a good posture for gratitude to take root." Another person, who entered the initiative from a desperate place, echoed this hope by noting an increase in gratitude "for the good now and to come." These reflections highlight the present focus with future hope that nurtures gratitude. Participants described a reality of gratitude that cannot be reduced to a list of things for which they are thankful. Much more, gratitude as an indicator of maturity connects to eschatological hope.

Other families alluded to the discipline of gratitude. One family cultivated gratitude by emphasizing the simple statement, "thank you," in their home. Another family described many points in a season of transition at which they had "to choose to be grateful, even when the complaints feel natural." God was teaching them to be "disciplined in gratitude." They also found that change in life could create a pressure that made it "very easy to hold tightly. . .and not be as free and giving."

One family's gratitude for all God has given them is conflicted by complaining and being anxious about the same. For instance, they are grateful for their children and their home, but they become anxious about all of the responsibility, and their stress can lead to complaining. As stated by the previous family, this family also found that when such frustrations arise, it easily thwarts their sentiment toward generosity and kindness.

Sources of stress, when viewed as gifts, can provide a perspective of sustained gratitude. Such a perspective supports generosity, as indicated by participant testimonies. Children were referenced as gifts to strengthen perspective and encourage ongoing responses of gratitude. One family explained how their "kids remind them of simple joy," which helps them "enjoy" life. Another couple confirmed that having "grandchildren has changed our hearts." They "are mindful of being joyful and thankful." Connected to these perspectives, these families described a freedom from things. One commented how possessions "lose their value unless the context is relational." So when they value things, it is because they value the relationships in view. This was stated in similar terms by another family whose growth in gratitude connected to a broader perspective of "new things for which to be thankful." They found that "possessions take on more value when given or shared." Another family believed they had a good attitude toward possessions because of knowing "we can't take it with us."

A global perspective is also very helpful. As one participant declared in facing financial struggles, considering "the plight of people worldwide, we live like kings! God provides!" Another offered, "I've gained some perspective in recent weeks about how much I do have."

Such perspective and contentment can impact how a family approaches their finances. One said, "[we are] content with what we have," and "[we] don't expect much. We give whatever we can–not saving as much for ourselves." This family spends cautiously in order that they might actually give more rather than save more.

While several participants expressed regret that they could not give more, one acknowledged that "we could give more to the church." Yet another person reported, in difficult circumstances, "I give more than I have sometimes."

The discipline of tithing was referenced by a few, one who mentioned tithing regularly, and another family who wrote: "We feel tithing is *very* important." Generosity as a discipline can be natural. One participant claimed that "giving is easy, for we know the blessings we have received, since possessions are not important to us." In fact, this family member loves to give "when you have not planned to do so."

The delight of generosity is also manifested by another family, who not only noted an increase in giving, but they also noted a deeper joy in giving as an outgrowth of the initiative: "Our giving (financial and spiritual) has increased, and there's a deeper joy in it. We find our heart is stirred as if it's our own experience as we listen to others share about ministering at the prison, praying for a family member to know the Lord, preparing for a [missions] trip. . .healing [that] someone's experienced, and whatever other testimonies came forth during this time."

Some participants began to see their receptive posture with generosity from others. One family noted, "at the moment we *receive* hospitality." Another stated: "So much of what we have is because of the generosity of others." Though limited in their ability to give financially, this family found "other ways in which we can be a blessing–such as service and using our talents and abilities."

Others found the initiative to nurture hospitality flowing from their being. One wrote "that God is showing me more joy as I learn to trust and hope." With hospitality, it "feels more natural for me and my family." On a practical note, one family mentioned that "we are hosting more family at times or able to serve family more because we are available."

The TKBF experience contributed to an understanding of the link between fellowship and gratitude and generosity. This connection emerged from the reflections of the participants. One individual directly linked his level of gratitude with fellowship. When alone, his gratitude is "squandered away." Another person also verified the connection by seeing how a lack of unity in the faith at home was hindering generosity.

One participant's gratitude progressed from an isolated virtue to something that had a context: "I am extremely grateful for my church community, and I am learning so much about God's heart and kingdom from those around me." Another individual put it succinctly: "constant fellowship leads to more" gratitude and generosity.

One family described the growth in their generosity during this period and its missional connection to the "going" of the church family:

> Another thing we found was that our giving (spiritual and financial) to those around us increased. We found ourselves feeling deeply invested in a friend's adoption, Zion's mission

trips, a friend ministering to a wayward teenage girl, a family fostering their niece, families growing and welcoming new life, and many other 'goings' of our church.

Rest → *Faithfulness*

Rest is elusive to families in pursuit of keeping pace with society. Since it is a reality of being before doing, families need to discern rest so they can implement it. A revelation of rest in the being of a redemptive family is essential for the family to be faithfully present throughout their current contexts of living, working, and playing. If a family only struggles to rest from work, then they may never progress to working from rest.

TKBF participants encountered this tension. One family commented, "Life seems to be a constant delicate dance back and forth over the line running between 'busy' and 'full.'" Fullness is working from rest, or being, and busyness is the tyranny of attempting to *do* rest in the midst of doing work.

One family felt that they were always catching up and had a hard time experiencing rest. Also consider a couple who finds themselves "always very busy." They believe it is good when it is with family, which is a lot. "But we don't do very well with our spiritual disciplines." This family also expressed room for growth with generosity and some wrestling with financial and family planning.

Spiritual disciplines themselves serve as junctions of being and doing, fueling a sense of fullness in the midst of activity. At the same time, they represent an opportunity to turn aside to stillness and quiet. Spiritual disciplines thrive when flowing from being, and they wane when oriented around striving to add one more thing to an already busy life. In Nouwen's words, ". . .prayer is not a pious decoration of life but the breath of human existence."[525]

---

[525] Nouwen, *The Wounded Healer*, 17.

A life integrated around mission calls for the practice of spiritual disciplines. One person was languishing in their Bible reading, but the preparation they had to do for leading a devotional while on a missions trip "lit a spark for me to continue that again." Another family member noted the connection to rest and spiritual disciplines while acknowledging their scarcity: "I find that the most restful places are in worship, corporate or alone, or alone in the word or in quiet meditation. Unfortunately, it happens far too little." For one person, an increase in satisfaction of rest had to do with better spiritual disciplines and being less busy.

From multiple testimonies, it is clear that TKBF at least raised awareness of the importance of rest as a missional characteristic. One family realized how "important issues are affected by our busy schedules." Another person acknowledged that while a struggle with rest continues, they are "much more *aware* of the need to be less 'busy.'" For another participant "running so thin" on activity, "one of my biggest prayers is that God teaches and leads me in 'de-cluttering.'"

Rest also relates to physical health and well-being. One couple credited the consociation period for providing encouragement to pursue a healthier lifestyle. Another individual also noted a renewed motivation for improved diet and fitness.

Though one person noted a slight decrease in their satisfaction with rest, it was qualified by growth as this person mentioned "re-learning, with new eyes" the meaning of rest. Still another referenced "learning a whole new definition of [rest]– even 'on the go.'" Another family expressed an increasing understanding of an integrated rest as fullness in life:

> This one we still are growing in. While there is great *joy* in continued fellowship and serving, we find ourselves often feeling very tired and trying to balance 'busyness' with purposeful involvement. At the same time, we've come to realize that feeling tired and weary is not such a bad thing! We're trying to not worry as much

> about feeling that way and trying to realize that
> seasons bring different levels of 'busyness' and
> it's more important to rest within that 'busyness'.
> We're learning rest isn't lack of 'busyness', but
> rest can be greatest and deepest amidst a very
> busy season of life.

Faithfulness in daily living flows from the alertness that results from rest. Thus, for one person, rest is valued for the purposes of being able to invest in others. Though adults may be more sophisticated than children at hiding the effects of tiredness, it is plain that emotions more easily affect the weary child and adult alike. Along these lines, one person noted how faithfulness at work required being diligent even when the feelings are lacking. Another applied faithfulness as being "faithfully attentive in each moment." Such alertness is countercultural to a society in constant motion and communication.

Faithfulness is sometimes underappreciated because it can be expected. Yet it is readily apparent when it is lacking. One family was thankful because a family member's "faithfulness at work has been noticed." Another family with young children, who also constantly work with children at church, indicated how faithfulness can feel unnoticed even by those carrying it out: "we often feel tired which doesn't bring forth great faithfulness. It's an 'in the trenches' lifestyle." They discovered consolation to be more than a model, but something they depend on for increased faithfulness: "Learning our great need for others during the initiative will, we believe, bring forth a greater faithfulness in our lives."

One family's alertness caused them to anticipate their need for rest. They found that proactively planning rest in advance was an effective way to be prepared to engage that activity with a missional mindset. In vocational faithfulness, this family was invigorated during the consociation period from being a bit bored at work to making the most of their opportunities.

Another family described faithfulness as wanting to "show up" in life. The activities they had in mind were as follows:

> It gives such purpose to each and every conversation, changing diapers, extended family dinners, going to work, reading to our kids, giving financially to God's work in the world, praying together as a couple, caring for our home, going to church, showing kindness to strangers, loving those who are difficult to love, and our nightly bed time routine as a family.

One participant realized that a faithful response to daily life views even missed opportunities as redeemable. He wrote the following about relational moments that he let pass by: "Even though I find myself missing opportunities, I am learning to go back later and follow up with the person, beginning with 'you know when you said. . .'"

Freedom → Going

Seeking out and exploring new contexts can be overwhelming. Freedom is a foundation from which redemptive families can both dream of new endeavors and persevere to overcome the challenges presented by such new opportunities. Such freedom includes receiving and extending forgiveness and repentance from sin. Freedom leads into healthy and holistic fellowship. Without freedom, families may still go, but the going can become more of an attempt to escape bondage, thus robbing them and those they serve of the blessings that could be realized if their going was in freedom.

The pairing of freedom and going is essential, because it involves others, which is necessary for connecting a family's brokenness with being a blessing. In addition, it is in being a blessing that the broken experience healing. Nouwen articulates this well:

> Christian leadership is accomplished only
> through service. . .the way out is the way in, that
> only by entering into communion with human
> suffering can relief be found. . .every Christian
> is constantly invited to overcome his neighbor's
> fear by entering into it with him, and to find in
> the fellowship of suffering the way to freedom.[526]

The testimonies of the families and individuals in The TKBF Initiative reveal this progression in being free to go. From the outset of the initiative, the aim has been to invite and inspire. Condemnation has no place in the work of the Spirit of God. The emphasis on being flowing into doing supports this freedom. As one participating family commented, the "TKBF outlook brings freedom from obligations, guilt, [and a] heavy sense of duties."

Reflections that reveal the progression from freedom into going include one person who explained his high degree of satisfaction in freedom: "I don't struggle a lot with forgiveness. . .I have done my best to forgive and seek forgiveness." This person is also looking to serve on the foreign field for an extended time. Another family's freedom has been hindered by struggling "with unforgiveness with members of our family and that has trickled down into our marriage." They continue to trust God for freedom and have learned that "wisdom comes a lot through conversation and just being in fellowship with others." Through such consociation, the family has "seen things" that they desire "to model in [their] own family or have heard things that have been meaningful and life-changing."

This family dreams of possibilities for going that span their new neighborhood to a distant land:

> I think the idea of going to the nations, especially
> the foreign nations, has become something that
> would practically be a desire that could be

---

[526] Nouwen, *The Wounded Healer*, 77.

fulfilled. Not only do we think that we could actually go with a family, but the need to go has been ever so increasing. We would love to go and give back because we know that we have been given so much. We would love to see our family go to [another country] some day and work with some of the orphanages there. [The father who himself was adopted from there would] like to share with the children that there is hope when things look very hopeless, because he has experienced those feelings himself.

One family member recited the addictions and behaviors that previously characterized the family, but do so no more. Even when not following God, He "has given [multiple members of the family] the gift" of freedom from crippling and long-term addictions. This pre-conversion freedom echoes Alan Hirsch's previously referenced concept of pre-conversion discipleship–God working in people's lives before they even decide to follow Him. One member of this family is now following God and explained, "It is a gift of hope for a better way. It was given when we weren't seeking gifts from a loving Father; we certainly did not deserve it. He just said 'Here, this is for you; love, God.' It was a dream come true even before I had the dream!"

Expanding upon true freedom from sin, the family member sees it as enjoying "life free from hidden agendas or ulterior motives." Such freedom equips this one with a vision of going to wrap "bits of truth in big bunches of love. . .and see what God does with it."

One family noted how the burden of sinfulness infringes upon their childlike freedom. As a family, their freedom has led to a life of going: "Life has become 'going,' making disciples of all nations. And we are willing to follow God wherever and to whomever He leads us."

With regard to freedom and the helpful presence of fellowship, one family was already learning "how everything we are/do is worship. . .Our church family helps us to live an integrated life in this regard." They further explained at the close of the initiative how "We've been finding that freedom comes from honesty and brokenness. A kingdom perspective brings great freedom." Seemingly connected to this freedom, the family noted that they are "seeing so much more of what we do as 'going.'" Their perspective indicates an important aspect of engaging new opportunities: Sometimes going continues through similar relationships and places but with a renewed vision for ministry.

Another individual, initially confused by trying to assess freedom, ended by noting the immense enjoyment experienced in "relationship and fellowship." Further, "many of my relationships have become more honest, which is *freeing*. I can see, though, how quickly my complaining, miscommunication, and unforgiveness can destroy my relationships."

This person has spent time among the nations and remains "so grateful for being able to go–supported and equipped." This same person also experienced a shift through the initiative toward seeing the need for fellowship and discovering identity with others, which compels the going.

One person's sense of freedom had to do with increased depth in relationships, including people at work. Initially, this person's going was "not as much of a focus recently." At the close of the initiative, a full level of satisfaction was reflected as this person went on an international missions trip and now viewed work as a place for going on mission.

Depth in fellowship has corresponded to depth in going for one family: "We have sensed an even deeper 'going' with all those around us. Even though we may not physically be a part of all these 'goings,' we feel invested and a huge part of Zion's thinking kingdom and being family."

One person, in their going through relational connections, is linked "with people all over the world." This includes making "friends with complete strangers." The person writes, "I may not be able to give to all, but I can pray." Another individual saw "much less striving" as part of the growth in freedom. Related to going, this person also has been in "weekly (or more) communication with people" in four different countries, each on a different continent. This continuous contact has given this person "a much more 'big picture' or global perspective" on all the missional characteristics. Going affects them all.

Freedom for one family meant "being more at ease with people and giving ourselves permission to play." This was helped by not getting "worked up about others' way of doing things" or the limitation people live under. This family also has found the freedom to go to the neighbors and the nations as converging dynamics, with going to the neighborhood at times "more stretching." Time in the community includes playing with their kids' baseball team and spending time in the evenings and weekends walking, biking, and interacting with neighbors. The family continues to stretch themselves in time and resources toward the nations as well.

An individual on the initial reflection saw going as basically non-existent and acknowledged a "very poor outlook" in this characteristic. At the end of the time, this same person expressed some growth in a "willingness" to work with current circumstances involving neighbors." Another was encouraged by the opportunities for going while stating that "there could be more 'going' on our end." Another couple concurred that they "could do more" with neighbors.

One person saw growth when abiding in Christ. The main focus on freedom for this person is being able to receive forgiveness because of being "so prone to wander." This participant is significantly involved in his neighborhood. In this he finds joy, and he is also praying for an opportunity "to go beyond the borders of Lancaster County." Such an endeavor was on another individual's heart, who referenced feeling "a little held back by having a child, but I'd *love* to go on a missions trip."

In being on the foreign mission field, one individual was very grateful for the opportunity to serve, and this person desired "to be open to where God has me 'go' in the future."

This person initially found it easier to go to the nations than the neighborhood but is also one who noted the initiative's help in reaching out to others beyond the normal reach.

In going from their neighborhood to the nations, one family is "learning to see one as the other and seeing and understanding how one [neighborhood] brings closer the other [nations]."

Consociation supports the persevering mindset necessary or going. One of the "biggest temptations" for one participant "is to 'stay' rather than 'go'–to remain comfortable rather than position myself as willing to go. Within my community context, I want to remain aware and keep a 'going' mindset rather than settling for what's easiest."

It is this type of alertness in "going" rather than "staying" that opens up daily life and its opportunities, not to mention the new doors that could open to people with such awareness. Perhaps it would be like seeing Jesus as Nouwen describes:

> You will find him in your own town, in your own family, and even in the strivings of your own heart, because he is in every man who draws his strength from the vision that dawns on the skyline of his life and leads him to a new world. IIt is this new world that fills our dreams, guides our actions and makes us go on, at great risk, with the increasing conviction that one day man will finally be free–free to love![527]

---

[527] Nouwen, *The Wounded Healer*, 22.

Chapter 21

Families Mobilizing in Mission

—⚬⚬⚬—

The TKBF Project provided a relational and theological context for both *Missional Family Wholeness* as a process and the virtues of *Missional Family Characteristics*. The participants' testimonies of missional wholeness and its characteristics demonstrate missional mobilization. In addition to starting something new, mobilization also includes, perhaps especially, encouraging greater awareness and action based on what is already at hand or in motion in the life of the family.

Missional wholeness itself leads to mobilization as being leads to doing. Wholeness is the healthy and sustainable way to be mobilized. As a measure of mobilization, the reflections recorded on wholeness and characteristics indicate the development within families and the individuals alongside of them. In addition, the participants' reflections confirm the validity of the elements used to define *Missional Family Wholeness* and *Missional Family Characteristics*. The reflections also directly and indirectly confirm the effectiveness of the family-with-family consociation model. These thick descriptions from participants' feedback form a qualitative foundation to support the principles proposed in this project for mobilizing missional families at Zion Church.

In addition to this qualitative analysis, I utilized a quantitative tool as a complementary approach to examine the model's effectiveness in mobilization. Specifically, Likkert items were utilized to facilitate assessment of each missional characteristic on the initial and follow-up reflections. These measured the participating family and individual's degree of satisfaction with the characteristic at the outset and conclusion of the initiative.

Though subject to the participating family's perspective, this quantitative tool allows for a measure of the family against itself. Measuring their degree of "satisfaction" preserved the invitational approach to the initiative by minimizing perceived expectations for improvement. In this way, families were invited to examine themselves without the pressure of evaluation or comparison that using terms like "growth" or "maturity" might have implicitly communicated.

Hence, the qualitative and quantitative approaches in this project are consistent with the literary, biblical, theological, and historical research of what constitutes the being and doing of a redemptive family. Being missional in community is a constant process of discernment and exploration. Effective mobilization and measurement works within this process. For TKBF, if participants indicated higher degrees of satisfaction in the elements of missional characteristics from the beginning to the conclusion of the project, then this would be further evidence of the model's effectiveness in mobilizing missional families at Zion Church.

The quantitative data was compiled and analyzed, and I have summarized the findings in four graphs below. The first two focus on the participating families, which were the focus group for this research. In addition, individuals, some single and some family members where the whole family did not participate, shared fully in the consociation and reflection process with the participating families. The second pair of charts reflects the data of all the participants combined.

Figure 3 compares the average degree of family satisfaction in missional characteristics on the initial and follow-up reflections. On a 1-5 scale, the starting place for satisfaction was over three for each characteristic. At the close of the project, they were all three and a half or higher on average, with three characteristics over four. The being characteristics of gratitude and rest were lower than the doing of generosity and faithfulness, which held true for both the initial and follow-up assessments. Interestingly, freedom was higher than going initially, and they were even when averaged from follow-up assessments. This graph also demonstrates visually that families grew in their satisfaction in every missional characteristic.

Figure 3.

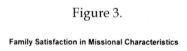

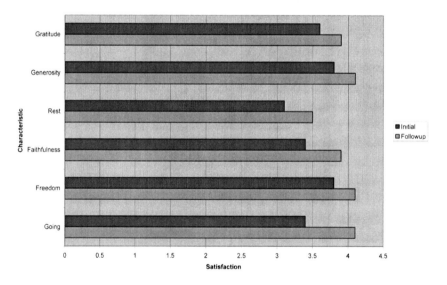

Figure 4 displays this increase of family satisfaction in each characteristic, based upon the average of family assessments, from the beginning to the end of The TKBF Initiative. Gratitude and going represent the largest increase, followed by rest and faithfulness, and then generosity followed by freedom. Four of the six increased by half a point or more.

Most significantly, every characteristic increased in family satisfaction during the three months of The TKBF Initiative.

Figure 4.

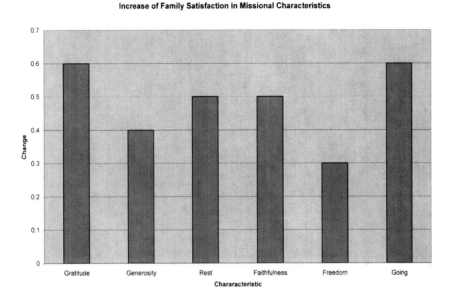

Increase of Family Satisfaction in Missional Characteristics

Figure 5 compares the average degree of satisfaction in missional characteristics on the initial and follow-up reflections for all of the participants–families and individuals. On a 1-5 scale, the starting place for satisfaction was over three for each characteristic except for rest, which was slightly under three. Consistent with Figure 3, at the close of the project, they were all three and a half or higher, with three characteristics over four. The being characteristics of gratitude and rest were lower than the doing of generosity and faithfulness (though only a one-tenth difference initially between gratitude and generosity), which held true for both the initial and follow-up assessments. Freedom was higher than going initially, and it was slightly less (one-tenth) than going on the follow-up average. As with Figure 3, this graph also demonstrates visually that all participants grew in their satisfaction in every missional characteristic.

255

Figure 5.

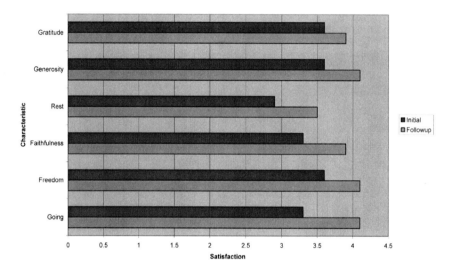

Total Participant Satisfaction in Missional Characteristics

Figure 6 displays this increase of total participant satisfaction in each characteristic, based upon the average of assessments, during the TKBF experience. It is visually the same as Figure 4, and statistically it is virtually the same with only slight differences of one-tenth lower averages in gratitude, rest, and freedom. Again, gratitude and going represent the largest increase, followed by rest and faithfulness, and then generosity followed by freedom. Four of the six increased on average by half a point or more. Again, the significance of the combined participants' growth in satisfaction remains the same as the families'–every characteristic increased in participants' satisfaction during the three months of TKBF.

Figure 6.

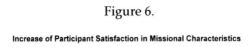

Increase of Participant Satisfaction in Missional Characteristics

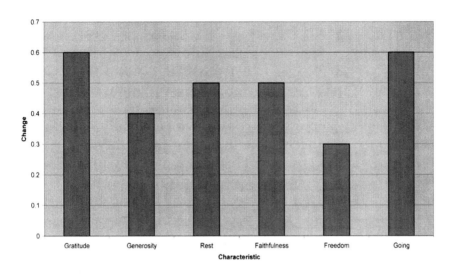

Hence, the qualitative analysis combined with the focused quantitative analysis confirms the presence of the elements of *Missional Family Wholeness* and *Missional Family Characteristics*. Further, the research confirms that the model for missional family mobilization through family-with-family consociation is effective for this congregation. All of this was evident through the storied living of the Zion Church of Millersville family.

More than statistics, the stories of missional mobilization abound in this congregation. One very special testimony took shape during the three-month TKBF experience that contains the ingredients of a mobilized church family, with the signs and wonders that only God can accomplish in His mission:

> During this time we were also concluding HIV testing for our youngest son, adopted from [Africa] 6 months ago. Our church family has walked through this adoption very closely with

us. After many ups and downs concerning his diagnosis, we were told that he is indeed HIV negative! This diagnosis came much to the [surprise] of the Department of Health and our pediatrician. HIV is a very complex disease, but the Department of Health had 'never seen a case like this, unexplainable,' so they told our pediatrician. Throughout a very long story of God's faithfulness and love toward our son (even while in the womb), we were fully able to receive this healing in his life and testify to it in our church body. This was a deep joy for us to celebrate and glorify God in this way with those who had prayed and labored to bring our son home.

Even while our son was in his mother's womb in [Africa] (months before we even knew about him), there was a specific prayer time about our family and future child led by a member of our church with a friend of his. During that prayer time, this woman (who was physically weak, recovering from surgery), had a sense that the Lord would heal our child. It blows us away to look back and see God's healing presence in our son's tiny life. When we got his referral, the name the Lord led us to give him was Abel Josiah Temesgen. . .Abel means *Breath*, Josiah means *Yahweh has healed*, and Temesgen means *Thanks be to God*. Our son's very name testifies to God's work in his little life. This perspective on belonging to God, life and healing, and gratitude has been awesome to be a part of. As we simply thought kingdom and were family (which for us involved a call to adopt a child who was HIV+ from [Africa]), God worked greatly along the way. We can't say we *specifically* prayed for any of these things, but we simply trusted God to write our story and use us in His kingdom. We never really even prayed for our son's healing; we simply said *yes* each step of the way, followed God's call, and trusted Him completely. We're still learning to walk in this way more and more.

And where it's really neat is how this all connects to our church body! They were thinking kingdom and being family right alongside us throughout this adoption journey. They encouraged us when we needed it and literally prayed our little boy home. So, to share this news with them was truly a great joy. How awesome is it when you see God work, but then to share that with brothers and sisters in Christ has to be the sweetest reward of all. It's so special to us that God brought all this to fruition during this three-month period.

Chapter 22

Project Evaluation and Implications for Ministry

⎯⎯⎯ ∞∞∞ ⎯⎯⎯

The approach for evaluating The TKBF Project focused on feedback from those invested and involved in the project– the facilitators and participants. By both soliciting and noting feedback from facilitators and participants, the evaluation of the initiative was informed and integrated to the whole experience from various perspectives. Any feedback provided by leaders in the church was through their roles as facilitators and participants. As already noted, Zion's accountability support partner offered strong evaluative feedback to the design and plan for implementation. His visit at the outset also helped frame the whole experience for the congregation.

In short, it is a qualitative evaluation of a qualitative project as informed by the words of the facilitators and participants themselves. This feedback was gathered through unsolicited evaluative statements added to the reflections, passed on through notes handwritten and electronic, and through comments shared with facilitators. Some of the feedback was also solicited through facilitators' field notes and a special Sunday School gathering at the end of the initiative for people to share about their overall experiences.

The congregation received The TKBF Initiative extremely well, and the feedback was overwhelmingly positive. This evidence comes first from the participants' descriptions and reactions to the experience of consociation. Next, they offered feedback regarding the teaching and reflection that undergirded the consociation among families. Finally, and perhaps most telling, people called for continued intentionality according to the mission of thinking kingdom and being family.

One person synthesizes the general perception by describing the consociation period as "a delightful time of fellowship." This does not mean everyone engaged fully from the beginning. Facilitators needed to help others navigate their questions and confusion. This included helping some adjust to the change in schedule by not having the regular Bible studies during this period. As anticipated, some did not understand what the initiative was about. For instance, one asked whether TKBF was only about mission work. Another facilitator observed individuals learning through this that "kingdom mission is more than overseas organized mission trips." This facilitator attributed initial stress encountered by a few as people not knowing "what they're 'supposed' to do."

The consociation experience took different forms throughout the church in terms of frequency, location, and the nature of the fellowship itself. Some were more group-oriented with a variety of activities, and others were highly relational, whether in large or small numbers. Looking back, only a couple facilitators referenced minor and personal adjustments in how they would coordinate next time, but overall, the focus throughout the feedback was not on the structure but the substance of the consociation.

One facilitating family member observed that people seemed to be "more connected" and vulnerable; they were taking it seriously, and they "seem to be craving it." Perhaps this level of engagement also supports another observation from this facilitator that the focused fellowship within Zion seemed to help people go beyond Zion. People were living "more intentional lives." An important part of this connectivity and intentionality for this facilitator was that participants appeared to better understand each other's sense of calling and mission.

Being intentional with consociation was both a continuation of what was already in place relationally and a commitment to new connections throughout the experience. One facilitating family spoke along with others in highlighting the value of following through on "scheduled times" together. Another facilitating family mentioned how the initiative provided a helpful framework for taking initiative with others. Another facilitating family described their experience as pretty fluid and informal without really needing a plan. Still another highlighted how consociation for kingdom purposes can become very natural, as it has been and continues to be the focus in family life. Summarizing the commitment and natural feel necessary for consociation, one facilitating family summarized it by stating that "intentionality strengthens the same relational muscles in various contexts." Muscles may be sore when put to a new use, but in time, the muscles strengthen and grow accustomed to the discipline. The effort becomes natural.

One participant anticipated long-term impact from The TKBF Initiative: "This whole experience hasn't been 'hyper' or 'super' spiritual, but rather it focused on forming relationship that would be cultivated and maintained for a lifetime." Some of this relational formation was already in motion, but TKBF helped advance it. One family appreciated this in how it "was an outflow of relationships that were already very much so established. This time only helped to make those relationships deeper." Another concurred: "For us, this time was not as much a start of something new, but rather a continuation and deepening. . ."

The intergenerational presence within consociation was affirmed as important for forming new relationships and nurturing existing ones. As one person put it, "having a mixed age group from twelve months to the 70–80s was wonderful." Specifically, the younger ones helped others relax and be with one another. Also, one facilitator noted how a couple of individuals who lacked father figures were able to interact with such people through the fellowship.

Participants in the experience who did not fill out the reflections still voiced strong support for the project. Our broad invitational approach permitted people to be a part of TKBF to varying degrees. Two such individual responses, one written and one spoken, speak to the impact of the initiative. One wrote, "Thank you for a fantastic three-month life-changing TKBF experience." After an initial lunchtime gathering, another person reflected how that time of fellowship made it one of the most special days of their lives. At the end of the initiative, this person expressed to me: "You have me hooked on this kingdom thing. . .we are going to keep meeting with our group!"

Consociation became the context through which participants experienced the perspective of thinking kingdom and being family. The teaching informed understanding through biblical theology, and the reflection process helped participating families make the connections.

The following comment reflects a consistent theme among participants: "Seeing the kingdom as much bigger than existing relationships expands my venue of 'family.'" Another family shared: "The ideas of God's family and His kingdom have gotten simpler and yet bigger to us during this time." It is interesting how an "initiative" can help people slow down and reflect, as confirmed by one facilitating family: "It was a great time to really stop, think, and reflect on our relationships with others and how we're thinking kingdom and being family."

One facilitating family "could not get over how much God was teaching people." This was evident through the informal discussion that surrounded the fellowship. The *missio Dei* includes His activity in teaching His followers.

One participant commented on how the teaching kept the congregation focused. He also mentioned how helpful it was to have different people share in the teaching. One of these voices who shared in the teaching was a missionary couple who visited Zion for the first time during this initiative. They encouraged the church in their follow-up note:

> We want to express our deepest thanks for the special love offering. . .This will be a huge help to us this summer in [Europe]. . .We thoroughly enjoyed our Sunday with you. What a great church family you have! We especially want to thank you for your heart for missions, both locally and around the world. You are making a difference. Blessings, blessings, blessings. . .

Lastly, indications for the project's effectiveness include the calls for continued intentionality based on what was set in motion. One facilitating family's sentiment expresses this excitement that was echoed by others: "TKBF was awesome! Hoping to have some get-togethers in future months."

Another facilitator provided this statement indicating resonance with the project and the necessity of its continuation:

> This initiative really matched my passion and my heart. I loved *knowing* that everyone from our church family was being specifically included in activities. Church can be a lonely place (the church in general, and even sometimes Zion). It was so exciting to look around on Sundays and see people talking to others who I never saw them talk to before. Good stuff, really good stuff. It filled my heart with joy. Thank you for choosing me to participate as a facilitator; I think it was more of a blessing to me than it was to the group. . .I also think that if we *don't* continue activities like this, we run the risk of causing people who just now started connecting to feel like 'projects'. . .and we absolutely cannot have that.

The TKBF experience parallels a finding in the SPE Peer Learning Project that "peer learning, in many *different* forms and models, produces energy for the pursuit of excellence in the practice of ministry."[528] Family-with-family consociation alongside of focused teaching and reflection is an effective way for mobilizing families at a local congregation. A key contribution of this initiative's success is that missional families can discern, within community, the way that God is redeeming their brokenness for the blessing of others. As Nouwen puts it, "When we become aware that we do not have to escape our pains, but that we can mobilize them into a common search for life, those very pains are transformed from expressions of despair into signs of hope." Churches need not strive (*doing*) to prescribe through their programs the whole process for this to occur or enough options for their families to participate in outreach. Rather, churches find freedom in *being* a hospitable community for its own families so as to nurture missional wholeness and its characteristics: "Hospitality becomes community as it creates a unity based on the shared confession of our basic brokenness and on a shared hope."[529]

During a visit to Peru, I met a man named Mario, whose testimony reflects this hope. Mario's son died at twenty-five years of age in 2005 of a brain tumor. Mario was not walking close to the Lord at the time, and the church sent an individual to wait with him through the grief over a year and half. During this time, Mario committed to serving the Lord in honor of his son, Jose. Mario now makes multiple trips a year with missions teams into Peru.[530]

An essential aspect of freedom in community is providing families the space and opportunity with one another to discern and design their missional response according to the Spirit's creativity rather than the prescriptions of programs. Churches pour significant time, energy, and resources into

---

[528] Marler, et al, 163.

[529] Nouwen, *The Wounded Healer*, 93.

[530] Interview with Mario Diaz, July 2013.

programs. TKBF highlights how churches can equip and release missional families to go where institutions cannot. TKBF confirms for families what the SPE project does for pastors: "Blessing pastors with freedom and the opportunity for creative thinking cultivates a lush learning environment. We are creative beings and can use both our imagination and intellect to take what is and see what can be. The result is that life-giving plans come together."[531]

Invitational and inspirational appeals help sustain the freedom of such intentionality. TKBF was not an initiative accomplished by the church staff. By connecting to dynamics of fellowship, teaching, and reflection already in motion, it was possible to encourage "active participation and personal 'buy-in,'" which are "critical element[s] in the creation of motivation for learning and pursuit of excellence in ministry."[532] Thus, The TKBF Initiative illustrates among congregants what the SPE project indicates as essential for pastors, namely the role of "participant *buy-in* and *ownership* developed through disciplined structures and skilled facilitative leadership."[533]

This provides more than an opportunity for a church's family ministry. It opens a way to mobilize the entire church as a family in mission together, with all of their unique capacities and opportunities. The TKBF Project fully included singles alongside of families, or families alongside of singles. This inclusion was not an afterthought or an accommodation; it was done by design to reflect God's redemptive family. The compartments that segregate stations in life, age groups, and genders too often de-humanize the people intended to reflect God's image as a complementary rather than uniform community. Thus, consociation was intentionally intergenerational as well as inclusive of singles and families in a variety of redemptive forms.

---

[531] Marler, et al., 106.

[532] Ibid., 170.

[533] Ibid., 169-170.

Singles and families alike described their process of developing missional wholeness and experienced increase of satisfaction in all the missional characteristics. The research's focus on families could readily shift to individuals in future studies. The increase in the degree of satisfaction in missional characteristics for individuals was slightly less than that of families. Further research could focus on supporting effective connections between singles and families in the church alongside of missional mobilization. TKBF at least demonstrates possibilities and positive results for individual and family consociation.

An urgency exists to inform and instruct discipleship initiatives on the value of intergenerational fellowship. It seems that the church is seeing the unintended consequences of age-segregated discipleship that Nouwen so aptly warned of: "If youth no longer aspires to become adult and take the place of the fathers, and if the main motivation is conformity to the peer group, we might witness the death of a future-oriented culture or–to use a theological term–the end of an eschatology."[534] Redeeming a missional form of discipleship through intergenerational relationships can restore hope to the church and through the church to those who are hurting and broken.

Potential exists for inter-disciplinary application of missional wholeness to a variety of leadership contexts. I completed an initial draft of this writing project while visiting Peru, and while there I effectively adapted and applied the concepts of *Missional Family Wholeness* and *Missional Family Characteristics* in teaching and encouraging a local team of missionaries and staff workers. The team consisted of families and singles. Given enough time, it seems reasonable that research similar to TKBF within one congregation could also be conducted within leadership teams in a variety of organizations. As evidenced in the review of literature for TKBF as well as the example below, parallels already exist between *Missional Family Wholeness* and other research-based processes for development. Consider as an example Daniel Goleman,

---

[534] Nouwen, *The Wounded Healer*, 33.

Richard Boyatzis, and Annie McKee's five discoveries of self-directed learning:

- The first discovery: My ideal self – Who do I want to be?
- The second discovery: My real self – Who am I? What are my strengths and gaps?
- The third discovery: My learning agenda – How can I build on my strengths while reducing my gaps?
- The fourth discovery: Experimenting with and practicing new behaviors, thoughts, and feelings to the point of mastery.
- The fifth discovery: Developing supportive and trusting relationships that make change possible.[535]

These discoveries are widely applied in professional leadership contexts. A caution must be considered when applying such insights as these discoveries and missional wholeness development within professional leadership teams. Often these teams consist of discerning and gifted individuals who can assess and criticize with ease. Nouwen offers this caution as contextualized for professional ministers:

> But the danger is that instead of becoming free to let the spirit grow, the future minister may entangle himself in the complications of his own assumed competence and use his specialism as an excuse to avoid the much more difficult task of being compassionate. The task of the Christian leader is to bring out the best in man and to lead him forward to a more human community; the danger is that his skillful diagnostic eye will become more an eye for distant and detailed analysis than the eye of a compassionate partner. . .professionalism without compassion

---

[535] Daniel Goleman, Richard Boyatzis, and Annie McKee, *Primal Leadership: Realizing the Power o Emotional Intelligence* (Boston: Harvard Business School Press, 2002), 111-112.

will turn forgiveness into a gimmick, and the kingdom to come into a blindfold."[536]

Mobilizing missional families is ultimately a labor of love for God and neighbor. It must never be packaged as anything else other than being led by the Spirit of God in the mission of God making disciples of all nations. Everyone has a family story of brokenness, and some have experienced redemption. This research, its implications, and continued work must always remain as redemptive endeavors rooted in the love of God.

Part Three Summary

The Think Kingdom–Be Family Initiative had many points of contact with the congregation. Throughout its introduction and implementation, great care was taken to use language and methods that inspired and invited participation. The gathering of facilitators and their preparation and continued service during the initiative became a solid foundation for engaging many in the congregation during the focused time period of three months.

The facilitators, church leaders, accountability support partner, and the participating families and individuals all illustrate "an ecology of partnerships" which helped accomplish the project.[537] Facilitators and those on their consociation rosters led the fellowship that occurred during the initiative. Church leaders did not prescribe what was to happen. Simply being intentional about spending time together effectively deepened current relationships and formed new ones. The fellowship shared throughout the church was intergenerational, which itself was a facilitating dynamic.

The sermons during TKBF supported three key areas of the initiative. First, the being and doing of God as understood in trinitarian relationality was the first month's focus.

---

[536] Nouwen, *The Wounded Healer*, 42.

[537] Marler, et al., 71.

Themes related to the kingdom of God to encourage thinking kingdom followed in the second month. The final month explored the practice of family in the New Testament and how it relates to contemporary culture. This encouraged being family. The teaching during Sunday School drew from Paul's understanding of the indwelling life of Christ in the Colossian community to explore the process that leads to missional wholeness and its accompanying characteristics. Sunday School also served to guide participants through the questions in the reflection exercises.

There were two reflection exercises participants worked through at the beginning and end of the initiative. These helped families synthesize their sense of TKBF wholeness and the application of its characteristics. We facilitated reflection during the initiative through corporate prayer and the sharing of testimonies in services, Sunday School, and during times of fellowship.

The TKBF Project aimed to identify elements for effectively mobilizing missional families at Zion Church. The reflections of the participants themselves bring clarity and confirm these elements while providing testimonies of this model's effectiveness in missional mobilization. This is evident from the qualitative analysis and further confirmed by the quantitative elements.

The mission of thinking kingdom and being family was revealed and integrated in the life of Zion Church over a period of years. This project synthesized the principles of the process and provided a way to mobilize families in redemptive wholeness and characteristics. With such evidence available from a three-month period, imagine the faithful presence of such a church sustaining the practice of missional mobilization.

Average-sized churches may find that Zion's story, with its mission to think kingdom and be family, inspires what is possible in churches without a large congregation and staff. Not only within the church, but especially through the church, meaningful expressions of faithfulness that reflect God's kingdom are possible from neighborhoods to the nations.

Perhaps TKBF will encourage larger churches at what is possible through intergenerational consociation among families and singles, with the result of empowering their families to reach beyond the program of the church to dreams that are possible for families in God's mission. The TKBF Project testifies of God's mission, not the performance of a particular church. God carries out His mission by His Spirit in His people throughout the earth. This research simply provided the opportunity to zoom in for a closer look at one church family grateful to be a part of His mission.

The Next Chapter. . .

Conclusory Remarks

———— ∞∞∞ ————

Thinking kingdom and being family has also become the mission for my family. Our own transformation from brokenness to being a blessing follows the example of our daughter, Victoria Grace. Her brief life has forever ruined my family for anything less than seeking God's kingdom first as a family, in the family of God, for the sake of the families of the earth. She has gone before us in belonging to Jesus in His dawn of resurrection and the hope of a new heaven and new earth. The words of Jerry Sittser resonate with my own heart:

> I am still not 'over' it; I have still not 'recovered'. . .Yet the grief I feel is sweet as well as bitter. I still have a sorrowful soul; yet I wake up every morning joyful, eager for what the new day will bring. . .Never have I felt as much pain. . .yet never have I experienced as much pleasure in simply being alive and living an ordinary life. Never have I felt so broken; yet never have I been so whole. Never have I been so aware of my weakness and vulnerability; yet never have I been so content and felt so strong. Never has my soul been more dead; yet never has my soul been more alive. What I once considered mutually exclusive–sorrow and joy,

pain and pleasure, death and life–have become parts of a greater whole.[538]

My vision is realized as described by Nicholas Wolterstorff: "I shall look at the world through tears. Perhaps I shall see things that dry-eyed I could not see."[539] In the midst of this project, my wife and I began to see clearly how our family could love the least of these by living among them. The doctoral training I have received is for others. As a doctor of the church, I plan to lead as a doctor for the sick, equipping leaders of the least of these through consociation, that we all might greet the dawn together. My family is among the mourners blessed by Jesus (Matt 5:4), and so we prepare to go as "aching visionaries."[540]

Along the way, I have become uncomfortable with aspects that do not seem to reflect the kingdom of God in my own cultural Christianity in a land of cultural Christianity, and I find myself increasingly zealous for the Father's mission. Hence, I trust that my family's life will be a testimony of God's victory by His grace, and that my words will be received in the spirit of what Nouwen describes as a "contemplative critic:"

> . . .I think that what is asked of the Christian leader of the future is that he be a contemplative critic. . .The man who does not know where he is going or what kind of world he is heading toward. . .will often be tempted to become sarcastic or even cynical. He laughs at his busy friends, but offers nothing in place of their activity. He protests against many things, but does not know what to witness for. But the Christian minister who has discovered in

---

[538] Gerald L. Sittser, *A Grace Disguised* (Grand Rapids, Zondervan, 2004), 198-199.

[539] Nicholas Wolterstorff, *Lament for A Son* (Grand Rapids: Eerdmans, 1987), 26.

[540] Wolterstorff, 86.

himself the voice of the Spirit and has rediscovered his fellow men with compassion, might be able to look at the people he meets, the contacts he makes, and the events he becomes a part of, in a different way. He might reveal the first lines of the new world behind the veil of everyday life. As a contemplative critic he keeps a certain distance to prevent his becoming absorbed in what is most urgent and most immediate, but that same distance allows him to bring to the fore the real beauty of man and his world, which is always different, always fascinating, always new. . .The Christian leader is called to help others affirm this great news, and to make visible in daily events the fact that behind the dirty curtain of our painful symptoms there is something great to be seen: the face of Him in whose image we are shaped.[541]

---

[541] Nouwen, *The Wounded Healer*, 43-44.

About the Author

M ark Jacob Coté is husband to Kristin, and dad to Caleb, Jacob, and Rachel. Mark and Kristin also have a daughter, Victoria Grace, with the Lord. Victoria's life and legacy is a testimony of God's victory by His grace through belonging to Him as His beautiful servant. As stewards of her testimony, Mark and his family rejoice in being God's children in His family and doing His work. Mark also serves as a pastor, teacher, administrator, leader, and coach. At Zion Church of Millersville, PA, he serves alongside his father, Pastor Stephen Coté. He has also served as Head of School at Lancaster County Christian School, PA. After graduating from Millersville University (B.A.) in 1999, Mark received a Master of Divinity from Regent University School of Divinity in 2002. He completed his Doctor of Ministry at Regent in 2014. His research focused on identifying elements that constitute missional families and how to effectively mobilize them. This vision for living as a redemptive family focused on the mission of the kingdom of God is expanding his own family's life and calling to include Pucallpa, Peru. As a doctor of the church, Mark's heart is to equip leaders of the "least of these" for the glory of God. To learn more, visit www.victoriasfund.com.

Bibliography

Arndt, William F., F. Wilbur Gingrich, and Frederick W. Danker, eds. *A Greek-English Lexicon of the New Testament and Other Early Christian Literature*, 3d ed., rev., Chicago: University of Chicago Press, 2000.

Allen, Leslie C. *A Liturgy of Grief: A Pastoral Commentary on Lamentations*. Grand Rapids: Baker Academic, 2011.

Balswick, Jack O. and Judith K. Balswick. *The Family: A Christian Perspective on the Contemporary Home*, 3d ed. Grand Rapids: Baker Academic, 2007.

Benson, Peter L. *All Kids Are Our Kids: What Communities Must Do to Raise Caring and Responsible Children and Adolescents*. San Francisco: Jossey-Bass, 2006.

Bowers, James P. "A Wesleyan-Pentecostal Approach to Christian Formation." *Journal of Pentecostal Theology* 6 (October 1995): 55-86.

Boren, M. Scott. *The Relational Way*. Houston: TOUCH® Publications, 2007.

Brown, Philip M. and John S. Shalett. *Cross-Cultural Practice With Couples and Families*. New York: The Haworth Press, Inc., 1997.

Brueggemann, Walter. *The Prophetic Imagination*. Minneapolis: Fortress Press, 2001.

——. *The Psalms and the Life of Faith*. Minneapolis, MN: Fortress Press, 1995.

Burguière, André, Christiane Klapisch-Zuber, Martine Segalen, and Françoise Zonabend, eds. *A History of the Family: The Impact of Modernity*, Vol. 1. Cambridge, MA: The Belknap Press of Harvard University Press, 1996.

——. *A History of the Family: The Impact of Modernity*, Vol. 2. Cambridge, MA: The Belknap Press of Harvard University Press, 1996.

Clapp, Rodney. *Families At The Crossroads: Beyond Traditional and Modern Options*. Downers Grove, IL: InterVarsity Press, 1993.

Collins, Kenneth J. *The Theology of John Wesley: Holy Love and the Shape of Grace*. Nashville: Abingdon Press, 2007.

Coontz, Stephanie. *The Way We Never Were: American Families and the Nostalgia Trap*. New York: Basic Books, 1992.

——. *The Way We Really Are: Coming to Terms with America's Changing Families*. New York: Basic Books, 1997.

Corbett, Steve and Brian Fikkert. *When Helping Hurts: How To Alleviate Poverty Without Hurting The Poor And Yourself*. Chicago: Moody Publishers, 2012.

Corbin, Juliet and Anselm Strauss. *Basics of Qualitative Research: Techniques and Procedures for Developing Grounded Theory*. 3d ed. Los Angelos: SAGE Publications, 2008.

Crabb, Larry. *Becoming a True Spiritual Community: A Profound Vision of What the Church Can Be* Nashville: Thomas Nelson, 1999.

————. *Connecting: Healing for Ourselves and Our Relationships.* Nashville: W Publishing Group, 2005.

Curran, Dolores. *Stress and the Healthy Family: How Healthy Families Control the Ten Most Common Stresses.* Minneapolis: Winston Press, 1985.

————, Delores. *Traits Of A Healthy Family.* New York: HarperSanFrancisco, 1983.

Foster, Richard J. *Freedom of Simplicity: Finding Harmony In A Complex World.* New York: HarperPaperbacks, 1981.

Flynn, James T., Wie L. Tjiong, and Russell W. West. *A Well-Furnished Heart.* Fairfax, VA: Xulon Press, 2002.

Garber, Steven. *The Fabric of Faithfulness.* Downers Grove: InterVarsity Press, 1996.

Gibbons, Dave. *The Monkey and the Fish: Liquid Leadership for a Third-Culture Church.* Grand Rapids: Zondervan, 2009.

Gilgun, Jane F., Kerry Daly, and Gerald Handel, eds. *Qualitative Methods In Family Research.* Newbury Park, CA: Sage Publications, 1992.

Goleman, Daniel, Richard Boyatzis, and Annie McKee. *Primal Leadership: Realizing the Power of Emotional Intelligence.* Boston: Harvard Business School Press, 2002.

Gottlieb, Beatrice. *The Family in the Western World: From the Black Death to the Industrial Age.* New York: Oxford, 1993.

Groome, Thomas H. *Christian Religious Education*. San Francisco: Harper & Row Publishers, 1980.

Hauerwas, Stanley and William H. Willimon. *Resident Aliens: Life in the Christian Colony*. Nashville: Abington Press, 1989.

Harper, Steven. *Embrace the Spirit: An Invitation to Friendship with God*. Wheaton, Il: Victor Books, 1987.

Hellerman, Joseph H. *When the Church Was a Family: Recapturing Jesus' Vision for Authentic Christian Community*. Nashville: B&H Academic, 2009.

Hiebert, Paul G. *Anthropological Reflections on Missiological Issues*. Grand Rapids: Baker Books, 1994.

Hirsch, Alan. *The Forgotten Ways: reactivating the missional church*. Grand Rapids: Brazos Press, 2006.

Hirsch, Alan and Debra Hirsch. *Untamed: Reactivating a Missional Form of Discipleship*. Grand Rapids: Baker Books, 2010.

Huneke, Douglas K. *The Moses Of Rovno: The Stirring Story of Fritz Graebe, a German Christian Who Risked His Life to Lead Hundreds of Jews to Safety During the Holocaust*. Tiburon, CA: Compassion House, 1985.

Hunter, James Davison. *To Change the World: The Irony, Tragedy, & Possibility of Christianity In The Late Modern World*. Oxford: Oxford University Press, 2010.

Johnson, Jan. *Growing Compassionate Kids: Helping Kids See Beyond Their Backyard*. Nashville: Upper Room Books®, 2011.

Johnson, Luke Timothy. *Prophetic Jesus, Prophetic Church: The Challenge of Luke-Acts to Contemporary Christians.* Grand Rapids: Eerdmans, 2011.

Karotemprel, S., K. Kroeger, F. González, A. Roest Crollius, W. Henkel, P. Giglioni, L. Boka Mpasi, and R. Marcias Alatorre, eds. *Following Christ in Mission.* Boston: Pauline Books & Media, 1996.

Kinnaman, David. *You Lost Me: Why Young Christians Are Leaving Church. . .And Rethinking Faith.* Grand Rapids: Baker Books, 2011.

Krallmann, Günter. *Mentoring for Mission: A Handbook on Leadership Principles Exemplified by Jesus Christ.* Waynesboro, GA: Gabriel Publishing, 2002.

L'Abate, Luciano. *Family Evaluation: A Psychological Approach.* Thousand Oaks, CA: Sage Publications, 1994.

Ladd, George Eldon. Ed. Donald A. Hagner, *A Theology of the New Testament.* Revised Edition. Grand Rapids: Eerdmans, 1993.

Lee, Helen. *The Missional Mom: Living With Purpose At Home & In The World.* Chicago: Moody Publishers, 2011.

Levison, John R. *Filled with the Spirit.* Grand Rapids: Eerdmans, 2009.

————. *Fresh Air: The Holy Spirit for an Inspired Life.* Brewster, MA: Paraclete Press, 2012.

Lewis, C.S. *The Silver Chair.* New York: Harper Trophy, 1953.

Lohfink, Gerhard. *Jesus and Community.* Philadelphia: Fortress Press, 1984.

Maachia, Frank D. *Justified in the Spirit: Creation, Redemption, and the Triune God.* Grand Rapids: Eerdmans, 2010.

Macchia, Stephen A. *Becoming a Healthy Church.* Grand Rapids: Baker Books, 1999.

Marler, Penny Long, D. Bruce Roberts, Janet Maykus, James Bowers, Larry Dill, Brenda K. Harewood, Richard Hester, Sheila Kirton-Robbins, Marianne LaBarre, Lis Van Harten, and Kelli Walker-Jones. *So Much Better: How Thousands of Pastors Help Each Other Thrive.* St. Louis: Chalice Press, 2013.

McNeal, Reggie. *Missional Renaissance: Changing the Scorecard for the Church.* San Francisco: Jossey-Bass, 2009.

Merriam Webster's Collegiate Dictionary. 10th ed. Springfield, MA: Merriam Webster, 1997.

Moore, Rickie D. "The Prophet as Mentor: A Crucial Facet of the Biblical Presentations of Moses, Elijah, and Isaiah," *Journal of Pentecostal Theology* 15(2). SAGE Publications, 2007: 155-172.

Myers, Jeffrey L. "Cultivate – Church Version: Mentoring for Parents." Draft Manuscript May 3, 2011. In author's possession.

Novak, Michael, Harold M. Voth, Archbishop Nicholas T. Elko, James Hitchcock, Mayer Eisenstein, Harold O.J. Brown, Leopold Tyrmand, Joe J. Christenson, and John A. Howard. *The Family: America's Hope.* Rockford, Il: Rockford College Institute, 1979.

Newbigin, Leslie. *The Gospel in a Pluralist Society.* Grand Rapids: Eerdmans Publishing Co., 1989.

Nouwen, Henri J.M. *In the Name of Jesus*. New York: Crossroad, 2000.

————. *The Wounded Healer*. New York: Doubleday, 1990.

Osmer, Richard R. *Practical Theology: An Introduction*. Grand Rapids: William B. Eerdmans Publishing Company, 2008.

Peterson, Eugene H. *The Contemplative Pastor: Returning to the Art of Spiritual Direction*. Grand Rapids: Eerdmans Publishing Co., 1989.

————. *Under the Unpredictable Plant: An Exploration in Vocational Holiness*. Grand Rapids: William B. Eerdmans Publishing Co., 1992.

————. *Working the Angles: The Shape of Pastoral Integrity*. Grand Rapids: Eerdmans Publishing Co., 1987.

Platt, David. *Follow Me: A Call to Die. A Call to Live*. Carol Stream, Il: Tyndale House, 2013.

————. *Radical: Taking Back Your Faith from the American Dream*. Colorado Springs: Multnomah Books, 2010.

Potter, Ellis. *3 Theories Of Everything*. Destinée Media: 2012.

Rainer, Thom S. and Eric Geiger. *Simple Church: Returning to God's Process for Making Disciples*. Nashville: B&H Publishing Group, 2006.

Romanowski, William D. Eyes *Wide Open: Looking For God In Popular Culture*. Grand Rapids: Brazos Press, 2007.

Roxburgh, Alan J. and M. Scott Boren. *Introducing The Missional Church: What It Is, Why It Matters, How To Become One.* Grand Rapids: Baker Books, 2009.

Saint, Steve. *Missions Dilemma: Workbook.* USA: I-TEC, 2009.

Scazzero, Peter and Warren Bird. *The Emotionally Healthy Church: A Strategy for Discipleship that Actually Changed Lives.* Updated and Expanded Edition. Grand Rapids: Zondervan, 2010.

Schultz, Glen. *Kingdom Education: God's Plan for Educating Future Generations.* Nashville: LifeWay Press, 1998.

Seamands, Stephen. *Ministry in the Image of God: The Trinitarian Shape of Christian Service.* Downers Grove, IL: IVP Books, 2005.

Settles, Barbara H., Suzanne K. Steinmetz, Gary W. Peterson, and Marvin B. Sussman, eds. *Concepts and Definitions of Family for the 21st Century.* New York: The Haworth Press, Inc., 1999.

Shenk, David W. *God's Call To Mission.* Scottdale, PA: Herald Press, 1994.

Sight & Sound Theatres®. *Jonah: Original Soundtrack Recording, Finale.* Don Harper, orchestrated by Jim Dellas. CD, 2012.

Sittser, Gerald L. *A Grace Disguised.* Grand Rapids, Zondervan, 2004.

Smith, James K.A. *Desiring the Kingdom: Worship, Worldview, and Cultural Formation.* Cultural Liturgies, Vol. 1. Grand Rapids: Baker Academic, 2009.

Smith, James K.A. *Imagining the Kingdom: How Worship Works*. Cultural Liturgies, Vol. 2. Grand Rapids: Baker Academic, 2013.

Snyder, Howard A. *The Community of the King*. Downers Grove: Inter-varsity, 1978.

Stetzer, Ed and Philip Nation. *Compelled: Living The Mission Of God*. Birmingham: New Hope Publishers, 2012.

Story, J. Lyle and Cullen I. K. Story. *Greek to Me*. J. Lyle Story, 2000.

Swinton, John and Harriet Mowat. *Practical Theology and Qualitative Research*. London: SCM Press, 2006.

Synan, Vinson, ed. *Spirit-Empowered Christianity in the Twenty-First Century: Insights, analysis, and future trends from world-renowned scholars*. Orlando: Charisma House, 2011.

Umidi, Joseph. *Transformational Coaching*. Virginia Beach: Xulon Press, 2005.

White, James M. and David M. Klein, *Family Theories*. 3rd ed. Los Angeles: Sage Publications, Inc., 2008.

Whitehead, James D. and Evelyn Eaton Whitehead. *Method in Ministry: Theological Reflection and Christian Ministry*. Lanham, MD: Sheed and Ward, 1995.

Wilhoit, James C. *Spiritual Formation as if the Church Mattered: Growing in Christ through Community*. Grand Rapids: Baker Academic, 2008.

Wilson, Marvin R. *Our Father Abraham*. Grand Rapids: Eerdmans, 1989.

Wolterstorff, Nicholas. *Lament for A Son.*Grand Rapids: Eerdmans, 1987.

Wright, N.T. *Simply Jesus: A New Vision of Who He Was, What He Did, And Why He Matters.* New York: HarperOne, 2011.

Yong, Amos. *Hospitality & The Other: Pentecost, Christian Practices, and the Neighbor.* Maryknoll, NY: Orbis Books, 2008.

Yong, Amos and Barbara Brown Zikmund, eds. *Remembering Jamestown: Hard Questions About Christian Mission.* Eugene: Pickwick Publications, 2010.

Appendix A

Introducing The Think Kingdom and Be Family Initiative

Sunday, March 3, 2013

Purpose

- To reflect within community on missional elements of *being* and *doing*
- To mobilize missional families and individuals accordingly

Background

- Function before form
- Vision: Jesus. . .Beholding, Building, Blessing
- Mission: Think Kingdom – Be Family
- The Story
- Koinonia
- Missional focus
- Real Talk Training
- Victoria's life/Mark's Doctor of Ministry

Description

- Time frame: April – June (begin on Easter!)
- Facilitating families/individuals cultivate koinonia connections with people at Zion (congregation-wide)
- Facilitators responsible to gather and reflect with several families/individuals assigned to them
- Focused and intentional process that may include a variety of activities, settings, and experiences

Tools

- Missional Family Wholeness
- Developmental process
- Missional Family Profile
- Characteristics of being and doing
- Established through biblical and literary research
- Missional Family Portfolio
- Compilation of two reflective exercises conducted at the beginning and conclusion of the initiative
- Family's testimony and mission statement

Missional Family Wholeness

- Revelation
- First and ongoing stage that initiates and sustains a family in mission
- Indwelling life of Christ and His kingdom
- Discerned through brokenness, relationship, prayer, and through Scripture
- The foundation of wholeness that will ultimately result in integration

Missional Family Wholeness

- Awareness
- General consciousness that flows from the revelation

- Increase in the thoughts and conversations about mission
- Continue to unpack and contemplate the meaning and implications of this new awareness based on the revelation

Missional Family Wholeness

- Motivation
- The bridge from revelation and awareness (being) into doing
- More than an increase in awareness, desires are actually changing
- Dreams emerge along the lines of mission
- Outings, work, vacations, recreation, hobbies, and relationships reflect changing motivation

Missional Family Wholeness

- Intuition
- Maturing motivation
- Instincts for blessing others
- Departure from simply doing good works to appease a guilty conscience
- The default position for a family's thought and action now becomes intuitively missional

Missional Family Wholeness

- Integration
- Focused aspect of wholeness (family life-focus)
- Mission is woven into the fabric of the family's lifestyle
- Choices, relationships, and activities reflect a natural focus on mission
- The family says "no" to things that cannot be integrated into this kingdom lifestyle

Missional Family Wholeness

- Lacking revelation = self-focused, lacking hope, idolatry, self-therapy
- Lacking awareness = overlook people and opportunities
- Lacking motivation = striving, weariness, performance-orientation
- Lacking intuition = may do harm with good intentions, poor discernment/judgment
- Lacking integration = dualism, hypocrisy

Missional Family Profile

- Family's being and doing
- Being: *gratitude, rest,* and *freedom*
- Being compels doing
- Doing: *generosity, faithfulness,* and *going*
- Shalom

Missional Family Profile

- Gratitude
- Ongoing posture of receptivity to God's grace
- Contentment and joy
- Worship is a family-experience that is integrated with lifestyle
- Key indicators that gratitude is lacking: complaining, criticism, and entitlement mindset

Missional Family Profile

- Generosity
- Characterizes commitments and actions
- Hospitality
- Finances
- Attitude towards possessions

Missional Family Profile

- Rest
- Reality of Sabbath integrated into family's lifestyle
- Spirit-baptism is known in spiritual disciplines such as prayer, fasting, contemplation, silence, and peace
- Healthy lifestyle including diet, exercise, sleep
- May be full of activity, but not "busy"

Missional Family Profile

- Faithfulness
- Redemptive responses to the current contexts in which a family lives
- Areas include rest, work, and play
- Obedience in little things
- Engagement with surrounding community (the neighborhood)

Missional Family Profile

- Freedom
- Burden of sinfulness as a lifestyle lifted (idolatry and unforgiveness)
- A quality of playfulness and delight
- Laughter and crying
- Sense of the presence of God in relationships
- No obsession for results
- No self-striving or religious performance

Missional Family Profile

- Going
- Opening new contexts and opportunities for mission
- Greater sacrifice once unburdened by self-preservation
- Distant communities (the nations)

Supplemental Tools

- Sunday School teaching on missional wholeness and profile
- Preaching on foundational themes
- Mark's dissertation proposal
- Exercises in *The Emotionally Healthy Church* by Peter Scazzero
- "Emotional/Spiritual Inventory"
- Book provided to facilitators during preparation

Preparation

- John's teaching on the heart of the initiative
- March 9 retreat
- Breakfast at 9 AM and continuing to early afternoon
- Facilitators invite those on their roster to participate
- March 19 final meeting with facilitators
- Presentation to the congregation at the Easter breakfast

Key Terms

- Initiative, project
- =/= program, small group
- Self-reflective assessment, process
- =/= evaluation, measurement of others, comparison with others
- Measurement is of the elements, not the people
- Q & A

Appendix B

TKBF Facilitator Orientation Retreat at Mark and Kristin's

March 9, 2013
9 AM – 2 PM

—∞∞∞—

9 AM – breakfast (baked oatmeal, muffins, OJ, fruit)

9:30 – 10:30 – Opening

- Walk around the neighborhood
- Prayer/Silent reflection/Bible reading
- Sharing of what God is placing on people's hearts from time with John and opening meditation

10:30 AM – 12:30 PM – TKBF Overview

- A <u>focused time</u> of <u>fellowship</u>, <u>teaching</u>, and <u>reflection</u> around God's calling to think kingdom and be family
  - <u>focused time</u>: Easter launch, April-June, gathering/connecting flexibility/frequency
  - <u>fellowship</u> – context (retreat/camp/mission trip dynamics) and content for connecting
  - <u>teaching</u> – Sunday school and sermons
  - <u>reflection</u> – review and revise initial and follow-up reflection exercises activities, initial reflections

handed out at Easter breakfast?, distribute books, explain facilitator field notes

12:30 – 1:00 – Lunch/Q & A (cold cuts, chips, carrots)

1:00 – 2:00 – Facilitator teams

- Review lists of people

Discussion on invitation to and nature of fellowship with the families and individuals on the list

Appendix C

Introducing The Think Kingdom and Be Family Initiative

Sunday, March 3, 2013

Purpose

- To reflect within community on missional elements of *being* and *doing*
- To mobilize missional families and individuals accordingly

Background

- Function before form
- Vision: Jesus. . .Beholding, Building, Blessing
- Mission: Think Kingdom – Be Family
- The Story
- Koinonia
- Missional focus
- Real Talk Training
- Victoria's life/Mark's Doctor of Ministry

Description

- Time frame: April – June (begin on Easter!)
- Facilitating families/individuals cultivate koinonia connections with people at Zion (congregation-wide)
- Focused and intentional process that may include a variety of activities, settings, and experiences

Tools

- Missional Family Wholeness
- Developmental process
- Missional Family Profile
- Characteristics of being and doing
- Established through biblical and literary research
- Reflection exercises
- Family's testimony and mission statement

Appendix D

TKBF Sunday School
and Sermon Schedule

—— ◉ ——

March 31 – Resurrection
SS: Breakfast orientation to TKBF
Key points:

- Centered vs. bounded set (centered around a deep well rather than fences)
- Distribute and introduce informed consent and questionnaires
- Due date for initial questionnaire: April 14

April 7 – *Mystery of the Mission (of TKBF)*
Scripture: Genesis 18; Supporting texts: Genesis 1; John 1
Sources/Illustrations: Icon of the Holy Trinity by Andrei Rublov (1425); *Ministry in the Image of God* by Stephen Seamands (chs. 1-2)
Key points:

- Relationality of the Trinity
- Humans created in God's image (relationality)
- Healthy components of relationality/family: full equality, glad submission, mutual deference (honor), joyful intimacy

SS (Mark) – TKBF Wholeness: Revelation; Colossians 1:1-12
Key points:

- Hearing from God in the midst of community and through experiences of brokenness
- Question 1 on the questionnaire

April 14 – *Model of the Mission (of TKBF)*
Scripture: Luke 3:21-22
Source/Illustrations: *Ministry in the Image of God* by Stephen Seamands (chs. 3-5)
Key points:

- God's being and doing is the basis for our being and doing
- Relationship of the Father and Jesus and Spirit: acceptance, sustenance, status, achievement
- Input from the Father leads to output through the Spirit
- Surrender, self-giving (barriers to overcome)

SS – TKBF Wholeness: Awareness; Colossians 1:13-20

- Seeing with new eyes the supremacy and centrality of Christ
- Question 2 on the questionnaire

April 21 – *Mutual Indwelling of the Mission (of TKBF)*
Scripture: John 17
Source/Illustrations: *Ministry in the Image of God* by Stephen Seamands (chs. 6-7)
Key points:

- Moving from old self into new self
- Indwelling within the Trinity
- Indwelling of God and man
- Indwelling with one another (unity): emphatic listening, intercessory prayer, team ministry, marriage intimacy

SS – TKBF Wholeness: Motivation; Colossians 1:21-24

- Reconciled and new through steadfastness; new desires
- Question 3 on the questionnaire

April 28 – *Mission of the Mission (of TKBF)*
Scripture: Acts 2
Source/Illustrations: *Ministry in the Image of God* by Stephen Seamands (ch. 8); Frogs or Lizards, including Seamands vineyard vision
Key points:

- *Missio Dei* (Mission of God)
- Acts about the mission of the Spirit
- Beyond comfort zones

SS – Mission trip report from Africa
TKBF Wholeness: Intuition; Colossians 1:24-27

- Indwelling life of Christ;
- Question 4 on the questionnaire

May 5 – *The King's Creation*
Scripture: Genesis 1
Key points:

- Understanding Creation from the Hebrew perspective

SS – TKBF Wholeness: Integration; Colossians 1:28-29

- Completion in Christ
- Question 5 on the questionnaire

May 12 – *The King's Battle*
Scripture: Genesis 3
Key points:

- Light vs. darkness
- Commitment to make creation new once again

SS – TKBF Characteristics; Colossians 2

May 19 – *The King's Court*
Scripture: Genesis 1:26-28; 12:1-3; Matthew 28:18-20

SS – TKBF Characteristics; Colossians 2

May 26 – *The King's Orders*
Scripture: Genesis 1:26-28; 12:1-3; Matthew 28:18-20

SS – TKBF Characteristics; Colossians 3

June 2 – *Family History: Part 1*
Scripture: Matthew 10:34-39
Source/Illustrations: *When the Church Was a Family* by Joseph Hellerman (chs. 1-3)
Key points:

- Family in the New Testament World
- Family re-defined by Jesus

SS – European missionary speaker

June 9 – *Family History Part 2: Family – A False Security..?*
Scripture: Matthew 10:34-39
Source/Illustrations: *When the Church Was a Family* by Joseph Hellerman (chs. 4-5)
Key points:

- Family in Paul's letters and in the Roman world

SS – TKBF Characteristics; Colossians 3

June 16 – *Family of Faith*
Scripture: 1 Peter 2:1-10
Source/Illustrations: *When the Church Was a Family* by Joseph Hellerman (ch. 6)

SS – South American missionary testimony

June 23 – *Family Fellowship*
Scripture: Acts 2:41-47
Source/Illustrations: *When the Church Was a Family* by Joseph Hellerman (chs. 7-9)

SS – TKBF Characteristics; Colossians 4

June 30 – *Family Reunion on the Mountain*
Scripture: Revelation 5
Illustrations: "One Day More" and "Epilogue" from *Les Misérables*
Key points:

- The mission to think kingdom and be family among families of the earth

SS – Testimonies from the TKBF Initiative

Appendix E

Informed Consent to Participate in
The Think Kingdom-Be Family Initiative
at Zion Church of Millersville, PA

———— ∞∞∞ ————

M ark Cote, a doctoral student at Regent University is conducting a study on elements for an effective model of family-with-family consociation to mobilize missional families at Zion Church of Millersville, PA. Mark Cote, a pastor at the church, has explained to me the purpose of this research and the intended outcome. I understand that I will be asked to submit my reflections as part of the church's Think Kingdom – Be Family Initiative. The degree of my participation in the fellowship, teaching, and reflection, through church life at Zion Church over a three month period, will be at my discretion. I will be invited to submit in writing my reflections to questions on thinking kingdom and being family at the beginning and end of the initiative. Completing these questionnaires should take a couple of hours or less. I understand that my anonymity with these responses will be preserved, meaning that my identity may be known to Mark, but will not be connected to my responses should any of my reflections be referenced in the publishing of any results of this study. I know that I may refuse to answer any question asked and that I may discontinue participation at any time.

As a self-reflective exercise, in the context of the church's fellowship and pastoral confidentiality, I understand that participation contains minimal risks. I am aware that I can seek further information about this study by contacting Mark Cote at markcot@mail.regent.edu.

I am aware that I must be at least 18 years of age to participate. If I have children who contribute to the family reflection, then I, as a parent, may or may not include their feedback with my own reflection at my own discretion. My completion and submission of the reflection activities signifies my voluntary participation in this project.

Appendix F

Initial Reflection Questions

—⊗∞⊗—

Family or individual (please circle)

Date:

*T*he *TKBF Initiative at Zion Church of Millersville is a focused time of fellowship, teaching, and reflection around God's call to think kingdom and be family. As you respond to the questions below, please share in your own words according to what is on your heart. Feel free to answer in whatever format is most comfortable for you (electronic, written, paragraph or list, verbally to a facilitator). Think of this like an interview and opportunity to share your family's story. If you want to add anything that is not connected to a question, feel free to write that as well. If any of your thoughts are written as part of Zion's story, this will be done while keeping it anonymous. Thank you!*

Background information about your family/yourself:

What has particularly been on your family's/your heart lately?

(For example: lessons learned through difficulty, reasons for hope, sources of inspiration that guide you, insights from others, life-shaping experiences)

How has what has been on your heart lately impacted how your family/you view(s) life?

(For example: blind spots, perspectives, attitudes)

In what ways are your family's/your desires affected by what has been on your heart and the resulting ways you view life?

(For example: what you look forward to, why you get up in the morning)

What influence has all of this had on your family's/your natural tendencies in terms of decisions or actions?

(For example: immediate reactions, patterns and habits)

How does what has been on your heart connect to your family's/your lifestyle?

(For example: sense of identity, what others see and say about you, direction in life)

Please indicate your level of satisfaction (1 low and 5 high) regarding the following characteristics in your family's/your life followed by your description of what this looks like in your life.

Gratitude (thankful, hopeful, joyful, worshipful, opposite of complaining)

low satisfaction   1   2   3   4   5   high satisfaction

Description:

Generosity (hospitality, expressing kindness, attitudes toward possessions, giving)

low satisfaction   1   2   3   4   5   high satisfaction

Description:

Rest (Sabbath, spiritual disciplines, peace, healthy lifestyle, opposite of busy)

low satisfaction   1   2   3   4   5   high satisfaction

Description:

Faithfulness (current opportunities at home, work, and play, "vocational commissioning")

low satisfaction   1   2   3   4   5   high satisfaction

Description:

Freedom (delight, play, laughter, wisdom, communication, forgiveness)

low satisfaction   1   2   3   4   5   high satisfaction

Description:

Going (new opportunities in the neighborhood and the nations)

low satisfaction   1   2   3   4   5   high satisfaction

Description:

Appendix G

Follow-up Reflection Questions

⸻ ∞∞∞ ⸻

Family or individual (please circle)

Date:

*T*he TKBF Initiative at Zion Church of Millersville has been a
focused time of fellowship, teaching, and reflection around God's
call to think kingdom and be family. This is a follow-up exercise in
order to reflect again on these questions at the end of this focused
time at Zion. As you respond to the questions below, please share
in your own words according to what is on your heart. Feel free to
answer in whatever format is most comfortable for you (electronic,
written, paragraph or list, verbally to a facilitator). Think of this
like an interview and opportunity to update your family's story
based upon the fellowship, teaching, and reflection over the past
three months. If you want to add anything that is not connected to
a question, feel free to write that as well. If any of your thoughts are
written as part of Zion's story, this will be done while keeping your
reflections anonymous. Thank you!

Describe your family's/your involvement and experience with The TKBF Initiative over the past three months:

What has particularly been on your family's/your heart during the past three months?

(For example: lessons learned through difficulty, reasons for hope, sources of inspiration that guide you, insights from others, life-shaping experiences)

How has what has been on your heart during the past three months impacted how your family/you view(s) life?

(For example: blind spots, perspectives, attitudes)

In what ways have your family's/your desires been affected by what has been on your heart and the resulting ways you view life?

(For example: what you look forward to, why you get up in the morning)

What influence has all of this had on your family's/your natural tendencies in terms of decisions or actions?

(For example: immediate reactions, patterns and habits)

How has what has been on your heart over the past three months connected to your family's/your lifestyle?

(For example: sense of identity, what others see and say about you, direction in life)

Please indicate your level of satisfaction (1 low and 5 high) regarding the following characteristics in your family's/your life followed by your description of what this looks like in your life.

Gratitude (thankful, hopeful, joyful, worshipful, opposite of complaining)

low satisfaction   1   2   3   4   5   high satisfaction

Description:

Generosity (hospitality, expressing kindness, attitudes toward possessions, giving)

low satisfaction   1   2   3   4   5   high satisfaction

Description:

Rest (Sabbath, spiritual disciplines, peace, healthy lifestyle, opposite of busy)

low satisfaction   1   2   3   4   5   high satisfaction

Description:

Faithfulness (current opportunities at home, work, and play, "vocational commissioning")

low satisfaction   1   2   3   4   5   high satisfaction

Description:

Freedom (delight, play, laughter, wisdom, communication, forgiveness)

low satisfaction   1   2   3   4   5   high satisfaction

Description:

Going (new opportunities in the neighborhood and the nations)

low satisfaction   1   2   3   4   5   high satisfaction

Description:

Appendix H

Think Kingdom and
Be Family Prayer

By Mike Shirley

Abba Lord Father,

You have created us in Your image and created a perfect world for us to live in. You gave us free will so that we could choose to love You, yet we were rebellious, and chose our own path, which led us away from the Garden and intimacy with You. Even so, Lord, Your Love for us was unwavering! You devised a plan to bring us back. You came to us in the Person of Jesus Christ. Even though You were met with distrust, betrayal, slander, brutality, and all kinds of ugliness that we had to offer You, You still loved us with an unending Love, and continued with Your plan. Jesus, Your only begotten Son, the only One without sin, separated us from our sin. To do this, Jesus would have to not only endure a painful death on a cross, but would have to receive Your entire wrath, that was due us. In doing so, the curtain of the Holy of Holies was torn and You made Yourself readily available to everyone. You reside in the hearts of those who call Jesus Savior and Lord. You have expanded Your Kingdom, from heaven to our hearts. So great is Your love for us!

Open our eyes and hearts so that we may know your very Character in ever-increasing ways. As we see You more clearly, we choose to love you. We no longer desire any path that would separate us from Your Love. We ask that You restore us back to Your Image, even if it means taking us through difficult trials and refining fires. We are willing to lay down our worldly ways. Selfishness, greed, lust, taking offense, and finger pointing are a few of the things that do not belong in the Kingdom. Purify us, Lord, that we may see You! Make us a righteous people that we may be used by You. Give us servants' hearts that we may serve those around us.

We are thankful, Lord, that You have given us each other. You call us Your children. You are our Father, Jesus is the oldest Son. We are Your Family! We ask for Your help and guidance as we walk together. We need Your very Presence in a real way whether it be when we celebrate together through triumphs, or it be when we cry together through tragedies. We ask that You hear us as we lift each other in prayer.

Lord we ask for revival in our hearts, in our households, and out to our neighbors from the communities which we live in, to the ends of the earth. We share Your desire that none be lost. We shed tears for the broken lives around us, who refuse Your Love. We remember how we were once broken, and how we were filled with Joy, as You rescued us. Lord we ask that You would burn in the hearts of the lost, and if at all possible, open doors so that we might impact them with Your Gospel message. Above all, may the Glory of Your Light shine in us, Your Family, so that those around us might find Hope in a world that is crumbling. We ask these things in Jesus' Name, Amen.

CPSIA information can be obtained at www.ICGtesting.com
Printed in the USA
BVOW04s0854100414

350102BV00006B/5/P